IMAGES
of America

SHREVEPORT
FACES OF THE PAST

IMAGES
of America

SHREVEPORT
FACES OF THE PAST

Eric J. Brock

ARCADIA
PUBLISHING

ISBN 978-0-7385-1416-1

Published by Arcadia Publishing
Charleston, South Carolina

Printed in the United States of America

Library of Congress Catalog Card Number: 2001097957

For all general information contact Arcadia Publishing at:
Telephone 843-853-2070
Fax 843-853-0044
E-Mail sales@arcadiapublishing.com
For customer service and orders:
Toll-Free 1-888-313-2665

Visit us on the Internet at www.arcadiapublishing.com

For my wife, Julie

CONTENTS

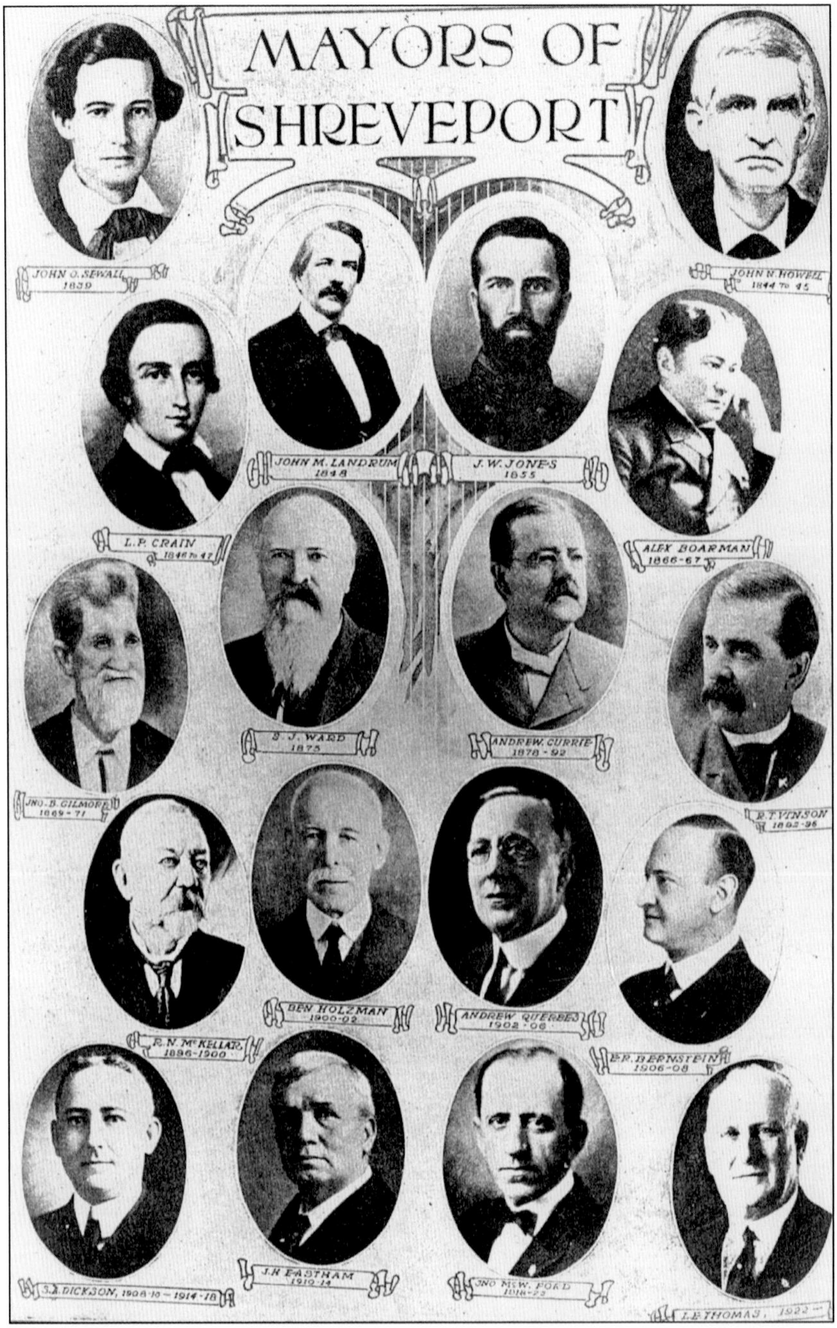

A collective portrait honors several of Shreveport's early mayors. City streets were named to honor Howell, Landrum, Jones, Holzman, Querbes, Bernstein, Dickson, and Thomas. Parks honor Currie, Ford, and Thomas. Boarman, who was the youngest mayor in the city's history when at age 27 he took office, later served as a federal judge; Ward later served as Caddo Parish sheriff. Landrum served in the U.S. Congress on the verge of the Civil War. Several of these men previously served on the city council or as commissioners; Thomas was a state representative before becoming mayor.

INTRODUCTION

Shreveport has a rich history, a history made by many thousands of men and women who have called this area home for nearly two centuries. There is no way, of course, to name them all, no way to show the faces of the myriad citizens who have each made their own marks, whether great or small, for good or ill, to the city's development.

This slim volume makes no pretense as to thoroughness. It would take a hundred times this many books and tenfold times that to adequately chronicle the people and personalities who have contributed to the Shreveport area's heritage and growth.

This book, rather, is a portrait of the citizens of the city's past painted small; it is a vignette of Shreveport's heritage as seen in the faces of those who helped create it. This is a book about the city, yes, but it is also a book about its people—the great and the unknown alike.

Here we see glimpses of faces that go with names we read and hear everyday: names of streets, of parks, of schools. Names of public buildings, names from history, names so commonly heard that we often forget they were once borne by individuals who lived. We are surrounded by monuments to the past, by public places named in memory of those who have gone before. In this book are some of the faces of those individuals. They are not studio portraits in every case—though in many cases that is all that exists—but also images of these individuals doing their jobs and living their lives.

Images depict everyday citizens going about their daily routines. We see a couple in a carriage on a downtown street, two men standing by a laundry wagon in what was once a suburb, women sewing in a garment factory, and a man plowing in the cotton fields outside town.

There is also much to be seen here of the city's rich cultural heritage, of its entertainment history, and of its religious and educational tradition. A plethora of musicians, painters, architects, sculptors, writers, and actors have all called Shreveport home. Their names resonate in our collective cultural psyche, their creations surround us wherever we look and listen, but their faces are often unfamiliar. It is hoped that this little book, at least to some degree, will change that.

And then there are the society leaders and the civic leaders. Not only mayors and other political figures are included but also those who found shelter for orphans and the homeless, those who crusaded for civil rights, and those who founded hospitals and schools.

Many who have contributed to Shreveport's rich heritage are not here. In some cases there are no pictures available; overall, it was simply necessary to choose a few who were representative of the many. Please know that if someone is not here whom the reader feels ought to be, it is not a slight or an oversight; it is simply economy of data and economy of space.

And so, with that, I offer to the present-day residents of the Shreveport area a collective portrait of the city's citizens from the very distant past to the very recent past and all that lies between.

—Eric J. Brock

One

Community Leaders

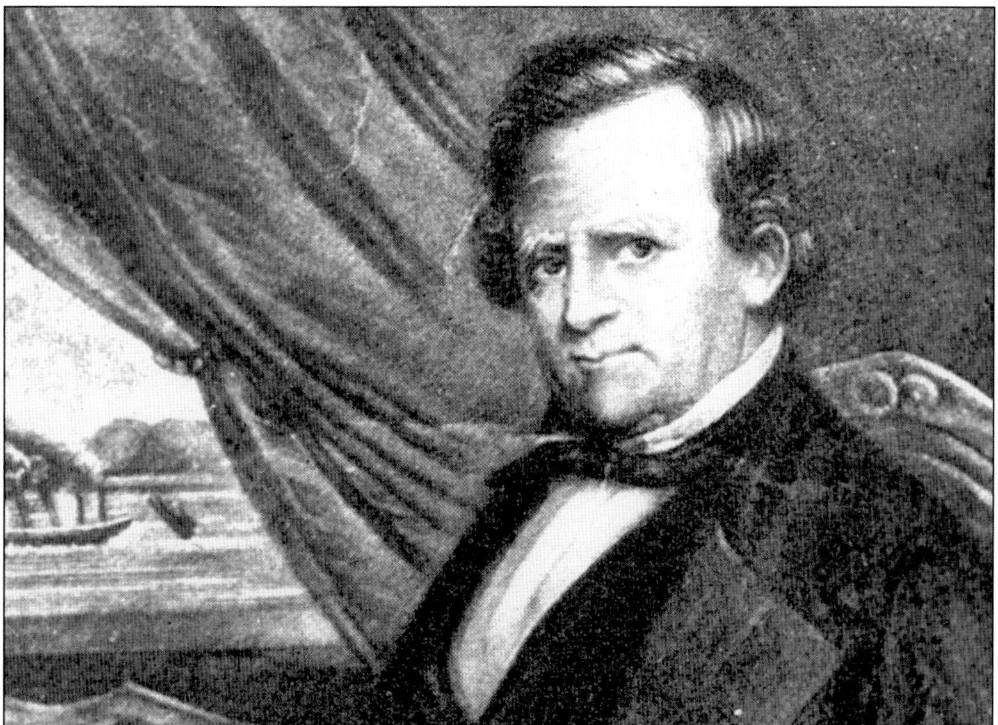

Capt. Henry Miller Shreve arrived at the site of modern Shreveport in 1833 to clear the Great Raft, a massive log jam which blocked the Red River for much of its route through Louisiana. Shreve began the project but would not live to see it completed. He would, however, live to see the founding of the city that bears his name: Shreveport, originally called Shreve Town, established in 1836 by the Shreve Town Company, a consortium of real estate speculators that included Shreve. Shreve never resided in Shreveport; he died in St. Louis in 1851 and is buried there.

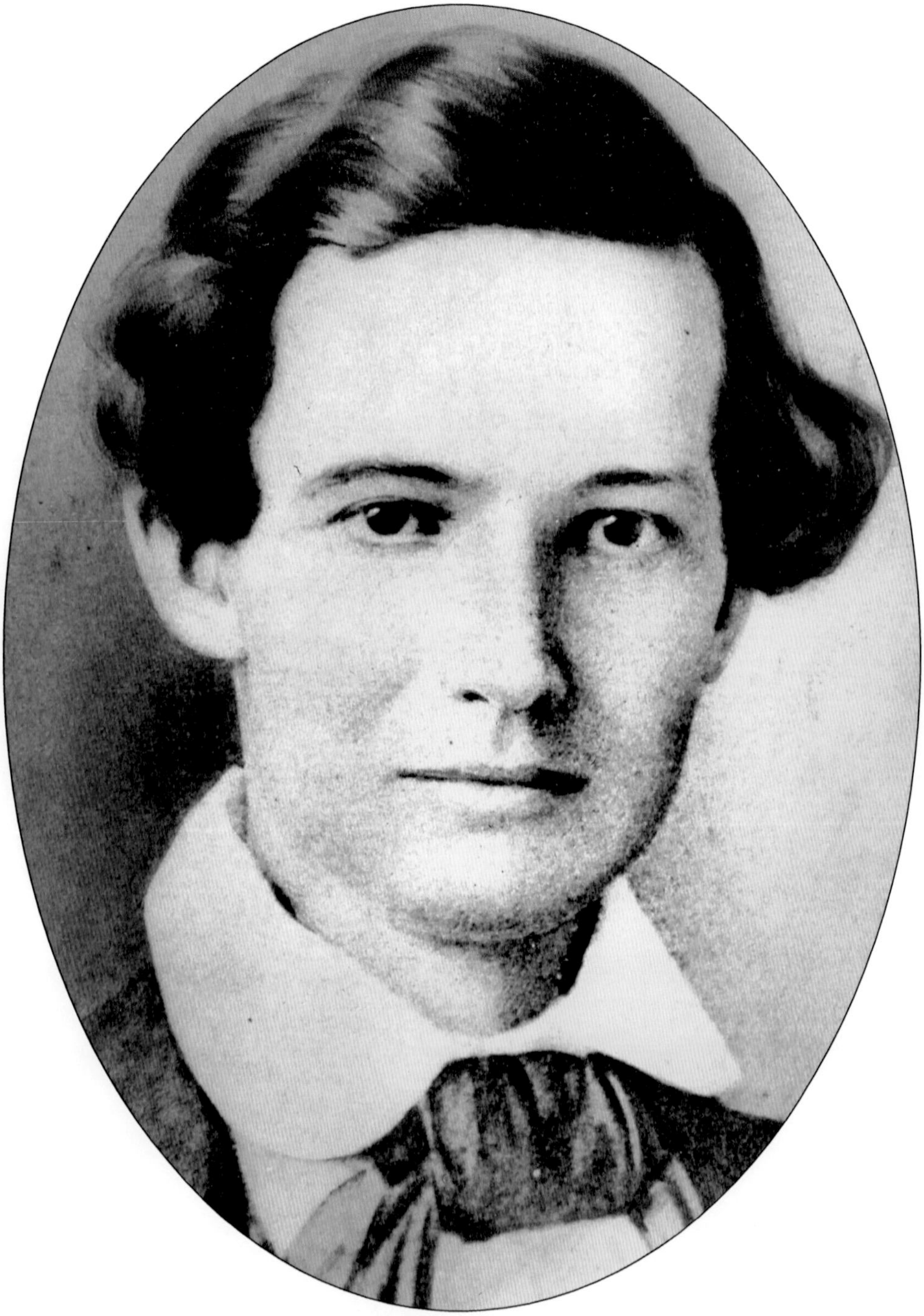

John Octavius Sewall, a native of Halowell, Maine, was Shreveport's first mayor. His term was cut short in 1840 when he was killed at age 33 in a duel at Elysian Fields, Texas. Legend holds that the duel was fought with a saloon kingpin named Wilson who resented Sewall's efforts to clean up the town. However, the known facts in the case indicate that Sewall's killer was one John Willson and that the cause may have been jealousy over Sewall's wife, Frances, later the wife of another mayor, Jonas Robeson.

An important figure in 19th-century Shreveport business was Benjamin May Johnson, who founded the city's first bank, Johnson's Exchange, in 1852. He was also involved in the establishment of the city's first electric plant and streetcar system.

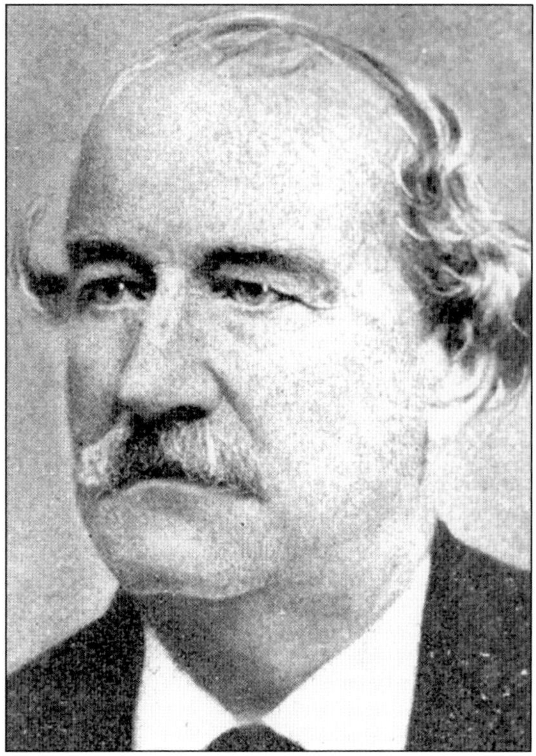

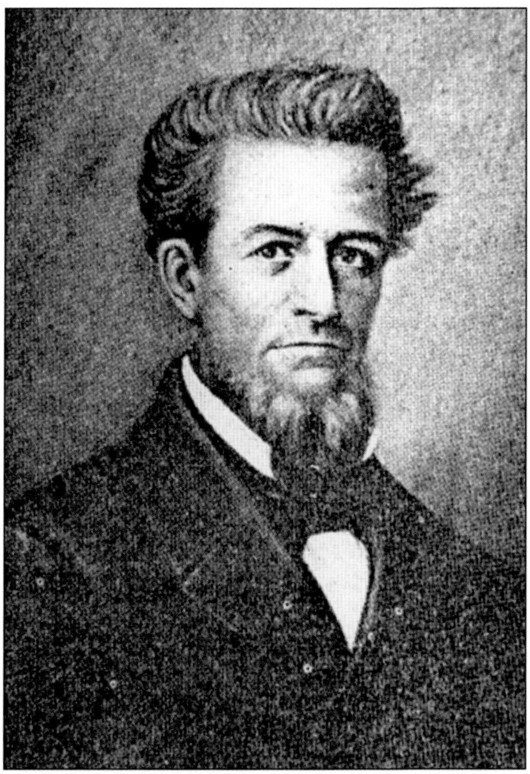

Gov. Thomas Overton Moore was the state's chief executive during the first half of the Civil War. It was during his term of office that the state government was moved from Baton Rouge to Shreveport, via Opelousas.

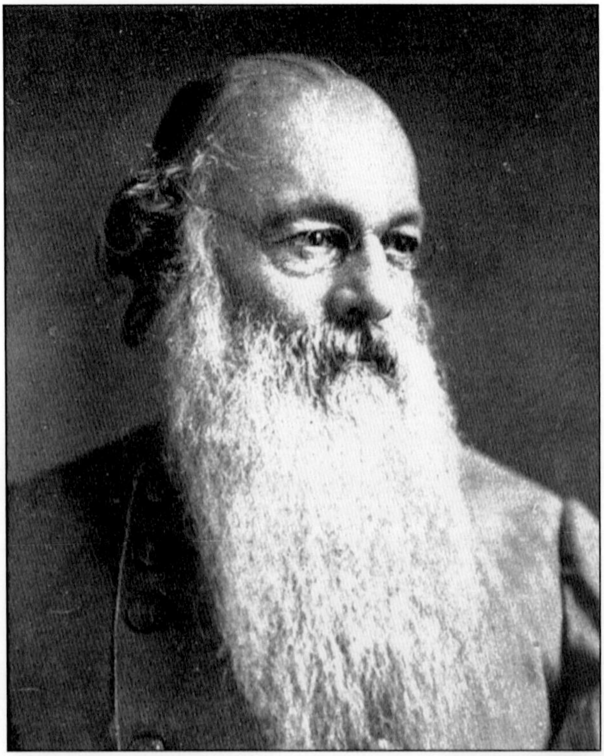

Gen. Edmund Kirby Smith was the commander of the huge Trans-Mississippi Department of the Confederate Army, headquartered at Shreveport, during the Civil War. The Trans-Mississippi Confederacy was the last major command of the South to surrender. That surrender occurred on May 26, 1865, almost seven weeks after Appomattox.

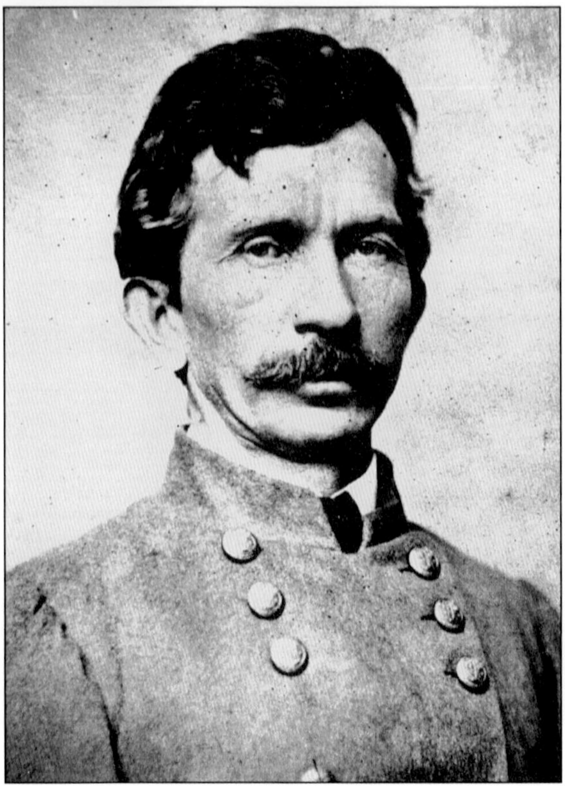

Gen. Henry Watkins Allen was the only governor of Louisiana to take the oath of office at Shreveport. He was also the state's only physically handicapped governor, having sustained major injuries in battle. Allen governed during the latter part of the war; his farewell address to the citizens of Shreveport before fleeing to Mexico at war's end became legendary. Allen Avenue and the Allendale neighborhood are named for him.

Gen. Richard Taylor, whose primary residence was at Shreveport throughout the war, was one of the South's important military leaders. The son of U.S. President Zachary Taylor and the brother-in-law of Confederate President Jefferson Davis, Taylor played an instrumental role in saving Shreveport from Union conquest.

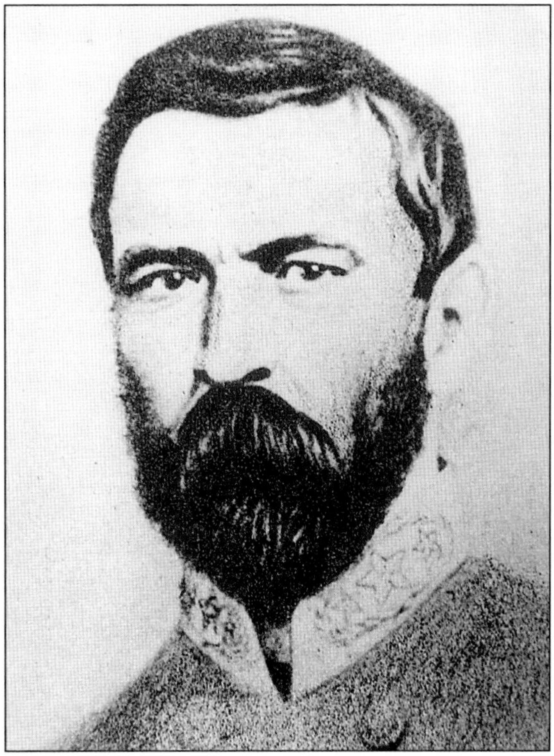

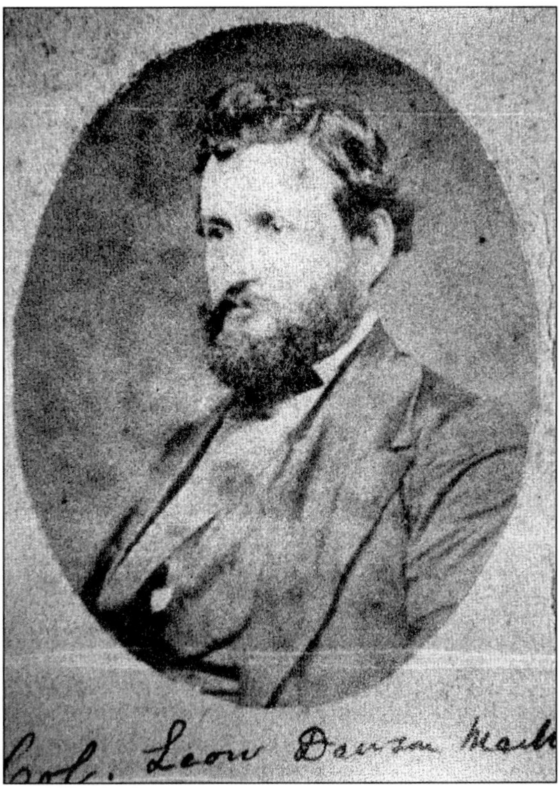

Col. Leon D. Marks, a Shreveport lawyer and newspaper owner, was one of only three Louisiana Jews to rise to high rank in the Confederate army. Marks suffered ultimately fatal injuries at Vicksburg but died at his Shreveport home after lingering for several weeks. Local camps (chapters) of the Sons of Confederate Veterans are named in honor of General Taylor and Colonel Marks.

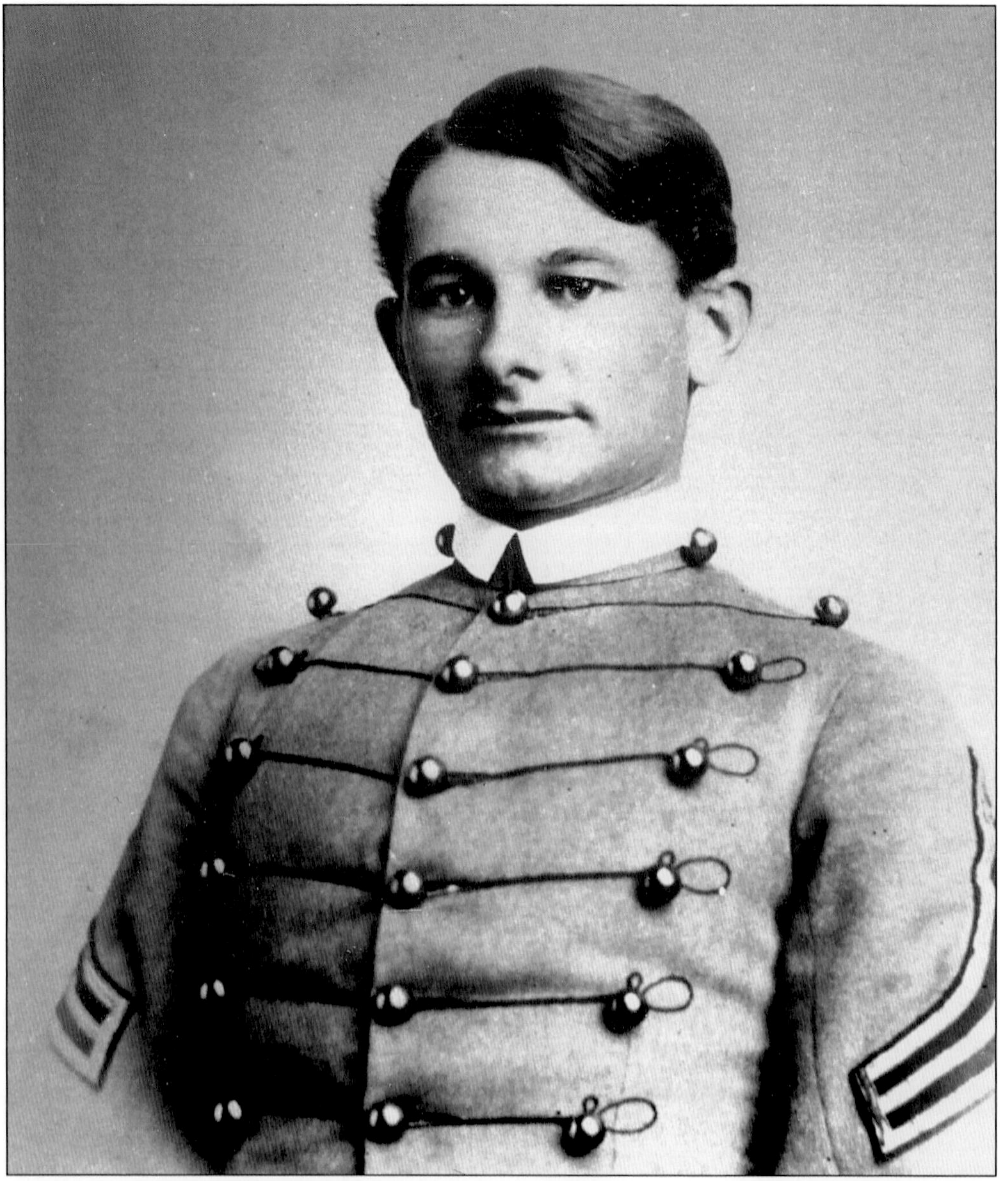

Lt. Eugene Augustus Woodruff, a Union veteran, became an unlikely hero in Shreveport during Reconstruction. Woodruff, a native of Iowa, was working with the U.S. Army Corps of Engineers clearing the partially re-formed log jam north of the city when Shreveport was stricken with an epidemic of yellow fever. The epidemic proved to be the worst in Shreveport's history and the third worst in American history. Rather than leave the city as ordered to do, Woodruff stayed to nurse the sick and dying. He fell ill and died of the disease at age 31. He was buried in Oakland Cemetery where a grand memorial was placed on his grave at public expense.

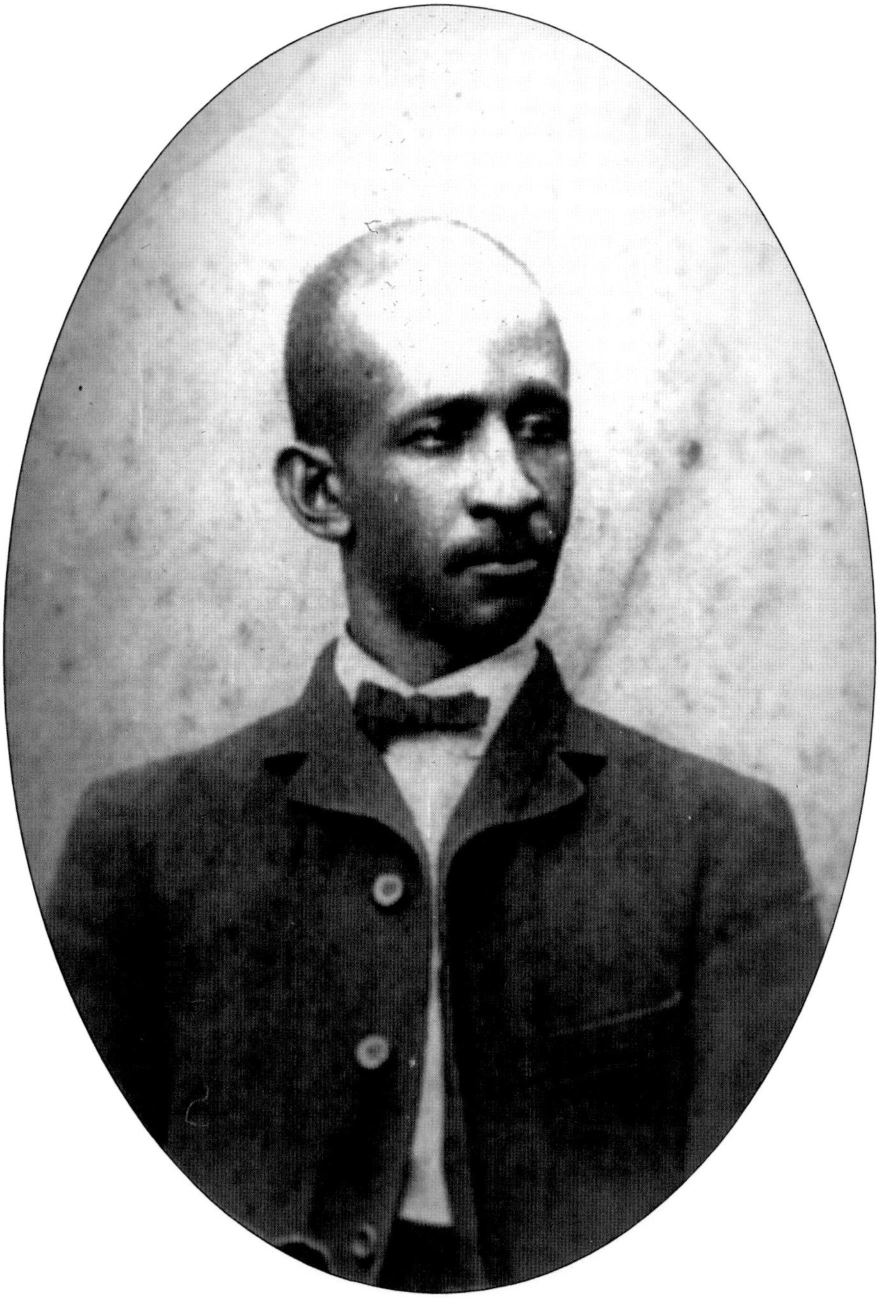

Lt. Gov. Caesar C. Antoine, a New Orleans native, was an influential figure in Reconstruction-era Louisiana. Born free, Antoine was educated in New Orleans and later moved to Shreveport where he operated a grocery and owned a cotton plantation. After the Civil War he served in several capacities in state government including acting governor for three weeks. The Shreveport Charity Hospital, first city hall, and city market were built with funds allocated by Antoine's office at his behest.

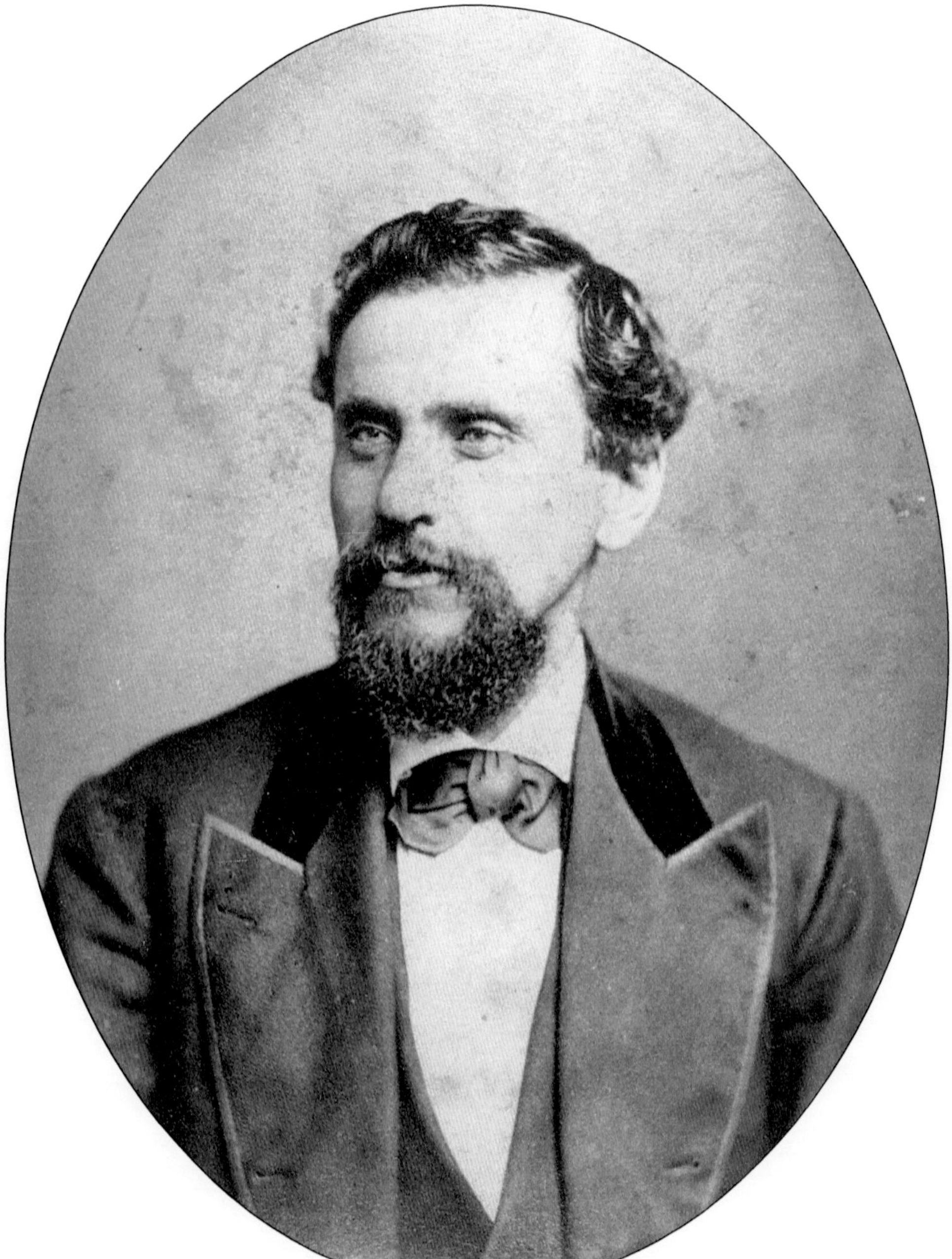

Capt. Simon Levy Jr., a native of Germany and a Confederate veteran, was a leading figure in Shreveport's post–Civil War economy. A co-founder of the Commercial National Bank, Levy also helped bring the KCS railroad through the city and kept the Charity Hospital open with funds from his own pocket when state funding was temporarily cut off. He was also the founder of the Columbia Club, Shreveport's first private social and dining club. Levy Street, which runs between Lakeshore Drive and Linwood Avenue, is named for him.

Capt. Peter Youree, a co-founder of the Commercial National Bank, was also one of Shreveport's leading late 19th and early 20th century builders. The Phoenix and Youree Hotels and the city's first skyscraper, the CNB Building at 509 Market Street, were his creations. He also helped found the electric streetcar system and was instrumental in getting the first traffic bridge built over the Red River. Youree Drive, one of the city's main thoroughfares, is named in his honor.

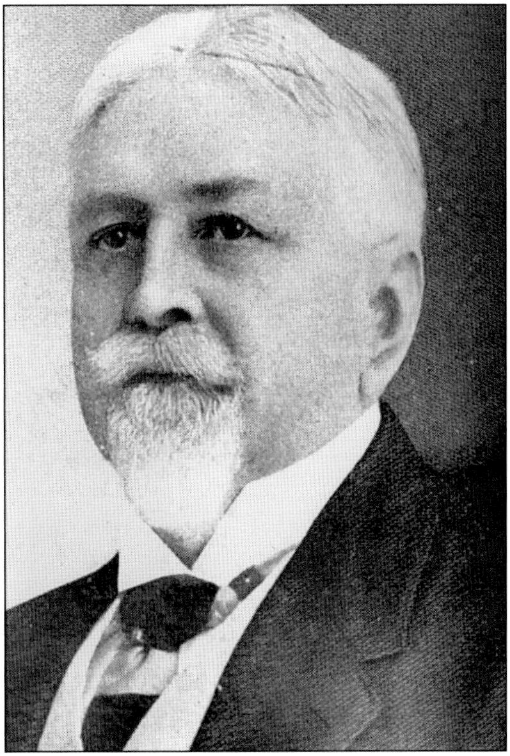

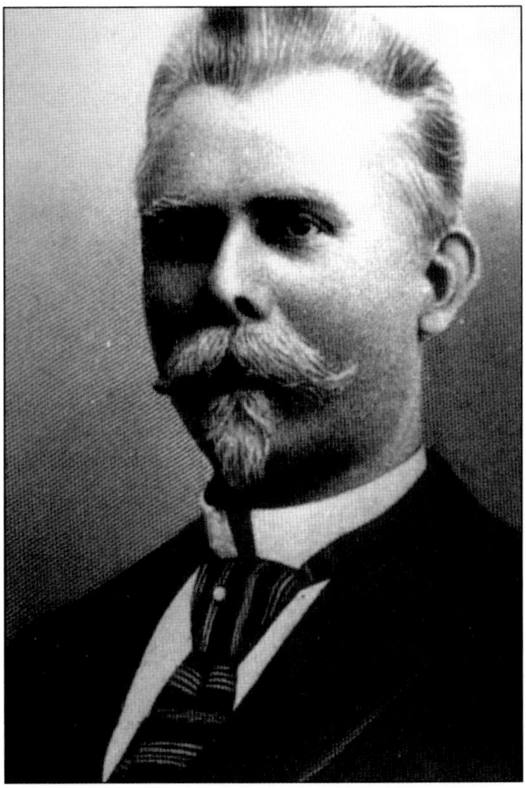

William Edenborn, once one of America's wealthiest men, made his home in Shreveport for many years and is buried at Forest Park Cemetery. He built the Louisiana Railroad and Navigation Company and the Louisiana and Arkansas Railroad. Edenborn Avenue in Metairie is named for him.

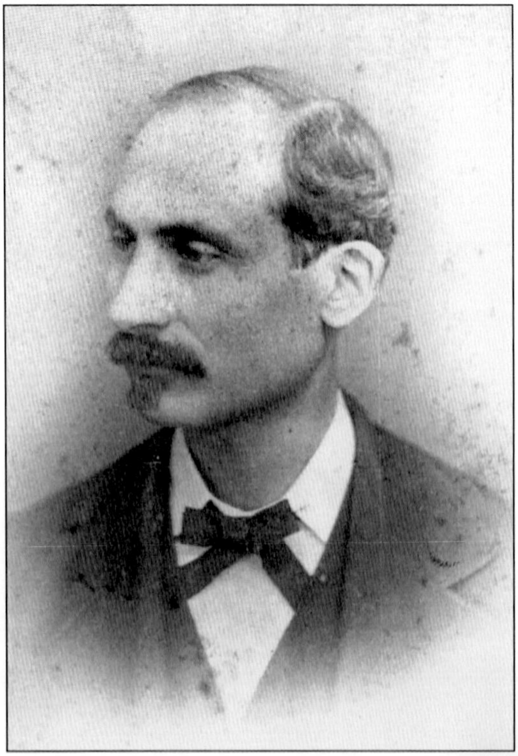

Emanuel Phelps, a native of Germany and Confederate veteran, was one of Shreveport's leading merchants for many years. A shoemaker, Phelps' shoe store became a major chain, with business all over America by the 1930s. His slogan, "Phelps Shoes are Good Shoes," was well known for decades and can still be faintly seen on old painted billboards on building exteriors.

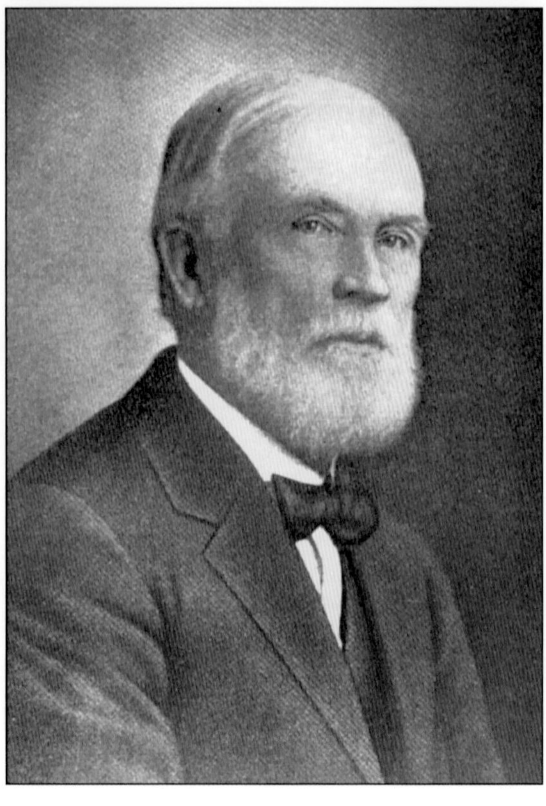

James S. Noel, planter, lumberman, and pioneer oilman, was a leading figure in the area's economy from the Civil War to his death in 1920. He built the Noel Methodist Church in Shreveport's Highland area and developed much of the area around Mooringsport, including the now-vanished town of Missionary on the Red River north of Shreveport.

Andrew Querbes, a New Orleans native of Basque/French heritage, came to Shreveport as a young man and entered the dry goods business. He also had interests in the Shreveport Ice and Brewing Company, helped found the State Fair, and was president of First National Bank. He twice served as mayor and was a member of the parish police jury as well.

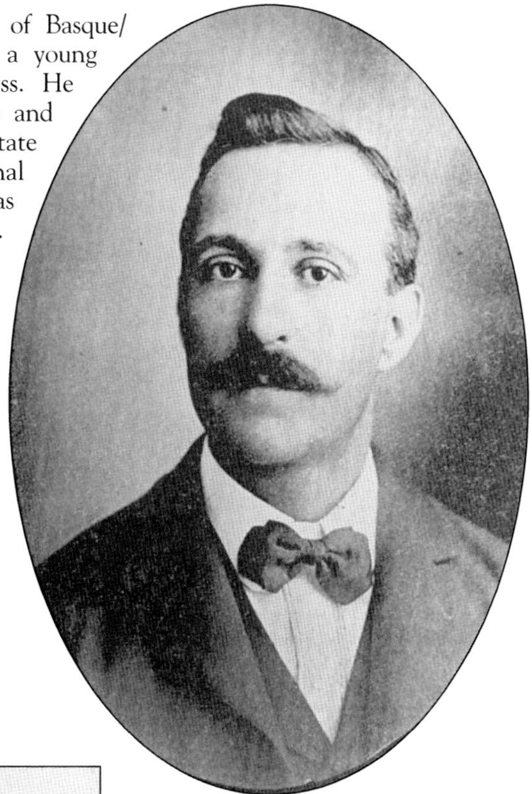

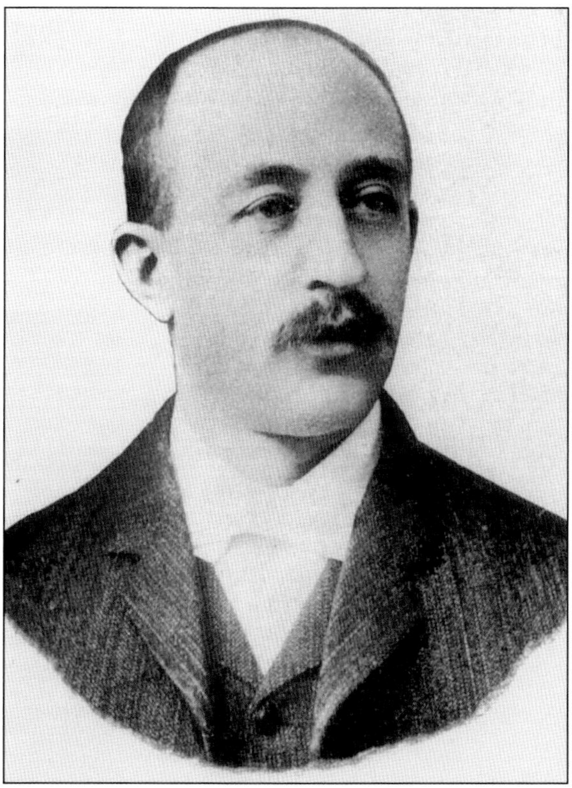

Justin Gras, a native of France and cousin to Mrs. Andrew Querbes, came to Shreveport to work in the grocery of his uncle, Justin Ricou. He later started his own grocery business and began to speculate in real estate. By the 1920s Gras was the largest landowner in Caddo Parish. He gave generously to his adopted community as well as to his home village in the Pyrenees, rebuilding its church after its destruction in World War I. He was well known both for his business acumen and for his generosity.

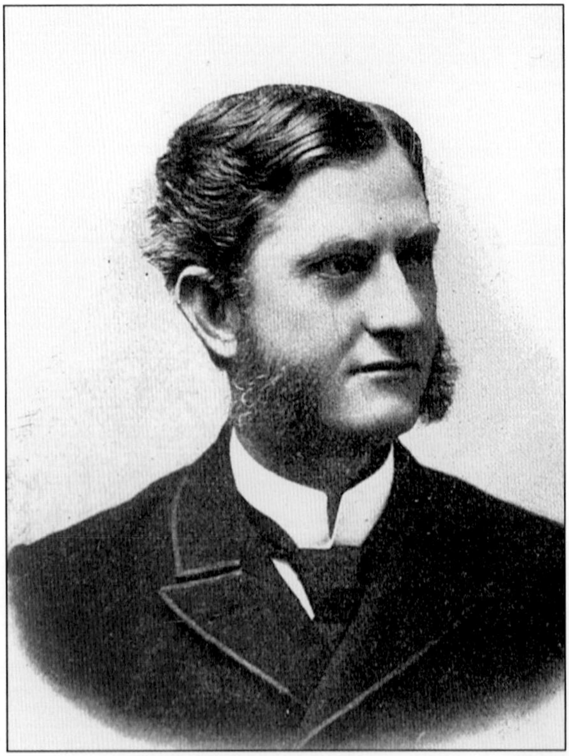

Newton Crain Blanchard, a Shreveport lawyer, was one of the state's most progressive early 20th-century governors. He served in the state legislature, the U.S. Senate, and on the constitutional conventions of 1879 and 1913. He is buried at Greenwood Cemetery. The suburb of Blanchard, on Shreveport's northern edge, is named for him.

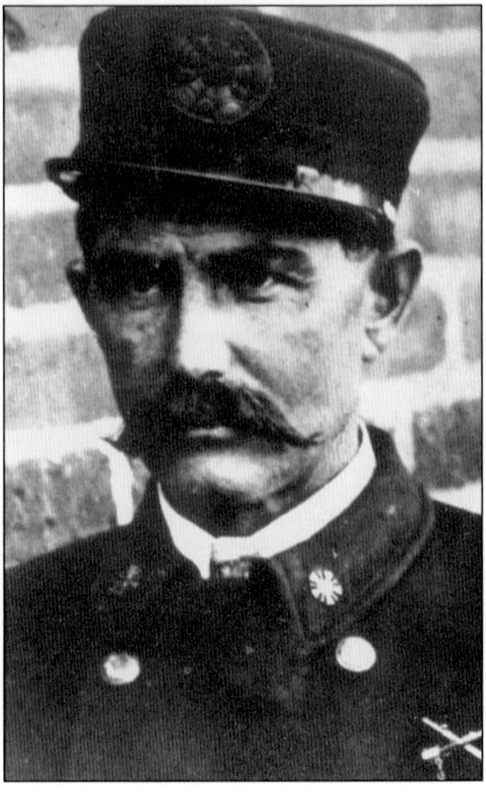

Chris O'Brien was the fourth fire chief of Shreveport's professional fire department, founded in 1891. He is credited with bringing the department into the modern age, introducing the first modern firefighting equipment and eliminating bucket brigades and the need for volunteer support. He served as chief for 21 years.

Dr. John Ira Schumpert (right) and his son Dr. Thomas Edgar Schumpert (below) were both noted Caddo Parish physicians. The elder was a surgeon in the Confederate army and later a state legislator. The younger Schumpert founded the Schumpert Sanitarium, today's Schumpert Medical Center, one of the largest hospitals in Louisiana. Dr. T.E. Schumpert also owned the first automobile in Shreveport. He died of tuberculosis in 1908. Father and son are interred in the Schumpert family mausoleum at Greenwood Cemetery.

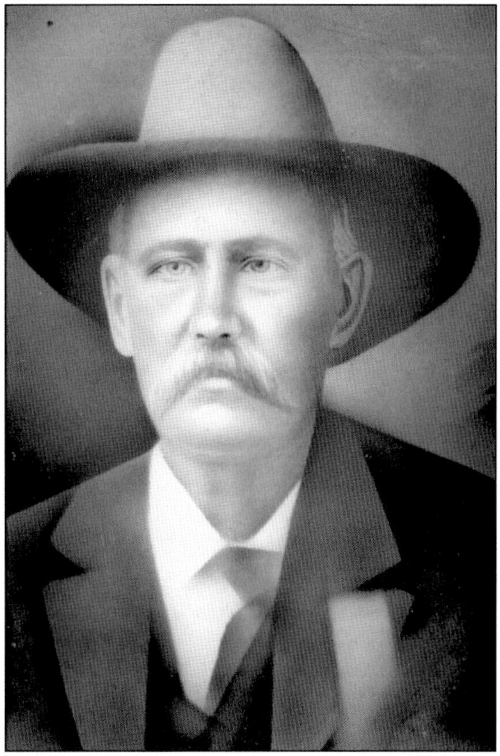

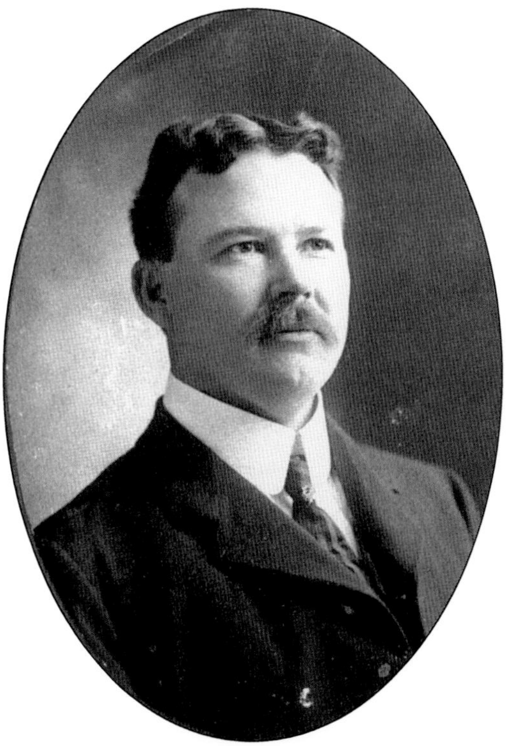

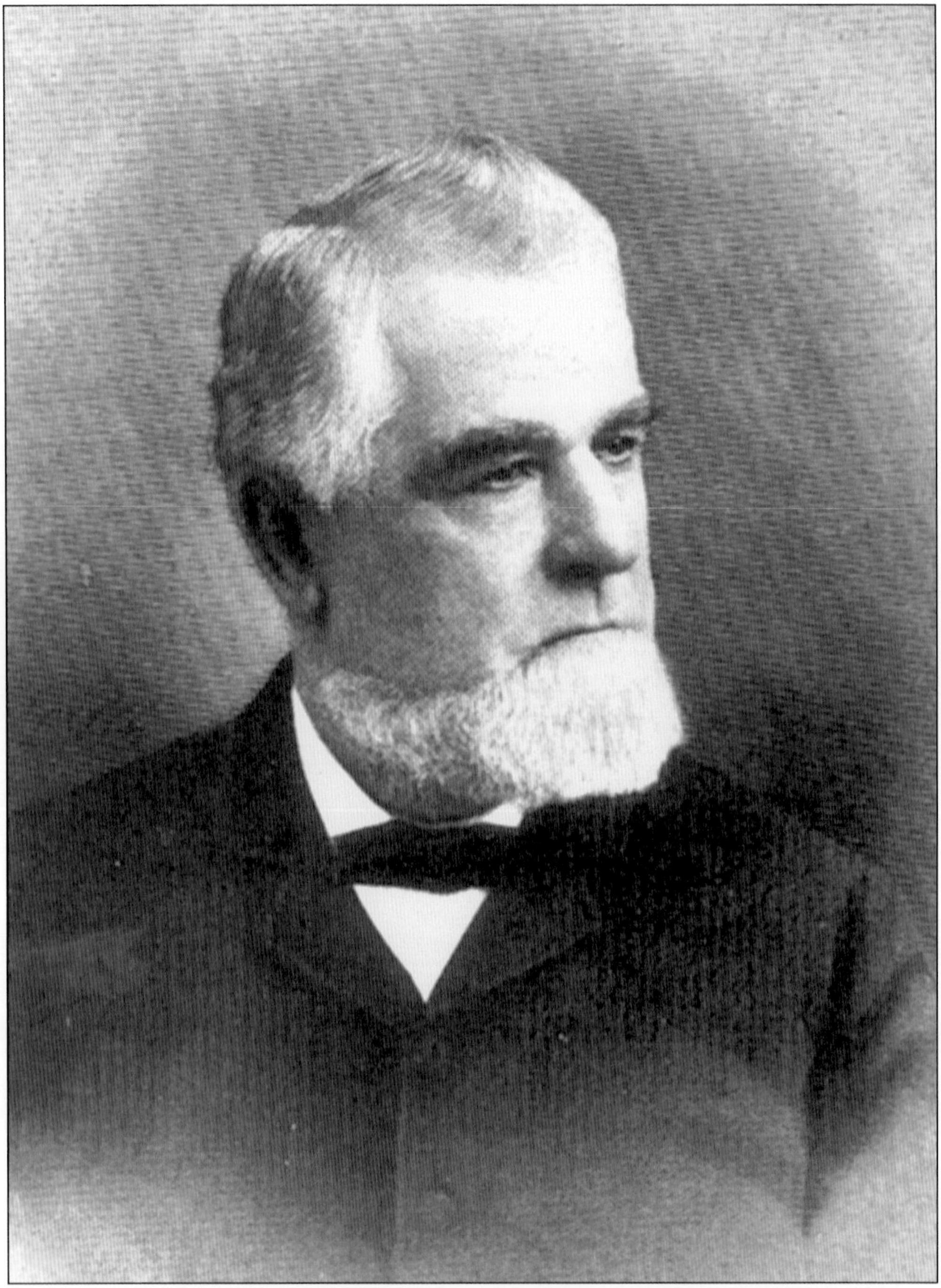

James Martin Foster, one of Caddo's largest planters, was also one of the state's most influential political leaders, making the careers of several congressmen and governors with his support and assistance. He also did much for Caddo Parish during his tenure on the police jury, including his work to establish the Caddo Parish School Board. The income derived from his public offices went to support the Genevieve Orphanage in Shreveport. Foster's "Curraghmuir" plantation is today the site of LSU Health Sciences Center, successor to the original Charity Hospital.

Sidney Levy Herold, a prominent Shreveport attorney, is perhaps best known for his successful state supreme court challenge to the unconstitutional practice of Bible reading in the public schools. His arguments later formed the core of the U.S. Supreme Court ruling removing public prayer from schools as violating the separation clause.

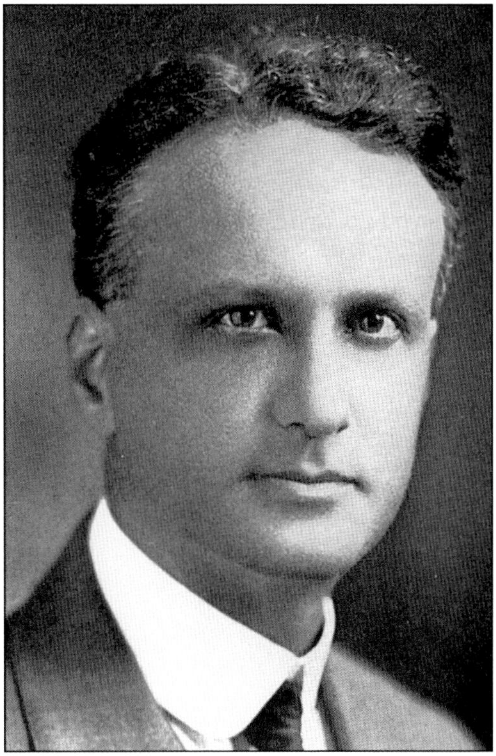

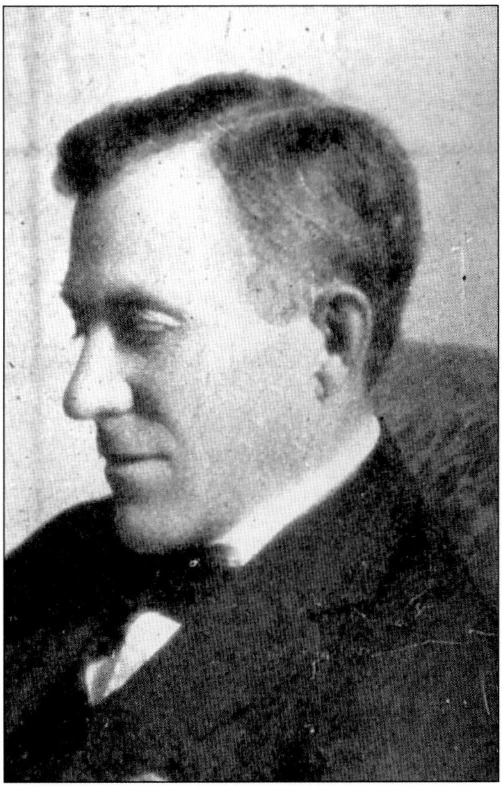

Albert Coldwell Steere was one of Shreveport's foremost real estate developers before his death in 1930 at age 50. Steere developed the South Highlands, Glen Iris, Broadmoor, Dixie Garden, and Hollywood neighborhoods as well as portions of Highland and other areas. A.C. Steere Elementary School and Albert, Coldwell, and Steere Streets in Broadmoor are named for him.

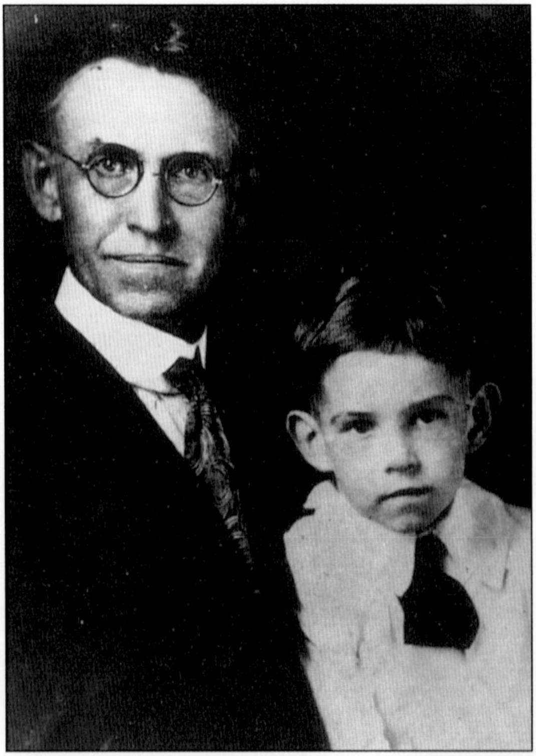

Burch Grabill is pictured with his son Bill in 1920. The elder Grabill established Grabill Studios in 1919 and his son followed in his footsteps as a photographer. Bill Grabill began his career at age 16 working for the *Shreveport Journal* as the paper's only staff photographer. Grabill Studios was responsible for more historic images of Shreveport than any competing photographer of the day. The firm remained in business into the 1980s.

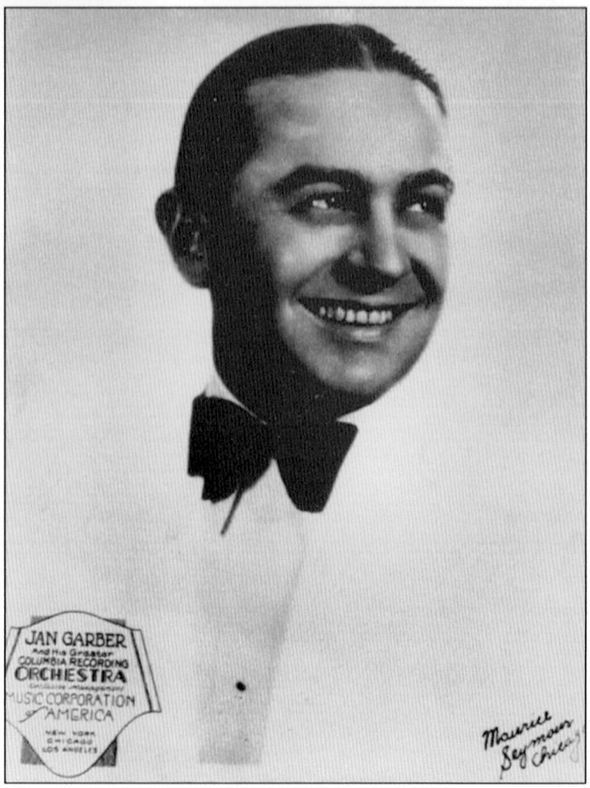

Big Band leader Jan Garber made his home in Shreveport after meeting a girl named Dorothy Comegys while performing on the rooftop terrace of the Washington-Youree Hotel in the 1920s. Dorothy would sometimes play with her husband's orchestra. Their daughter also became a band leader in California. Garber's band had one of the most distinctive sounds and was one of the most popular orchestras of the big band era.

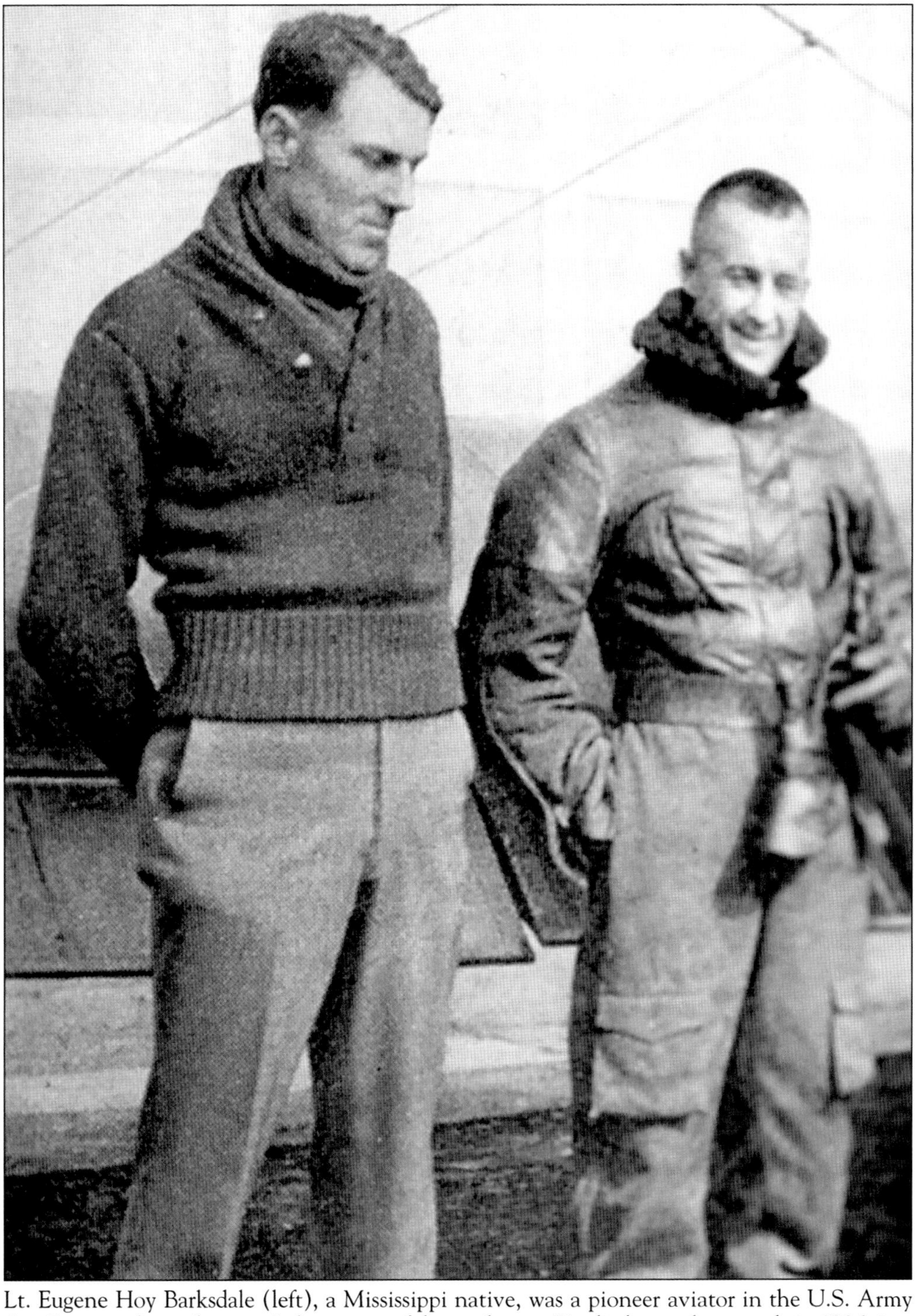

Lt. Eugene Hoy Barksdale (left), a Mississippi native, was a pioneer aviator in the U.S. Army Air Corps and was the army's first successful parachutist. He died in a plane crash in 1926, just three months short of his 29th birthday. When the Department of the Army decided to locate a new air field at Shreveport in 1928 it was named for Barksdale. Opened in 1933, Barksdale Army Air Field became Barksdale Air Force Base in 1947.

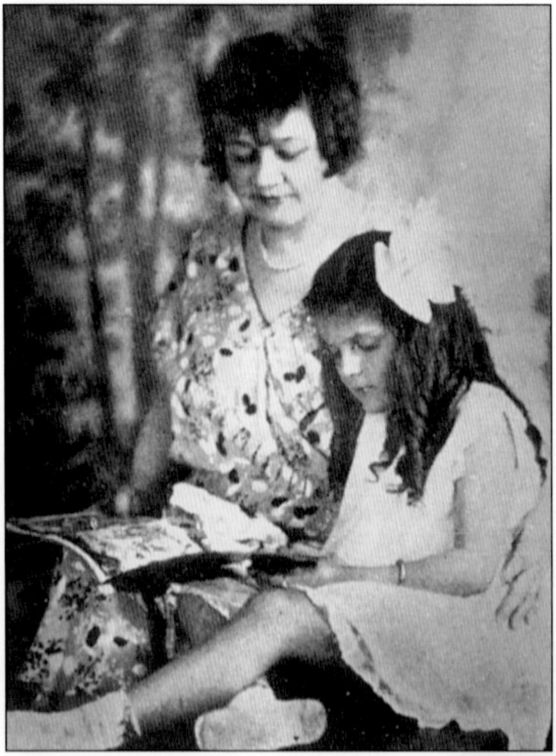

Adah Vinson DeLay, daughter of Mayor Richard Tucker Vinson and widow of *Times* editor Cyril Scott DeLay, was one of Shreveport's important early 20th-century philanthropists and a pioneer social worker. She was responsible for placing hundreds of orphaned and abandoned children in loving homes and outfitted the baby ward at Charity Hospital from her own pocket. Though raised in a well-to-do family, she died penniless in 1933 at the age of 64, having given all of her fortune to help needy children.

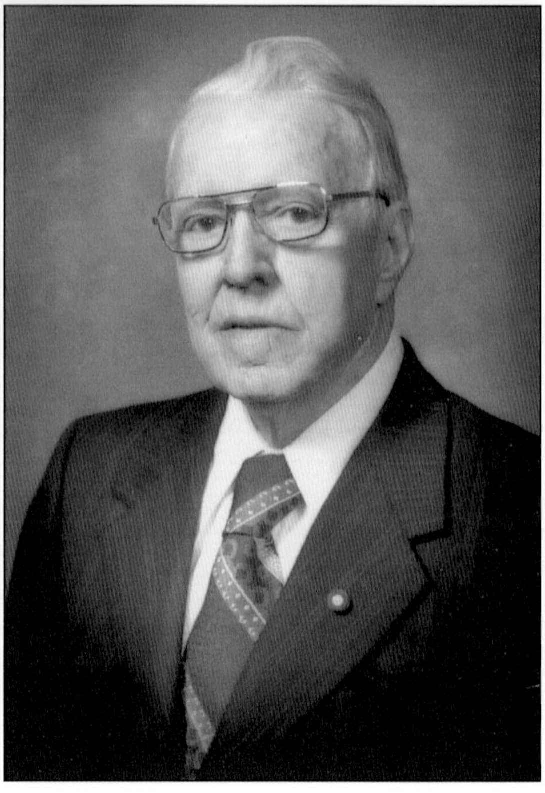

Dr. Willis Butler, for many years coroner of Caddo Parish, was an internationally known pioneer in the field of drug addiction maintenance. His work with morphine addicts in the 1920s and 1930s was the prototype for modern methadone treatment. Seen here in a 1977 photograph, Dr. Butler died in 1991 at the age of 103.

Huey Pierce Long, a Shreveport Lawyer, served as Railroad Commissioner of Louisiana and later as governor and U.S. Senator. He was one of the most influential figures in American politics in the early 1930s and was considered a strong opponent to FDR in the presidential race of 1936. He would have been, had he not been assassinated in Baton Rouge in September 1935. The photo below shows Long (third from left) with his wife and Bossier Parish dignitaries at the dedication of the Dixie-Overland Highway (Highway 80) in 1928.

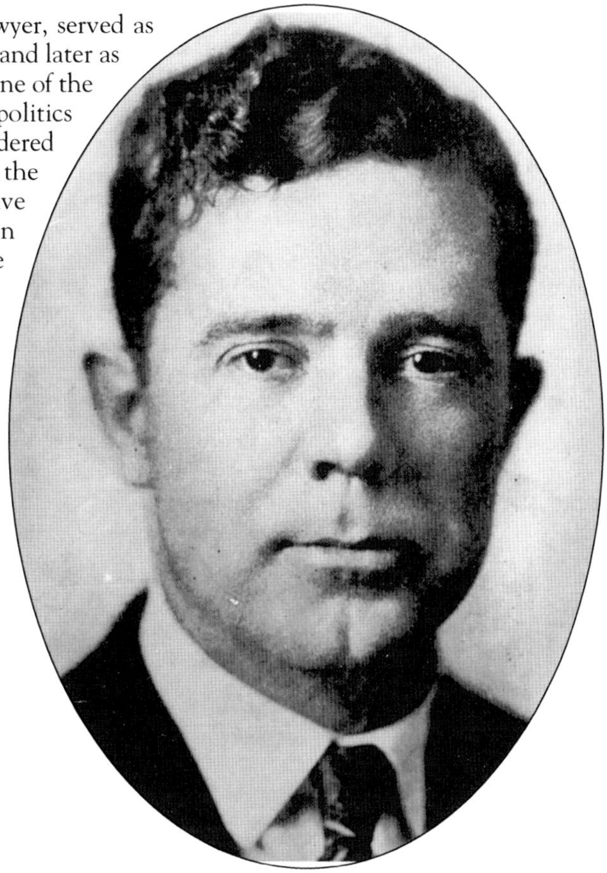

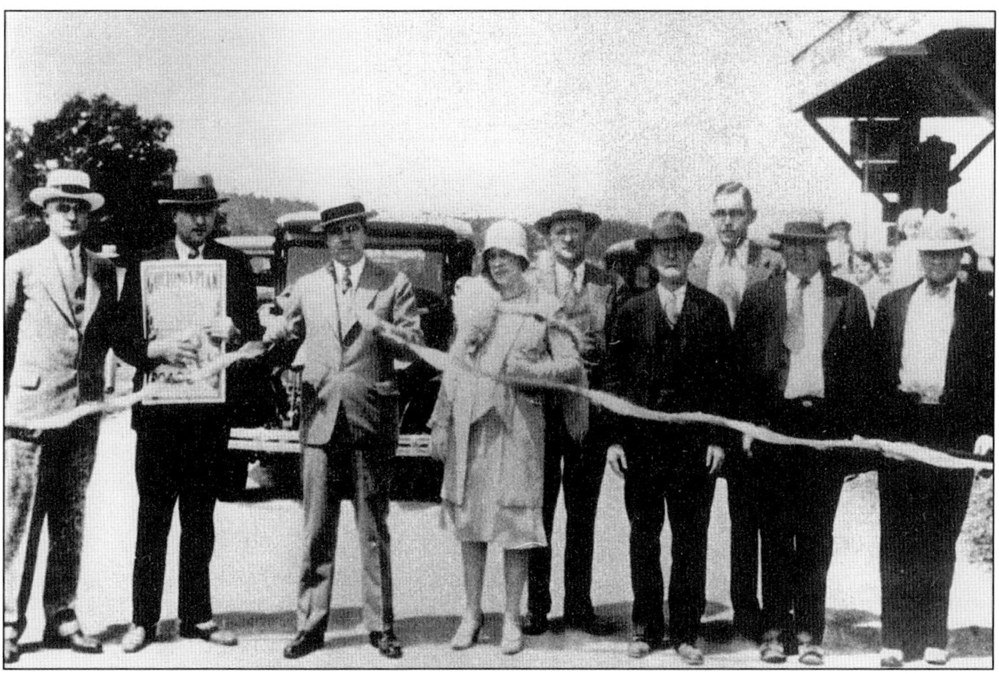

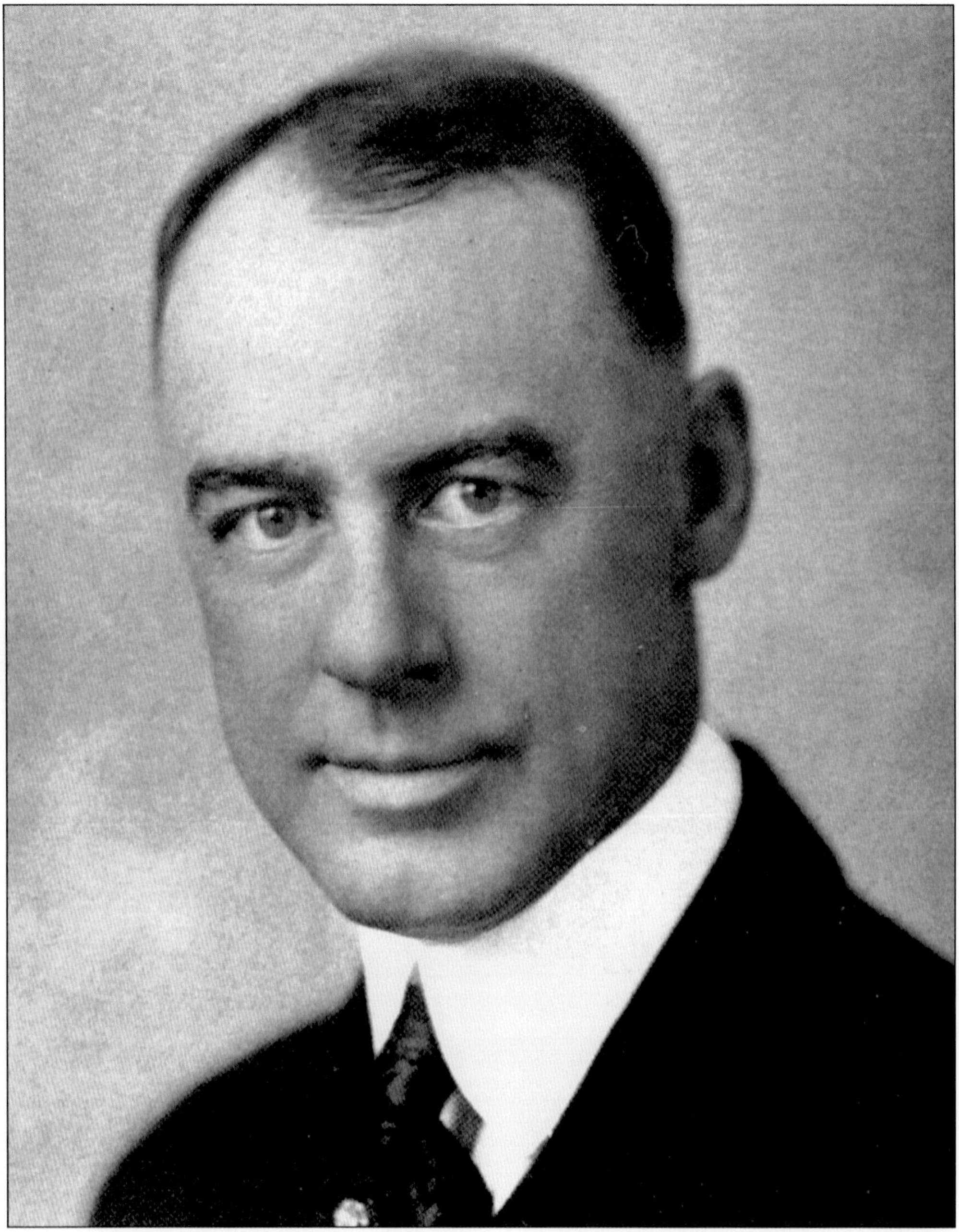

William Kennon Henderson was one of the most influential Shreveport businessmen of the 20th century. Owner of the Henderson Iron Works, founded by his father, Henderson's enterprises included the first auto dealership in the city (1907), radio (he founded KWKH radio—the call letters are his initials), banking, real estate, and other ventures. Henderson made and lost several fortunes during his influential career. He was known nationally for his radio broadcasts, which included his famous anti-chain store crusade. The FCC was established partly in response to complaints about the massive wattage being used to power his broadcasts, which could be clearly heard as far away as Canada. He died in 1945 and is buried at Greenwood Cemetery.

Sheriff Thomas Roland Hughes was well-known and well-liked but is perhaps best remembered today because of Huddie "Lead Belly" Ledbetter's song "Mr. Tom Hughes's Town." Sheriff Hughes served from 1916 to 1940 during which time he participated in the hunt for Bonnie and Clyde, the capture of the infamous "Butterfly Man" murderer of Shreveport (both in 1934), and oversaw the last execution in Caddo Parish. He died in 1965.

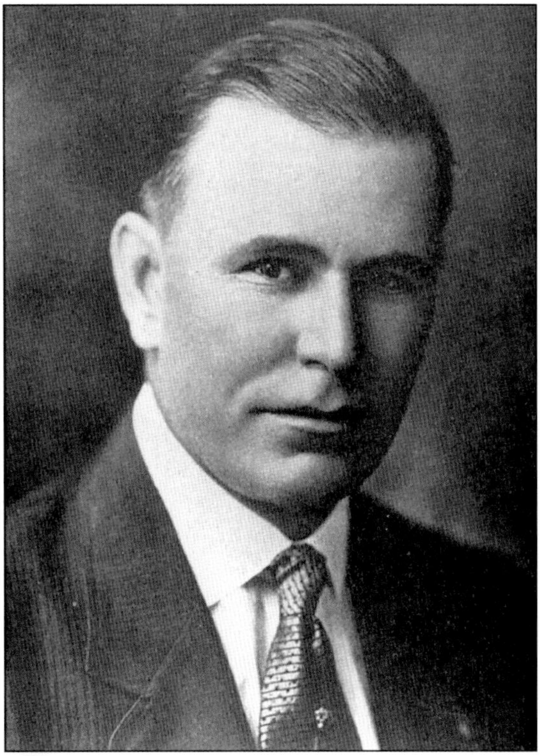

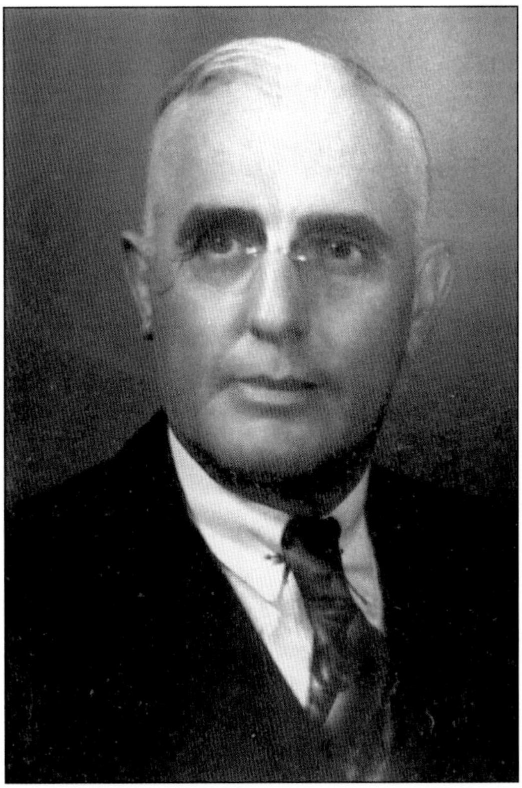

Samuel Guy Sample was one of the city's leading business figures of the early 20th century. In addition to being in the fertilizer and cotton seed oil business, Sample was also involved in the lumber business and in banking. A director of Commercial National Bank from 1909 until his death in 1943, Sample also served as the bank's president in 1921.

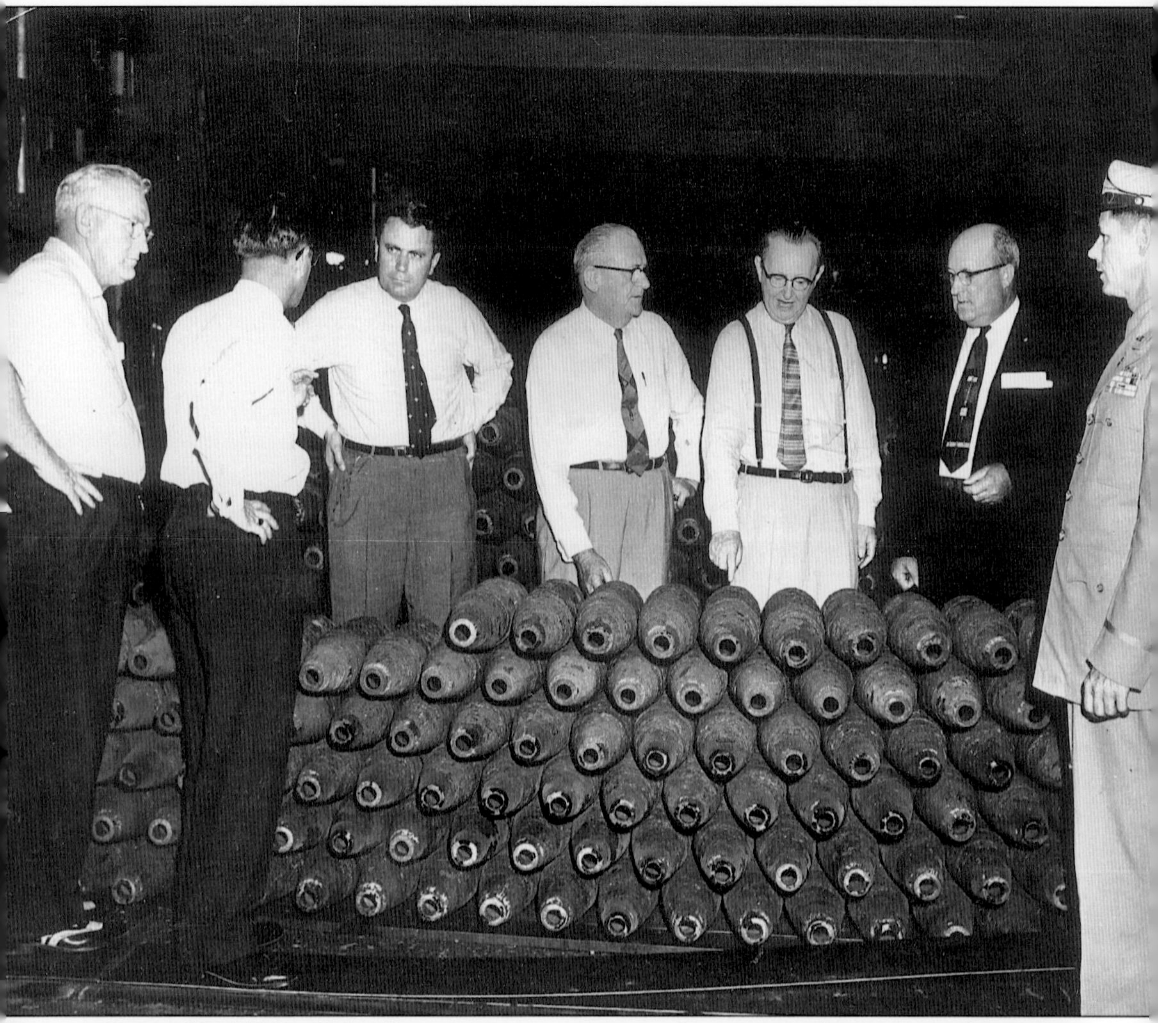

During World War II the Shreveport area saw tremendous growth, due in no small measure to the presence of Barksdale Army Air Field, Fort Polk, and several munitions factories, the largest of which were the Brewster and Beaird Companies. These companies built many of the bombs that fell on Nazi Europe. Here Congressman T. Overton Brooks (fifth from left) looks over shells being readied for the war effort.

Among the many thousands of servicemen stationed at Shreveport during World War II was actor James Stewart, seen here during an interview at Barksdale Air Force Base.

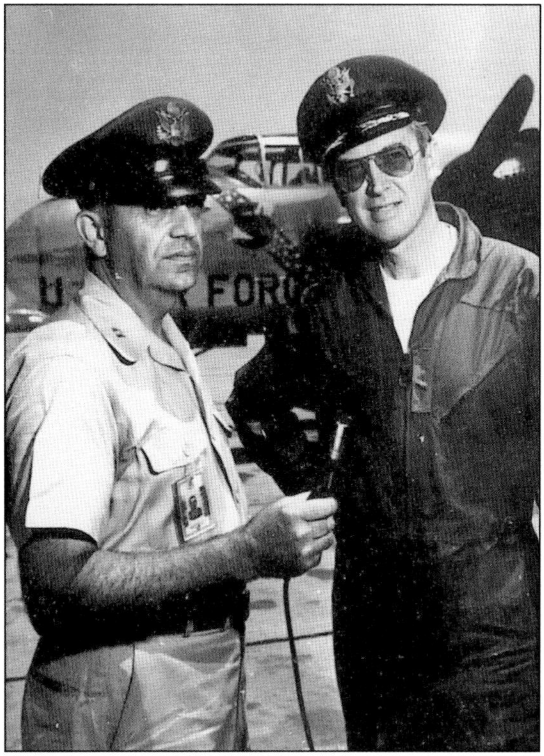

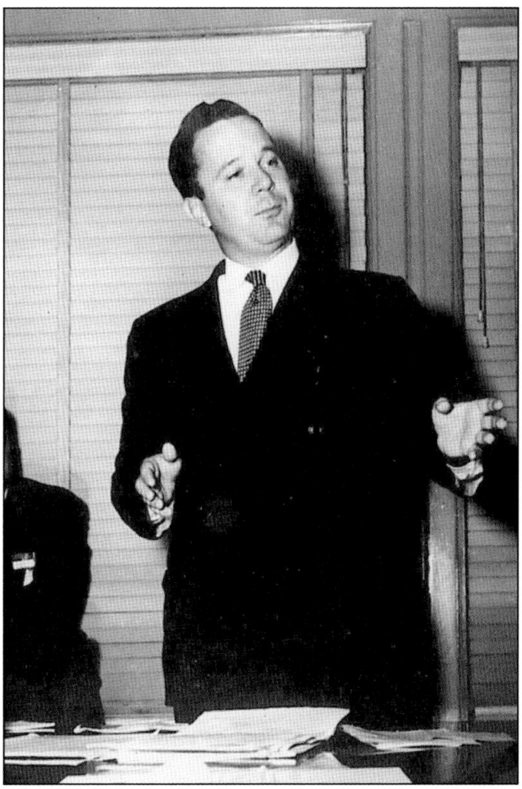

Sen. Russell Long, son of Huey P. Long and a Shreveport native, took office in 1949 and remained in the Senate until his retirement in 1987.

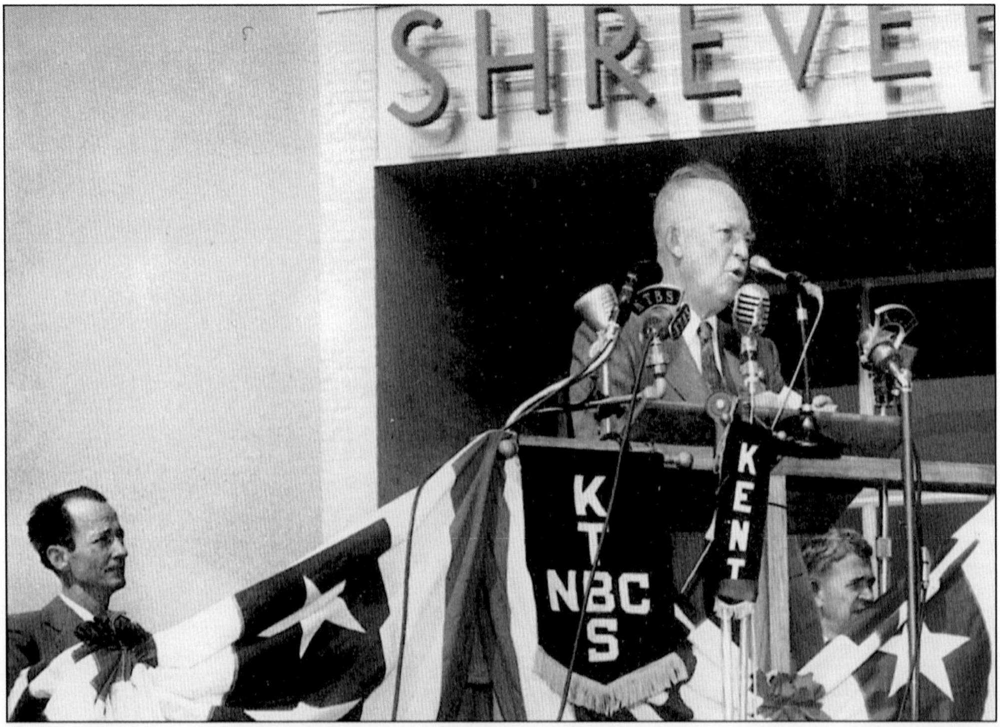

(Above) Mayor Clyde Fant was one of Shreveport's longest serving mayors (1946–1954 and 1958–1972). Here he listens to President Eisenhower during a campaign stop at the Shreveport airport. Fant Parkway is named in his honor. (Below) Mayor James Gardner served from 1954 to 1958 and was the third youngest mayor in the city's history and youngest during the 20th century (elected at age 29). He served as a state representative before becoming mayor and as a city councilman after. He is seen at left being made an honorary Caddo Indian.

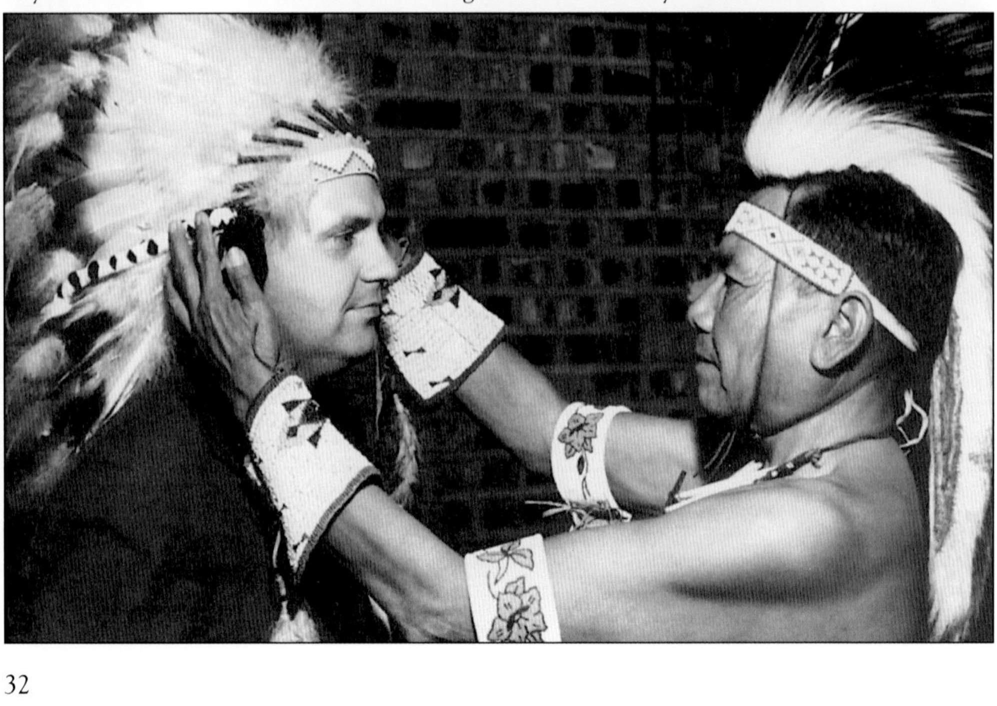

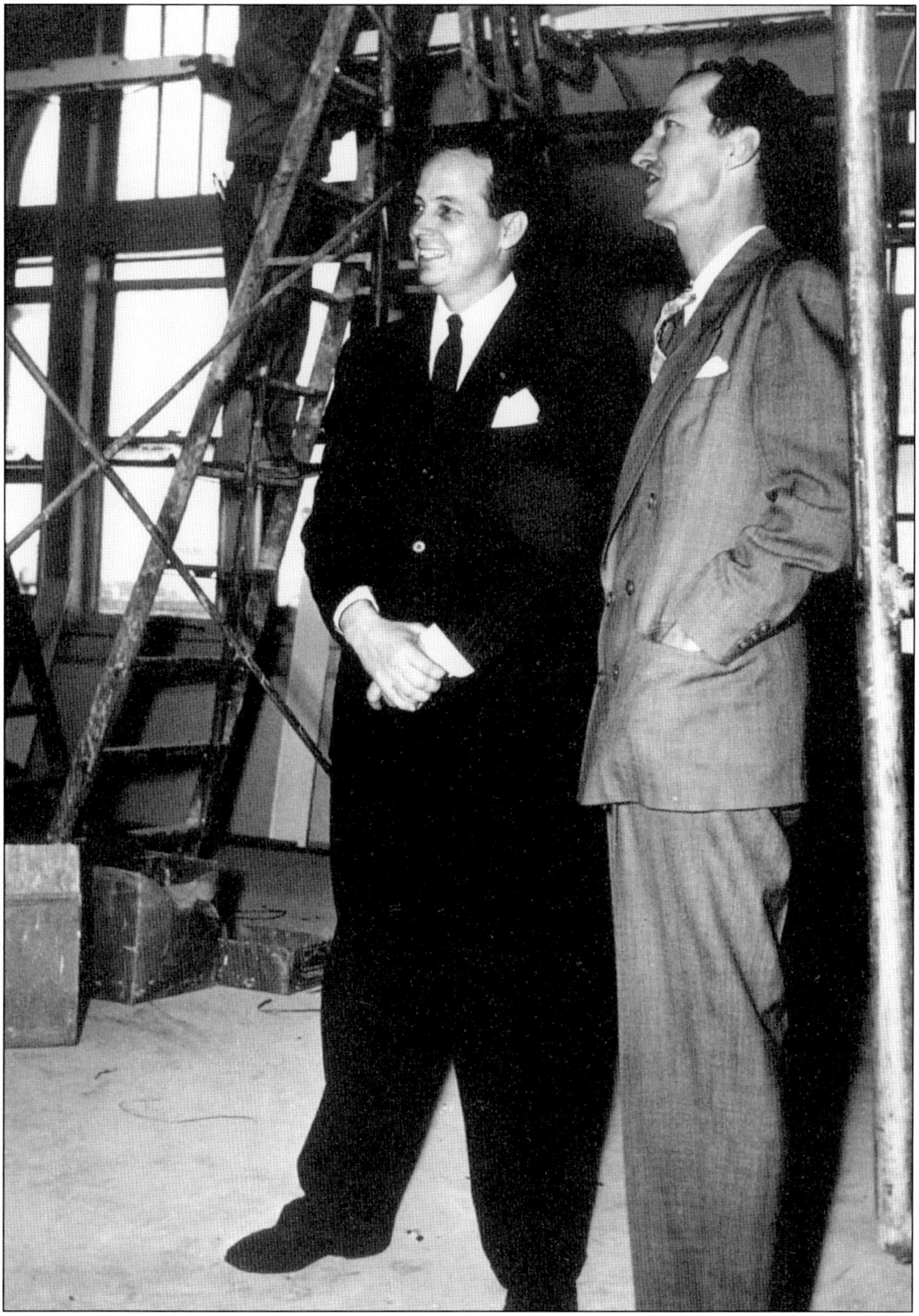

Mayor Fant (right) confers with New Orleans Mayor deLessups "Chep" Morrison during remodeling at Shreveport's old city hall, at the northwest corner of Milam and Louisiana Streets, about 1950. City hall would move to Texas Avenue at Murphy Street in 1954 (now the police complex) and to 500 Travis Street in 2000.

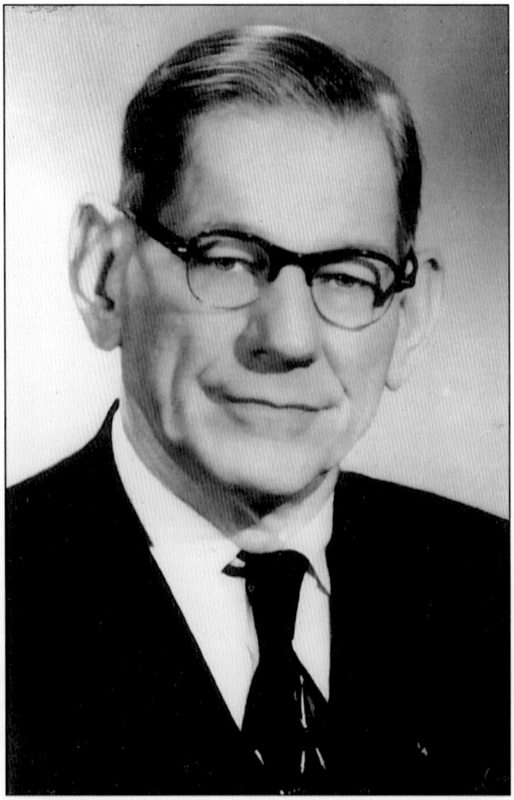

(Left) Joseph Howell Flournoy served as Caddo Sheriff from 1939 to 1966 and was considered one of the most innovative sheriffs in the department's history. His father, Pat Flournoy, and grandfather, Alonzo Flournoy, had also served as sheriffs of Caddo Parish. (Below) As the civil rights struggle heated up during the 1950s and early 1960s, law enforcement was not always on the side of justice. In 1963, Rev. Harry Blake of Mt. Caanan Baptist Church, a field representative for the Southern Christian Leadership Conference (SCLC), was seriously beaten by the police after a meeting at Little Union Baptist Church on Milam Street.

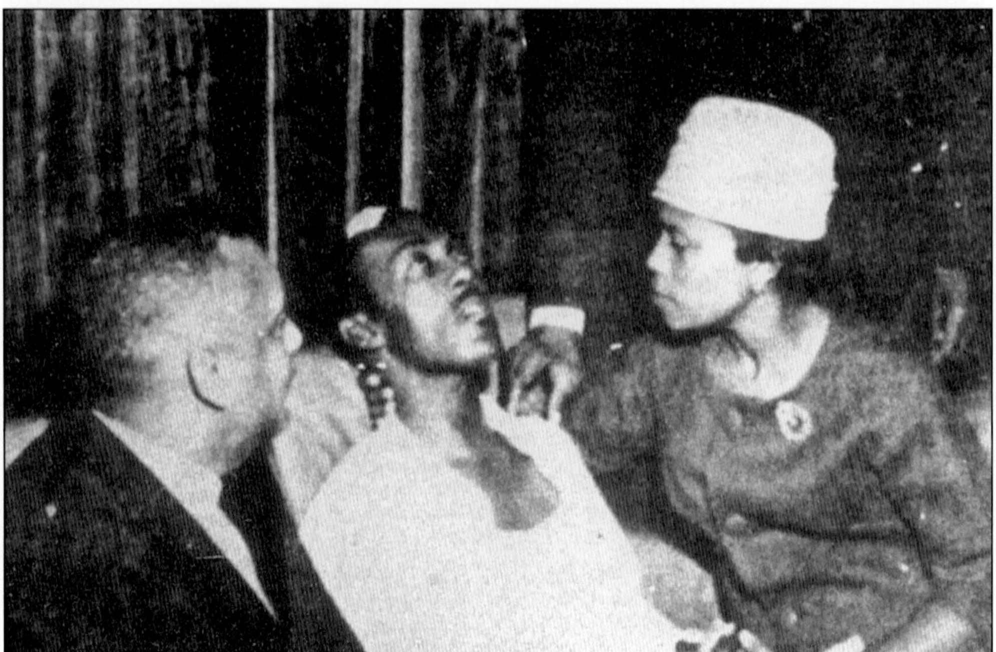

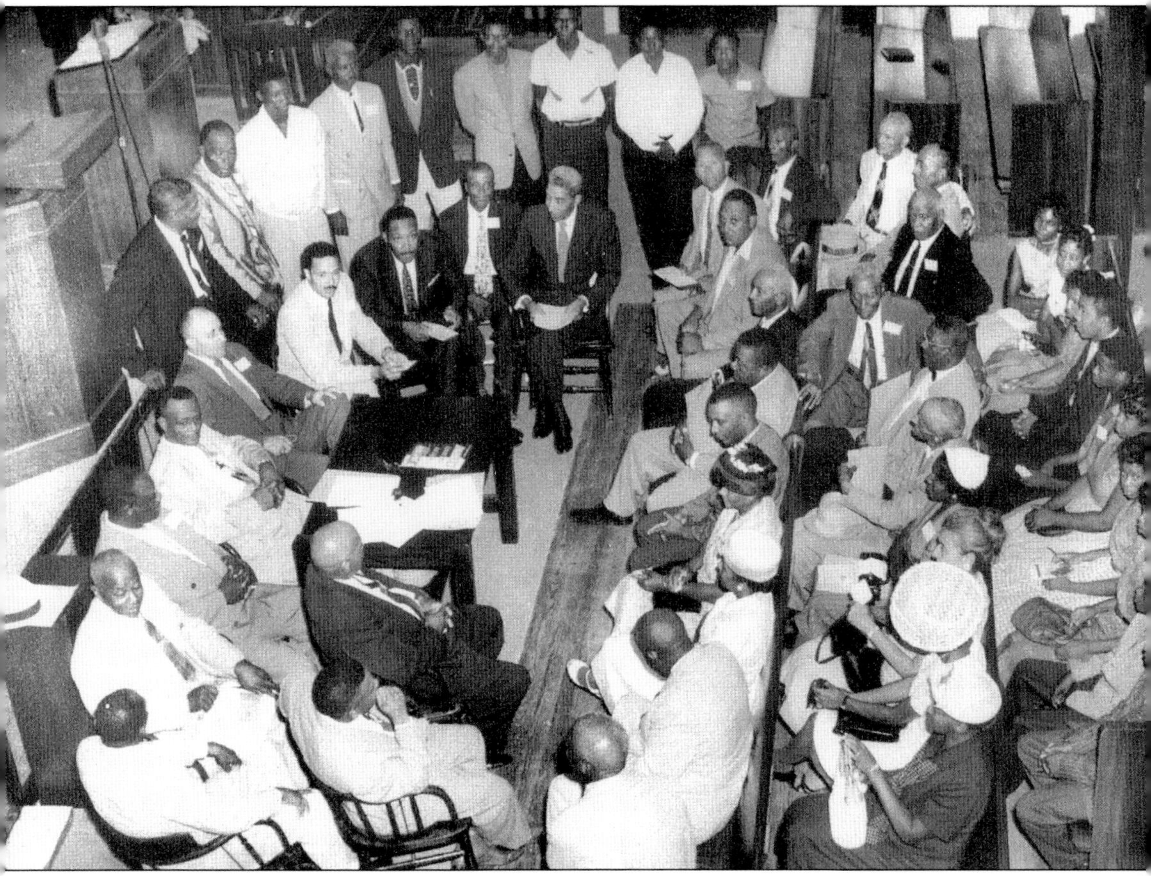

On August 14, 1958, Dr. Martin Luther King Jr. spoke at Shreveport's Galilee Baptist Church during a workshop on voting rights. Over 500 people attended the meeting and almost all the vehicles parked outside were ticketed or vandalized (despite being across the street from the police station). Dr. King, who was president of the SCLC, was invited to Shreveport by Dr. C.O. Simpkins, who was then a vice president of the SCLC and president of the United Christian Movement. Dr. J.T. Stewart, pastor of Galilee, asked King to speak there after Avenue Baptist Church refused, fearing retribution. Dr. Simpkins recorded the whole speech—the earliest King speech to be taped in its entirety. Here Simpkins (in light jacket with dark tie, upper left-hand quadrant of photo) is seated next to King (dark jacket, holding a paper; he is to the right of Simpkins).

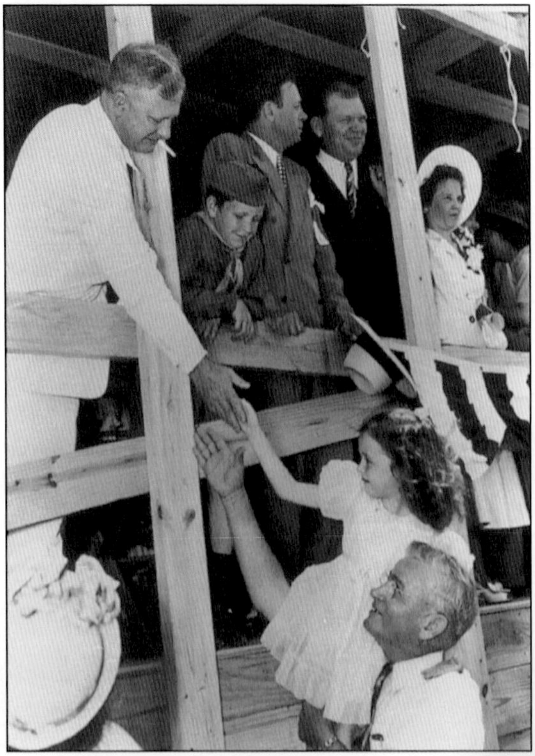

(Left) The flamboyant Gov. Earl K. Long, younger brother of the late Gov. Huey P. Long, greets local citizens in 1948. Another governor, Jimmie Davis, stands to the right of the boy scout next to Long. Long's wife, Blanche, is at right in the light dress and hat. (Below) Prince Tiao Savang of Cambodia (right) visits his friend Jean Despujols of Shreveport. Despujols had been an artist for the French government in Indochina in the 1920s and 1930s. His work was widely published and he was the recipient of numerous awards. He died in Shreveport in 1965 and is buried at Greenwood Cemetery.

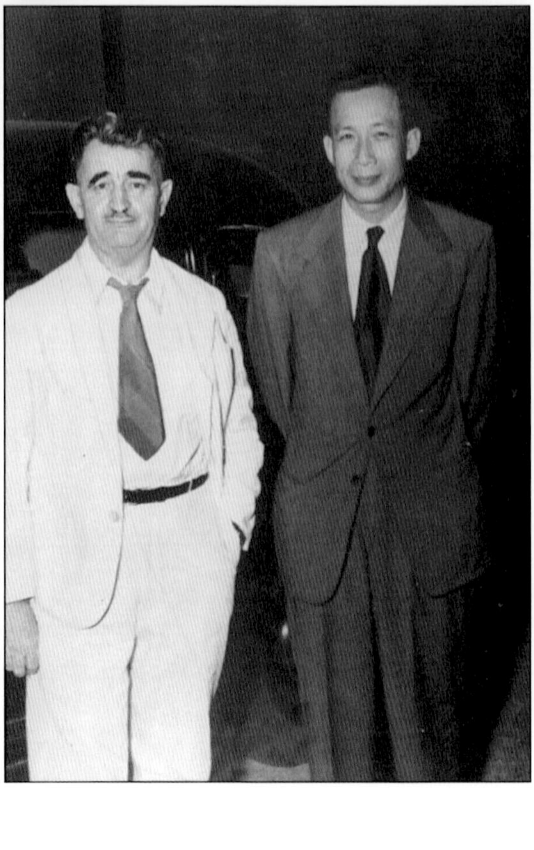

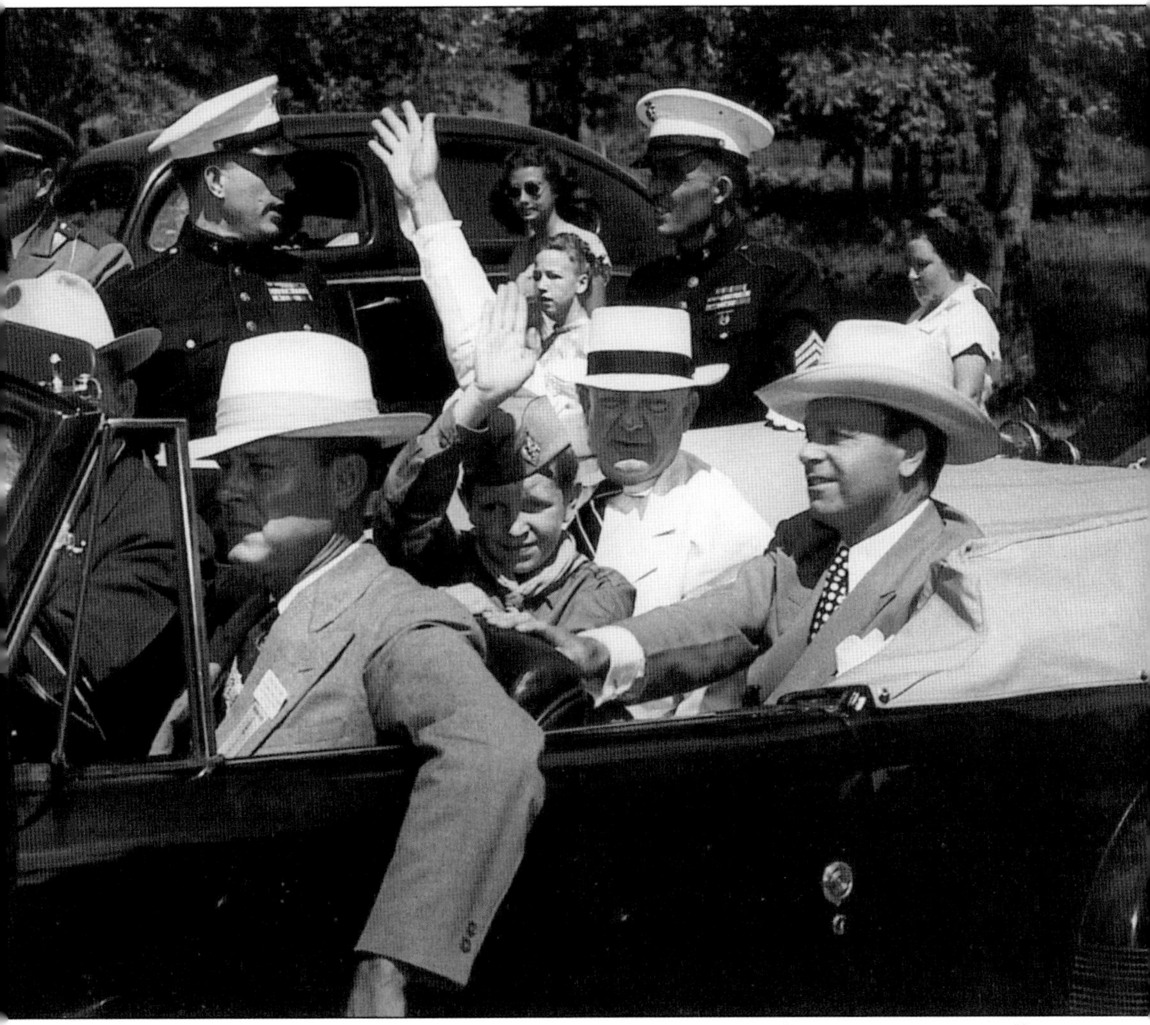

Outgoing governor Jimmie Davis (right) and incoming governor Earl Long, returning to office after an eight-year absence, greet crowds in May 1948. In 1960 Davis would return to the governor's mansion, succeeding Long, who died that same year. Louisiana governors who called the Shreveport area home were Thomas Overton Moore, Henry Watkins Allen, Newton Crain Blanchard, Ruffin G. Pleasant, Huey P. Long, James Houston Davis, Robert F. Kennon, and Charles "Buddy" Roemer.

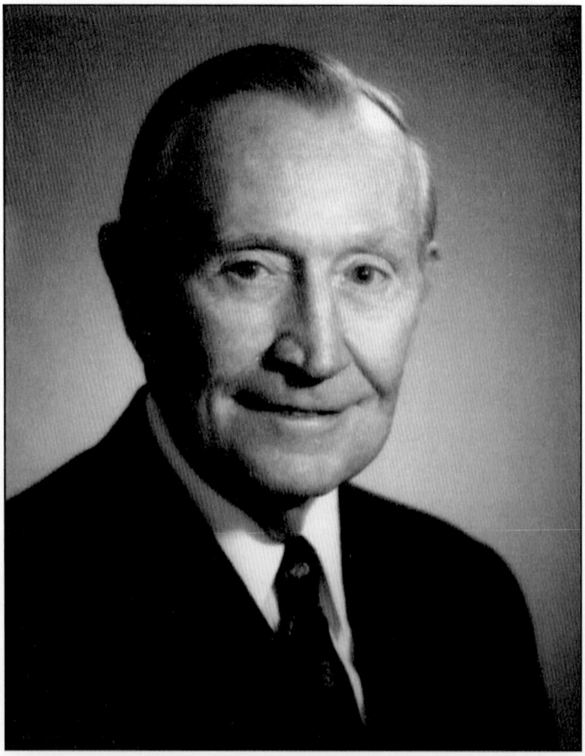

One of the most significant 20th-century Shreveport developers was Noah Oscar Thomas. N.O. Thomas laid out and developed large tracts of real estate in the city including sections of Pierremont, South Highlands, Glenwood, Madison Park, and Broadmoor as well as all of Sunset Acres and sections of west Shreveport. The present city hall was built by Thomas for First Federal Savings and Loan Company in 1980–1981 and is still often referred to as the N.O. Thomas Plaza.

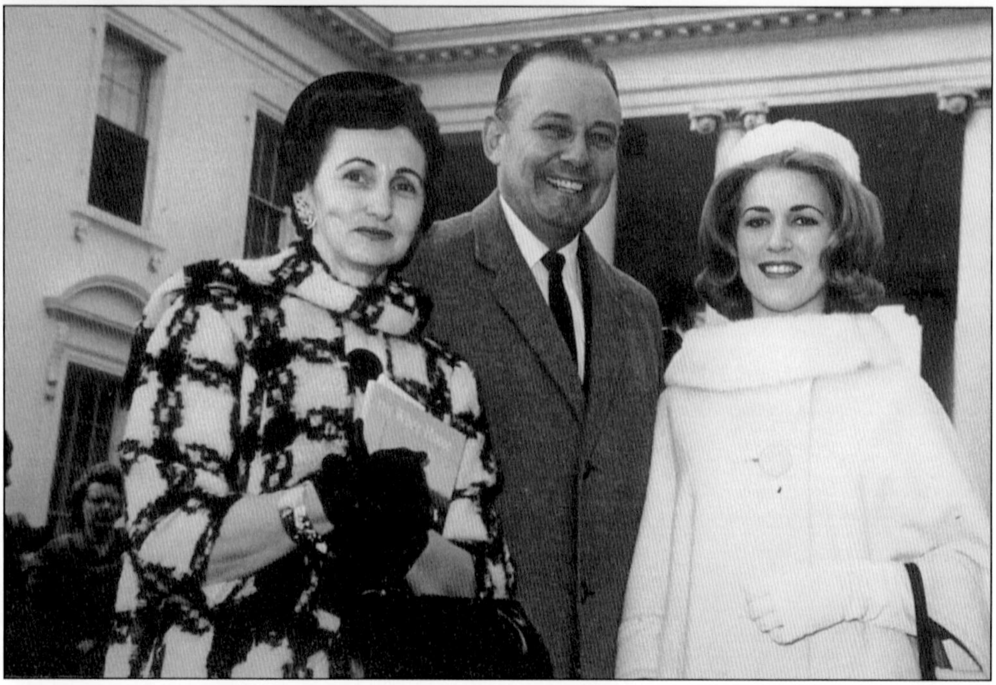

Congressman Joe D. Waggonner represented the Fourth District from 1963 to 1981. Here he is seen in front of the White House in Washington, DC, with his wife and Miss Dianne Catanese of Shreveport in February 1963.

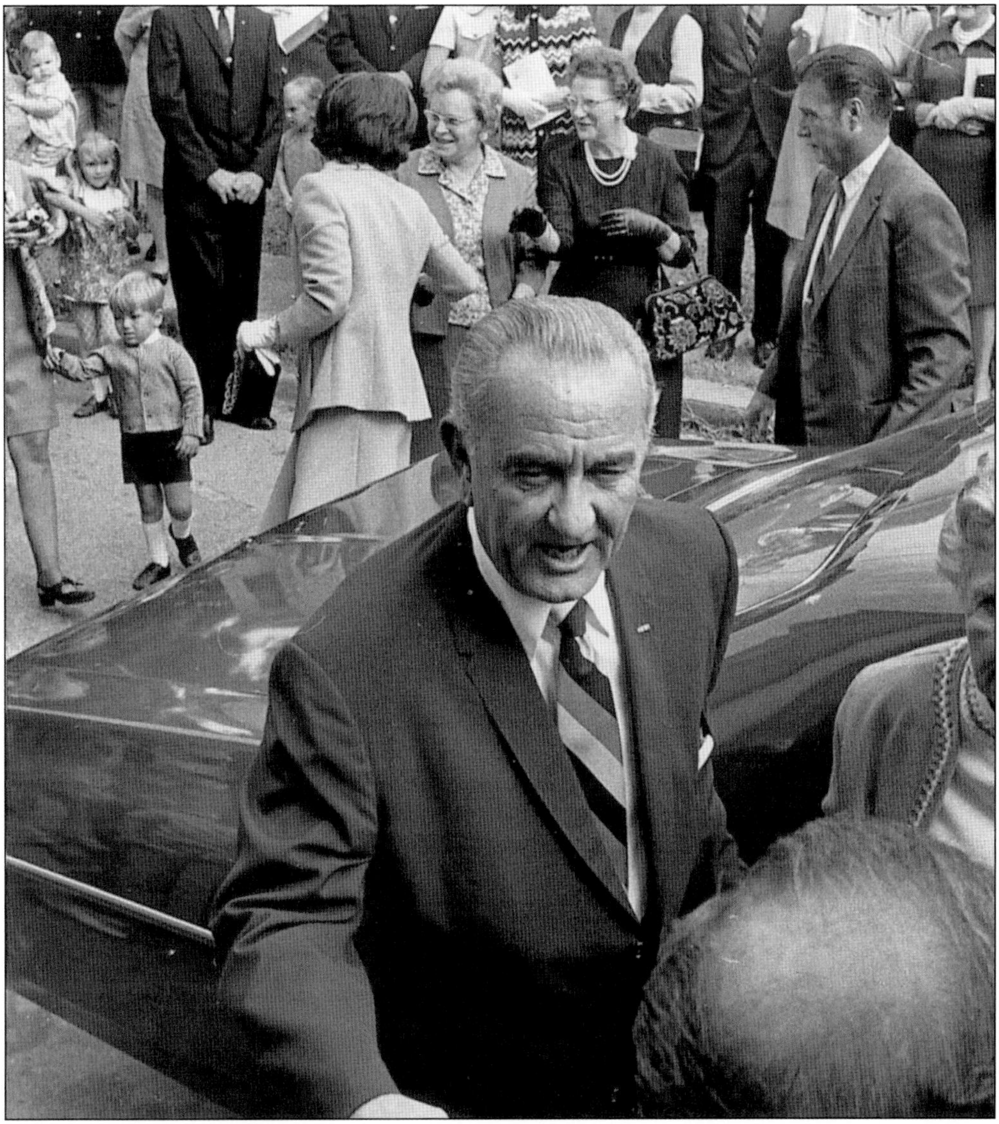

President Lyndon B. Johnson, whose wife Ladybird was from Karnack, Texas, just west of Shreveport, greets well-wishers on a visit to Shreveport in October 1969. Many presidents, including all who served in the second half of the 20th century, have visited the city—several on multiple occasions.

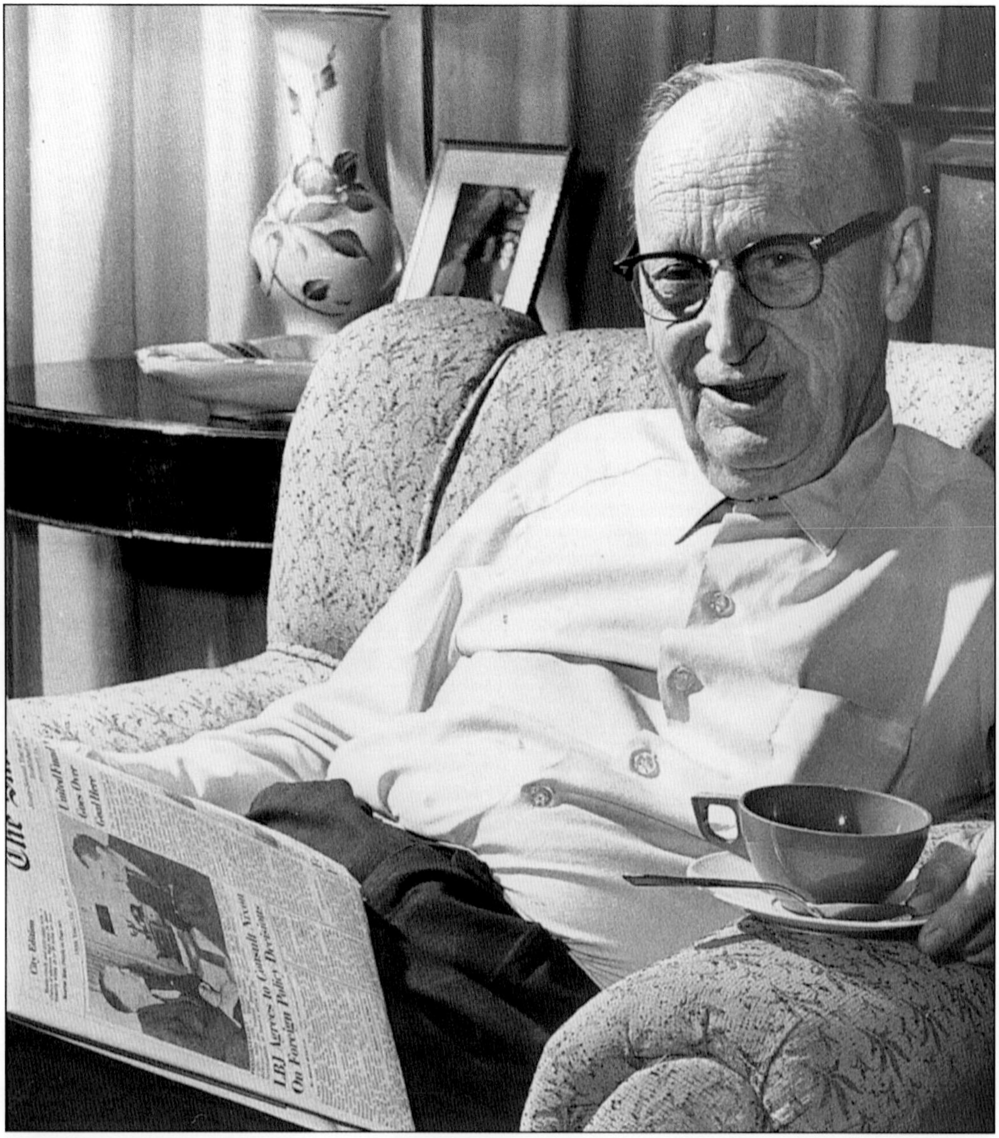

John Thomas Scopes, the Tennessee teacher who was prosecuted (and persecuted) for teaching evolution in his public school classroom in 1925, later became a petroleum geologist and relocated to Shreveport where he lived until his death in 1971. Scopes is seen here during a rare interview in 1968 at his home on Moss Point Drive, along the south shore of Cross Lake.

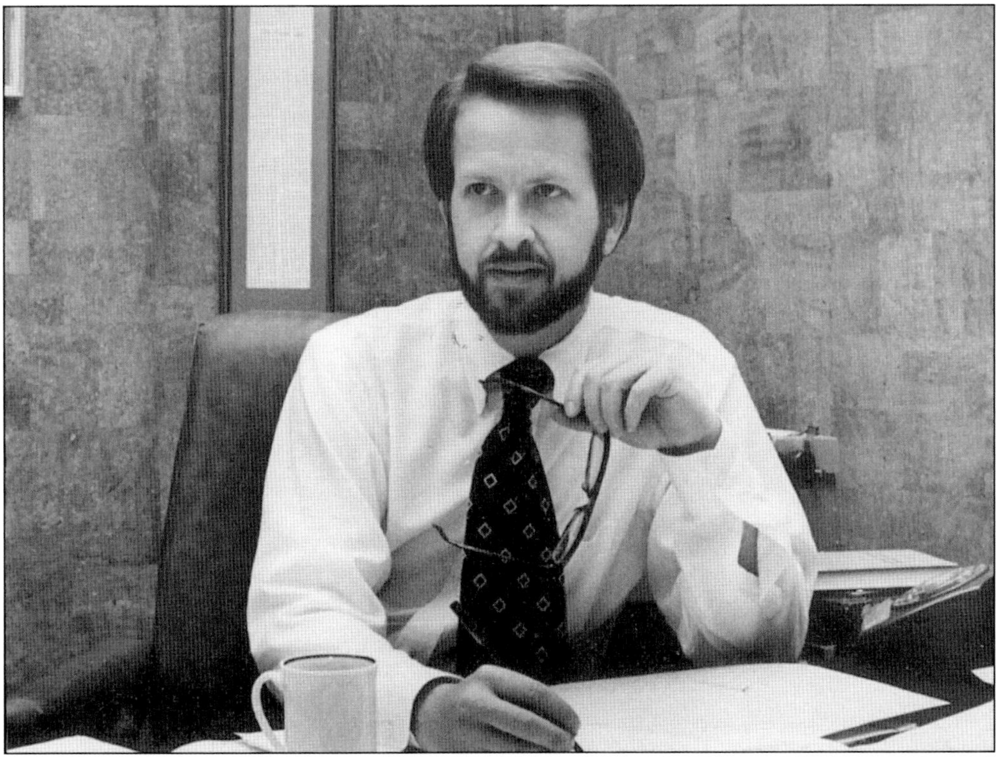

A number of notable journalists have come from Shreveport. Among these are Jim Montgomery (above), editor of the *Shreveport Times* for many years and later editor of the *Shreveport Journal*, and Paul Greenberg (right), a nationally syndicated editorial columnist and Pulitzer Prize winner. Other noted journalists who have lived in this area are Pulitzer Prize–winning reporter John Craig Flournoy and television commentator Larry King, a New Yorker who resided in Bossier City in the early 1970s.

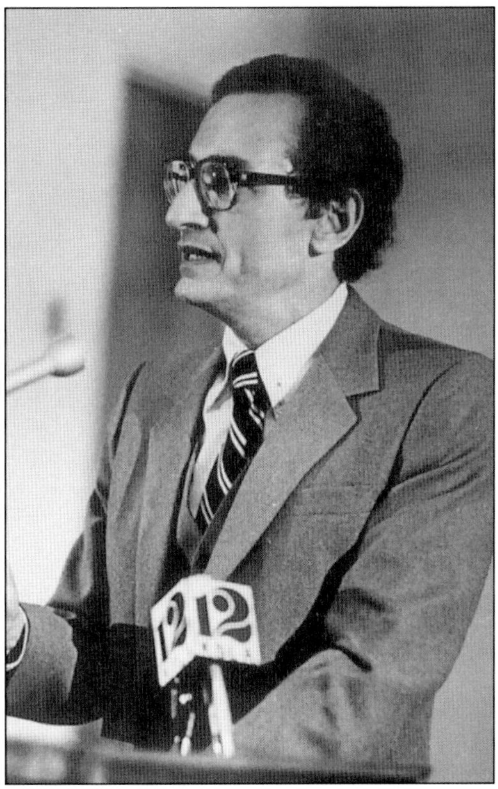

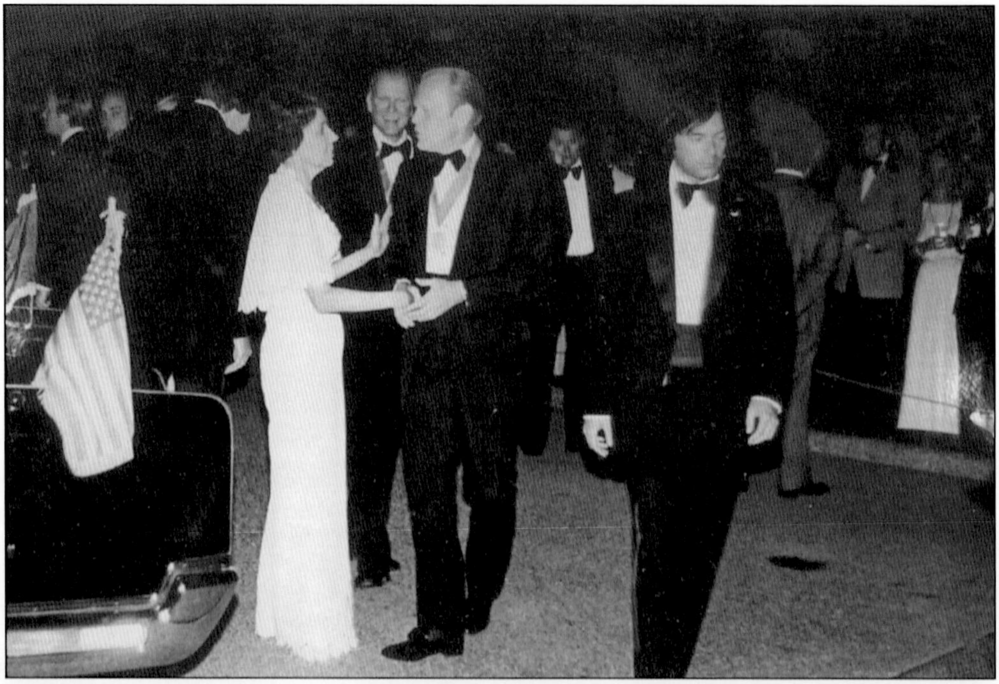

President Gerald R. Ford's April 1976 visit to Shreveport was marked by a reception at the home of oilman Dalton Woods on Ellerbe Road. Ford was made an honorary member of the Holiday in Dixie Ambassadors Club and is seen here wearing the Ambassadors medallion.

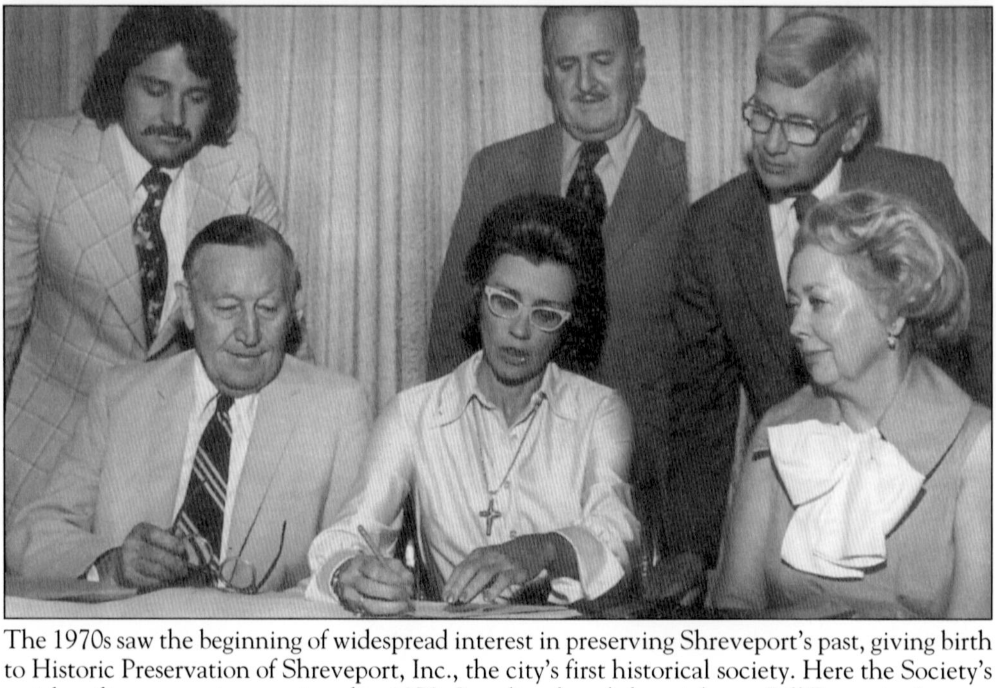

The 1970s saw the beginning of widespread interest in preserving Shreveport's past, giving birth to Historic Preservation of Shreveport, Inc., the city's first historical society. Here the Society's articles of incorporation are signed in 1973. Standing from left to right are Bill Fountain, Jacques Steineau, and historian Goodloe R. Stuck. Seated from left to right are N.O. Thomas, Barbara Railsback, and Louise Querbes.

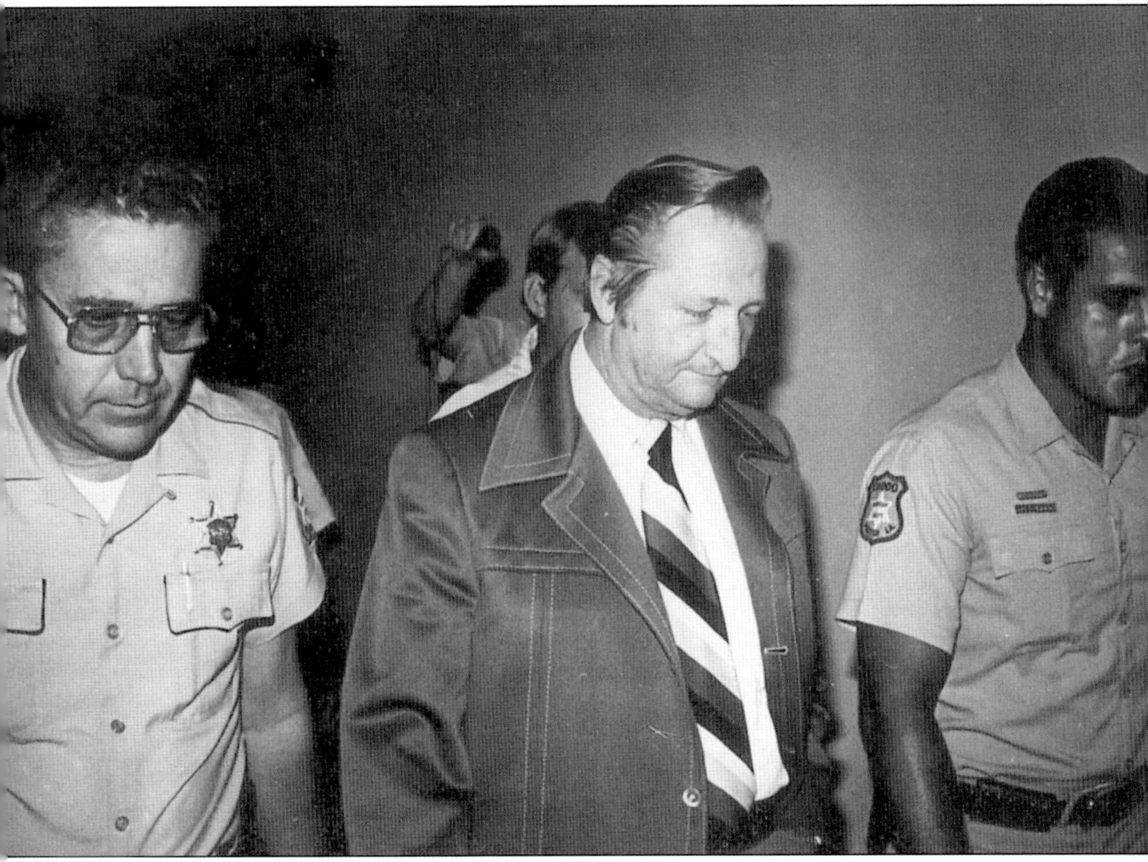

George D'Artois, who started out as a sheriff's deputy and ended up a political boss, saw his notorious career come to an end with his arrest on August 6, 1976 for conspiracy to murder Shreveport ad man Jim Leslie. Leslie, who was threatening to expose D'Artois, was gunned down in Baton Rouge a short time earlier. D'Artois was then, ironically, Commissioner of Public Safety for Shreveport. He was at the same time feared, loathed, and by many admired for his brutal tactics in keeping crime rates low. The same tactics, however, were used to build his career and influence the careers of those around him for good or ill. He was particularly disliked in the black community for his violent and successful repression of the civil rights movement in Shreveport. D'Artois, here flanked by deputies Bob Poston (left) and Lee Roy Coleman (right), never went to trial. He died of a heart attack in 1977 at the age of 52.

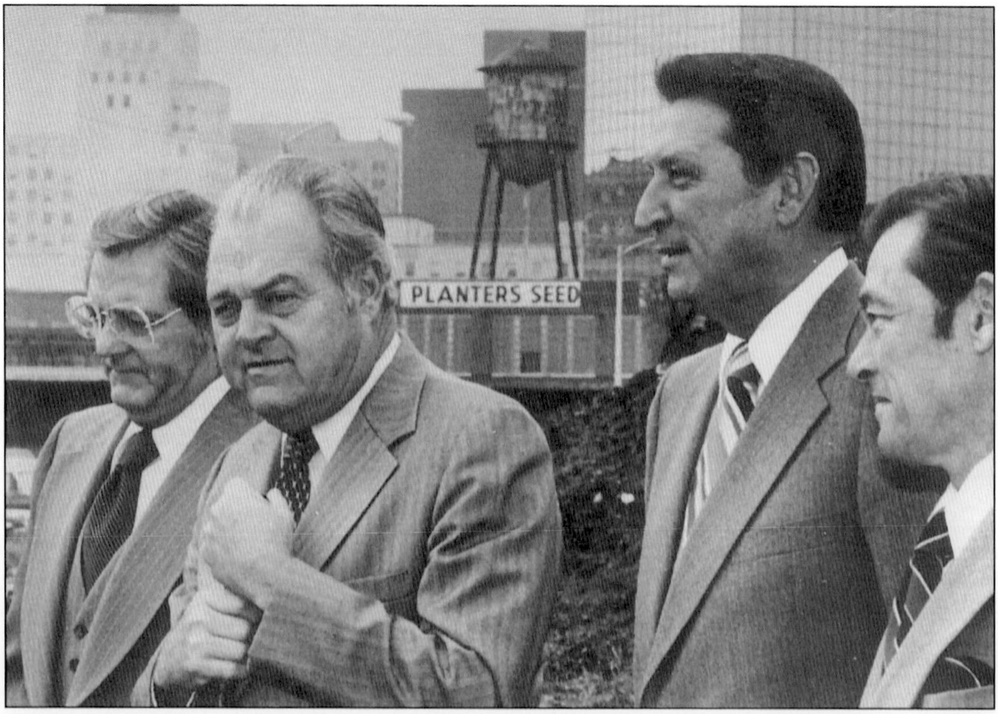

Pictured from left to right, Mayor-elect Bill Hanna, Mayor L. Calhoun Allen, Commissioner (and later Sheriff) Don Hathaway, and attorney Billy Guin gather on the riverfront to break ground for a new Exposition Hall on November 21, 1978. The Expo Hall was later renamed as a memorial to Mayor Allen.

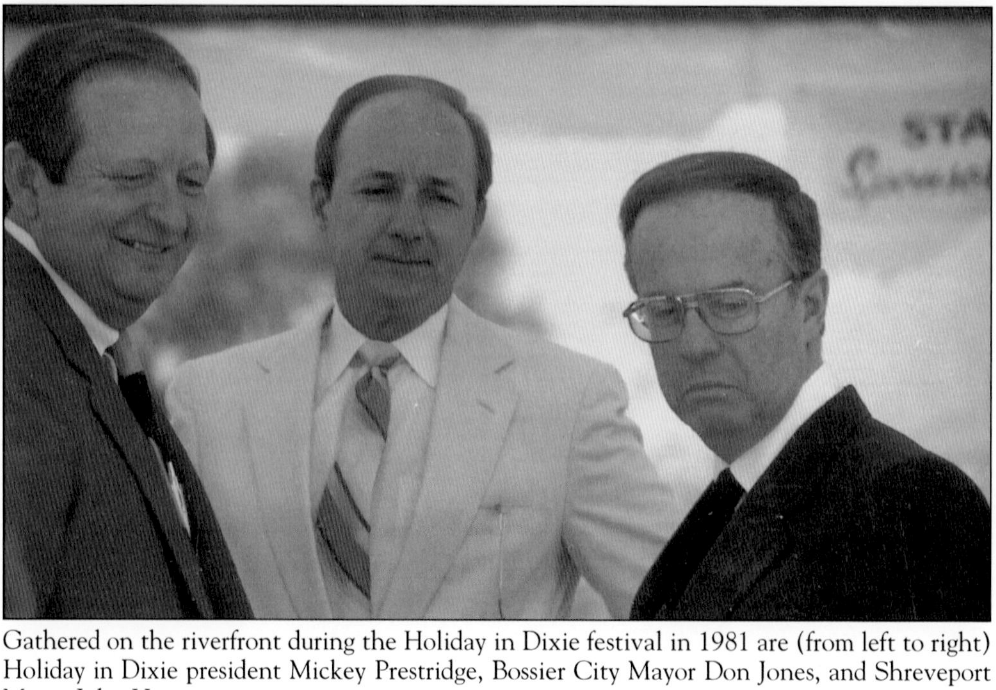

Gathered on the riverfront during the Holiday in Dixie festival in 1981 are (from left to right) Holiday in Dixie president Mickey Prestridge, Bossier City Mayor Don Jones, and Shreveport Mayor John Hussey.

Judy Gallagher Purgeson (later Durham) was executive assistant to Mayor John Hussey in the early 1980s and a decade later became chief administrative officer of Caddo Parish. She was forced from office on trumped up charges of malfeasance but was later exonerated. The incident did irreparable harm to her career and cast doubts on the credibility of the Parish Commissioners who had pushed for her removal, arguably, in order to further their own political agendas.

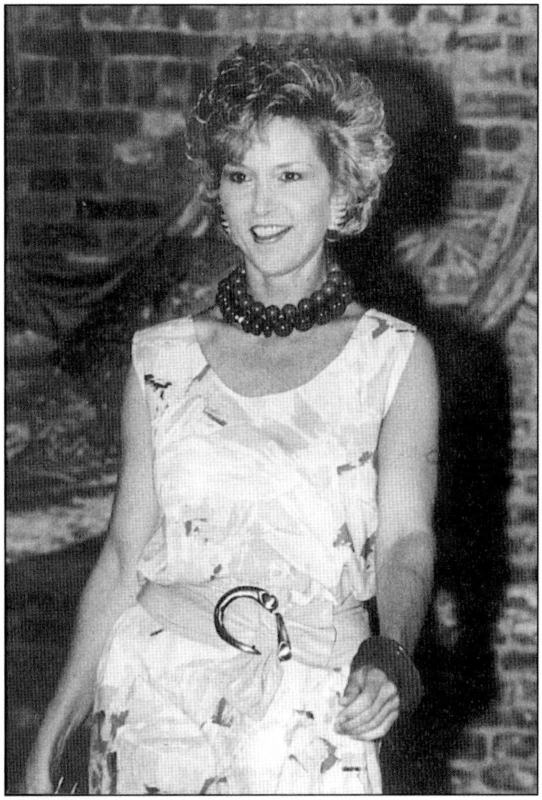

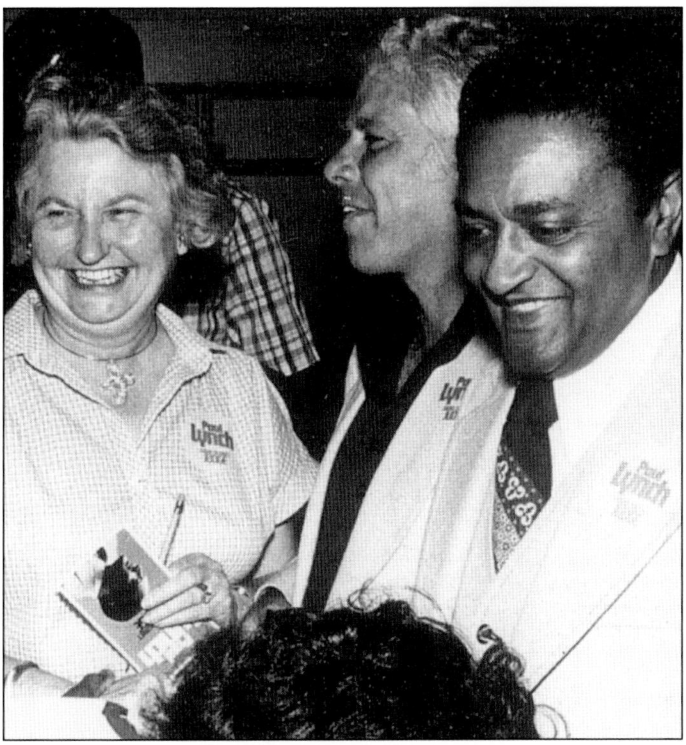

In 1978 former Assistant U.S. Attorney Paul Lynch (left) became the first black district court judge in Shreveport's history. He died suddenly at age 47 only four years later. Here he is seen with supporters State Senator Virginia Shehee and local businessman Donald Zadeck (center) at his victory party. The Paul Lynch Park in north Shreveport is named for Judge Lunch, who is buried at Carver Cemetery in southwest Shreveport.

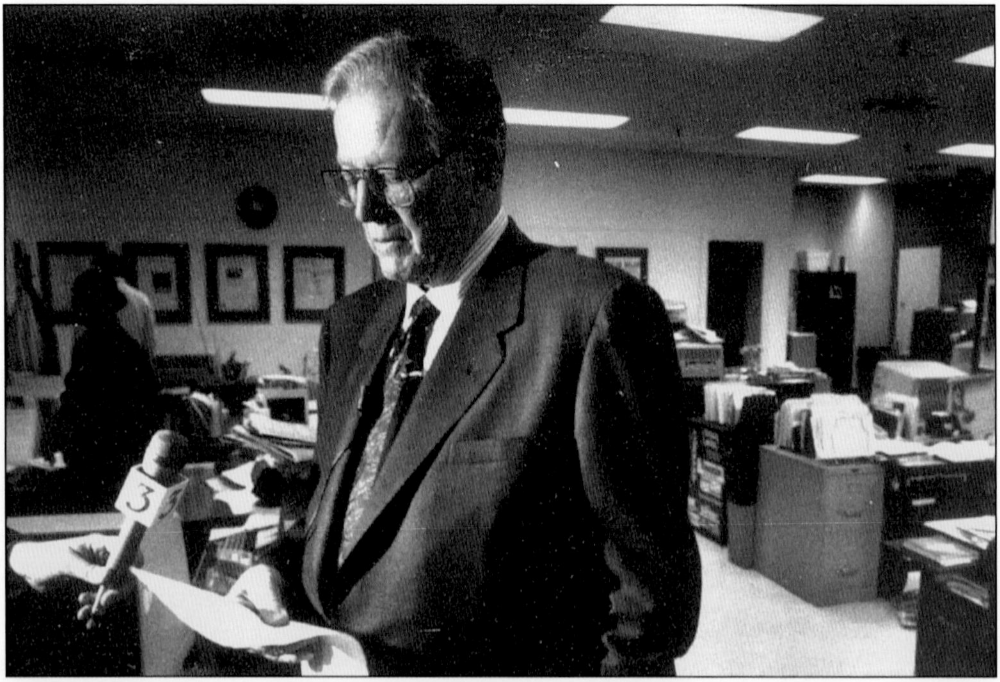

Among outstanding influences in Shreveport's business and cultural life in the late 20th century are the names of Dr. Charles T. Beaird (above), and James "Sunny" Noel (below). Beaird, publisher of the *Shreveport Journal* from 1976 to 2000, is widely recognized for his civic contributions. Noel donated his huge collection of nearly 400,000 books to LSU in Shreveport as the nucleus of the Noel Memorial Library. The collection includes many rare and extraordinary volumes.

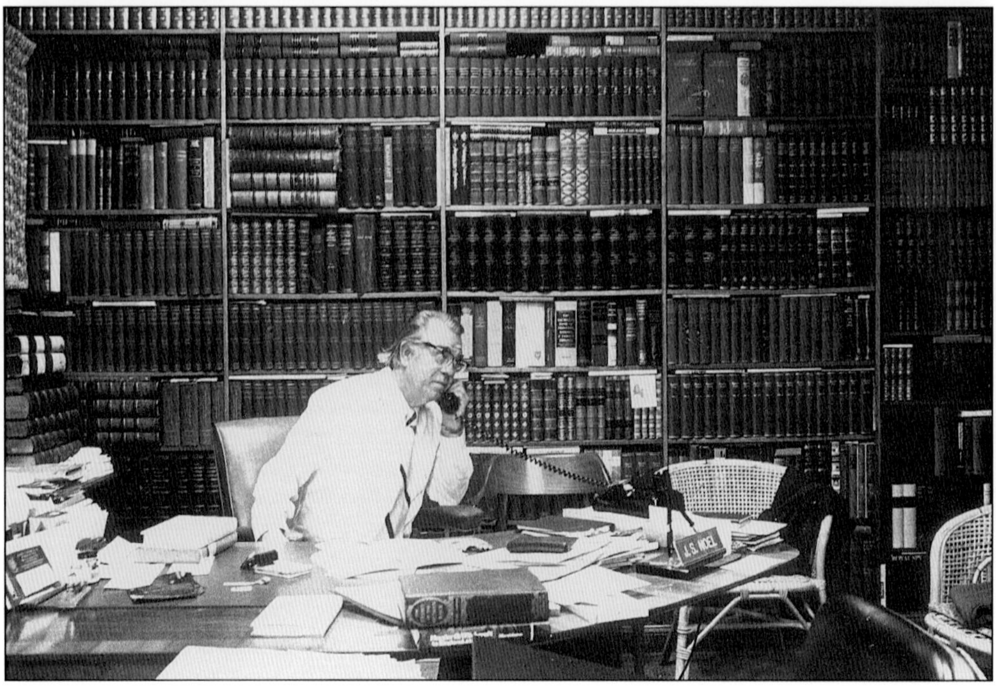

Robert Oakley of Shreveport has served as U.S. Ambassador to Zaire, Pakistan, and Somalia. Other ambassadors from Shreveport include George Williamson (Costa Rica, Honduras, Guatemala, Nicaragua, El Salvador), Baxter Rand (Venezuela), William A. Seay (Bolivia), and Richard H. Jones (Lebanon).

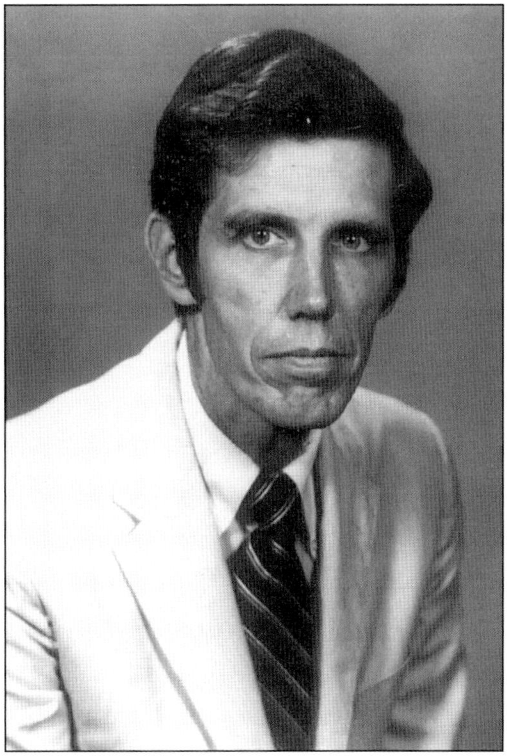

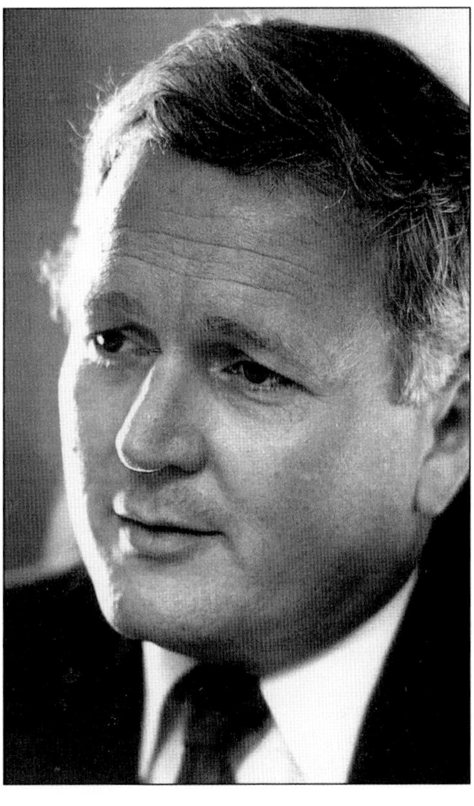

Flamboyant local attorney N. Graves Thomas was a champion of the underdog as well as a proponent of historic preservation and urban renewal, putting his own office in a meticulously restored Victorian cottage located in a highly ghettoized neighborhood. On Memorial Day 1987, Thomas, then 40, was struck by lightening and killed while boating on Lake Bistineau. An urban legend almost immediately developed that he had stood up in the boat and challenged God to "take me" when lightning struck. According to the testimony of all eyewitnesses present, however, this never occurred. Unfortunately, the legend, which was picked up by national media, still persists.

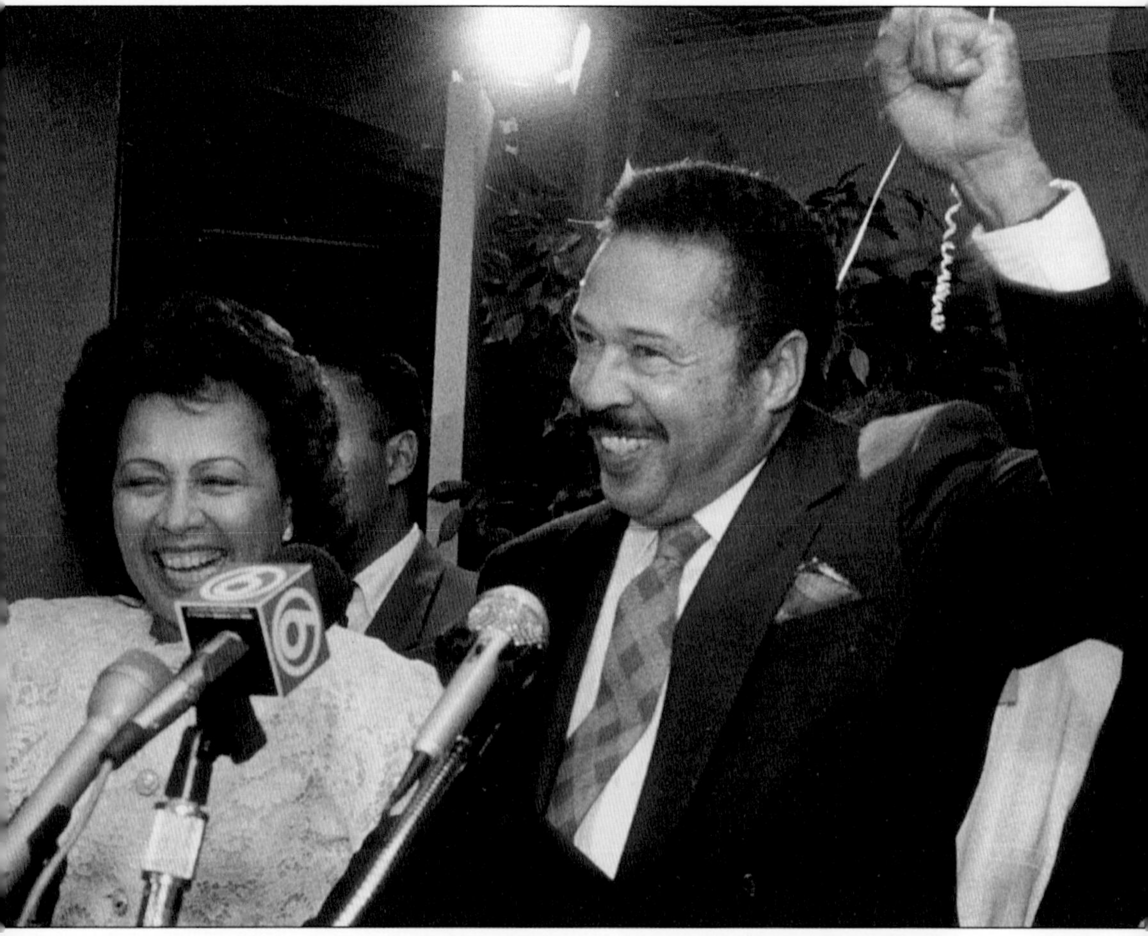

Dr. C.O. Simpkins (right) was the first black Shreveporter to run for office after Reconstruction, making an unsuccessful bid for the Caddo School Board in 1953. A nationally prominent civil rights leader, Simpkins was a vice president of the SCLC and founder of the United Christian Movement. He was a close friend of Martin Luther King and Ralph Abernathy and brought them as well as other civil rights leaders to Shreveport in the 1950s and early 1960s. Following two bombings of his homes in 1962, Simpkins left Shreveport for New York, returning in 1987. In 1990 he ran for mayor, making it to the runoff from a large field of contenders. He was narrowly defeated by Hazel Beard, the city's first female mayor. A year later Dr. Simpkins won a seat in the State Legislature. Here he is seen with his wife, Dr. Elaine Simpkins (left) upon learning he had made it to the runoff in the mayoral election.

Hazel Beard, the first woman to serve as mayor of Shreveport, held office from 1990 to 1994. She was succeeded by Robert W. "Bo" Williams, the city's first handicapped mayor, who served from 1994 to 1998. Both also served on the city council before becoming mayor.

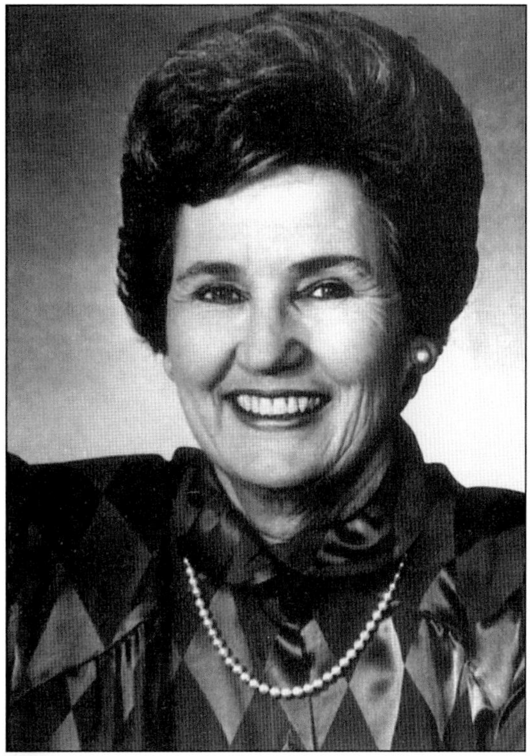

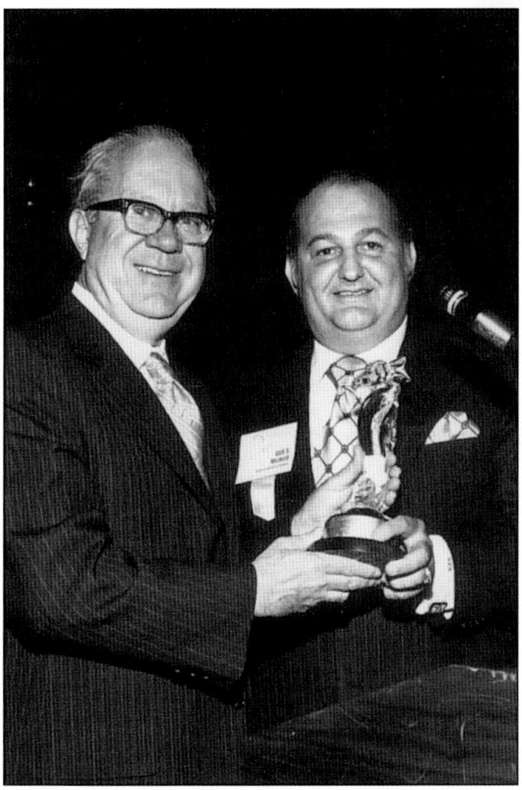

Sen. Russell Long (left) is pictured with Shreveport businessman Gus Mijalis. Mijalis, an owner of Farmer's Seafood Company, is presenting Long with the National Fisheries Institute's "Man of the Year" award in 1978 (see page 31).

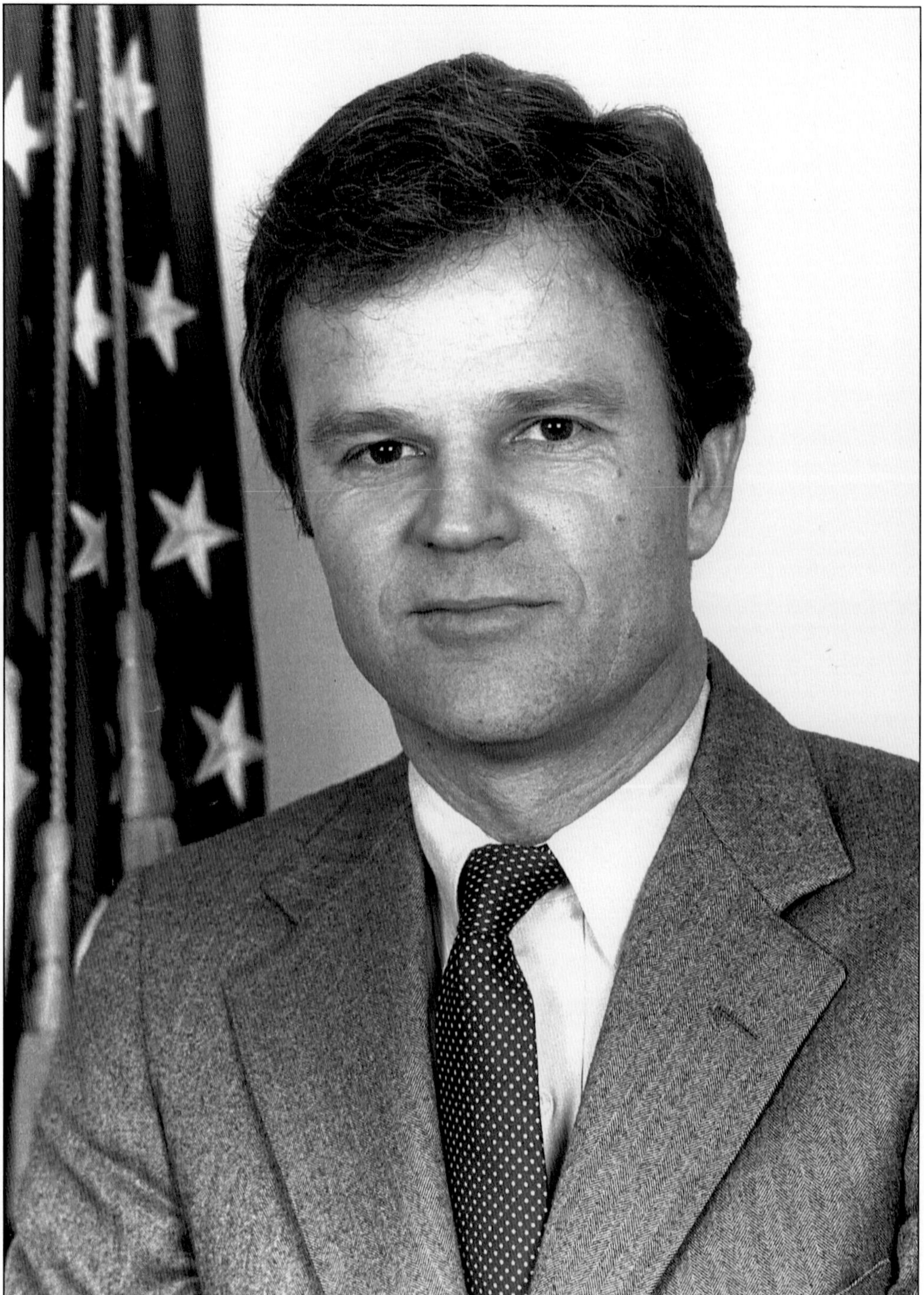

Gov. Charles "Buddy" Roemer grew up in Scopena in Bossier Parish, just across the river from Shreveport. Roemer was a popular governor, balancing the budget of a state on the brink of bankruptcy and espousing progressive causes. He served for only one term, however, from 1988 to 1992.

Two

Education and Religion

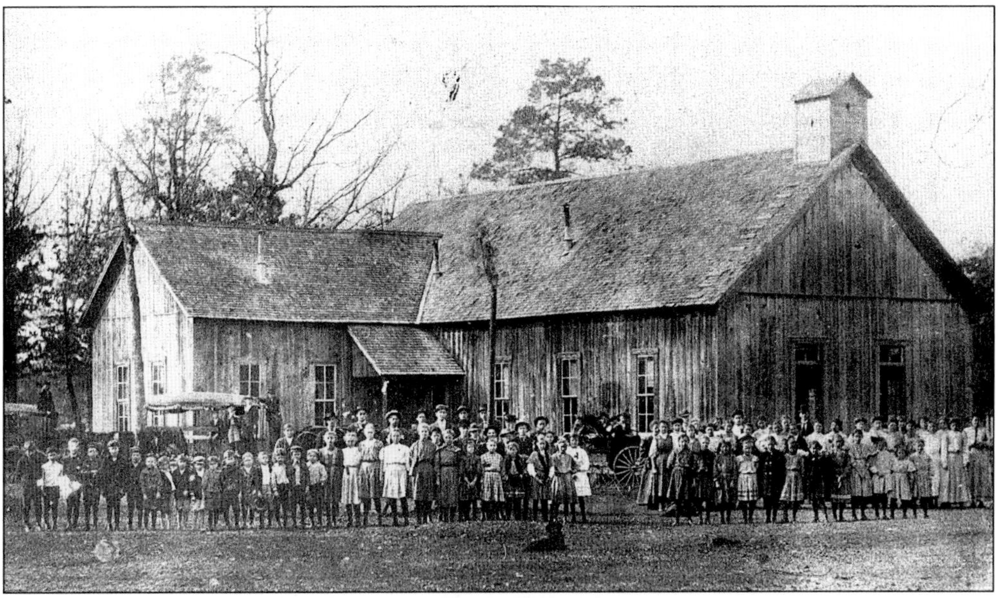

The Alden Bridge School was located in Bossier Parish, just northeast of Shreveport, and is seen in 1908. This school is typical of early schools both rural and urban, with every grade represented under one roof. The form of the school derives from traditional church forms since churches often operated most schools prior to the establishment of public education here in the late 19th century. Large as they were, many of these early schools had only one or two rooms. By the beginning of the 20th century few such buildings remained except in rural areas like the lumber mill village of Alden Bridge. More than 90 pupils and several teachers (as well as one dog) gathered for this photograph, which could as easily have been made a half-century earlier.

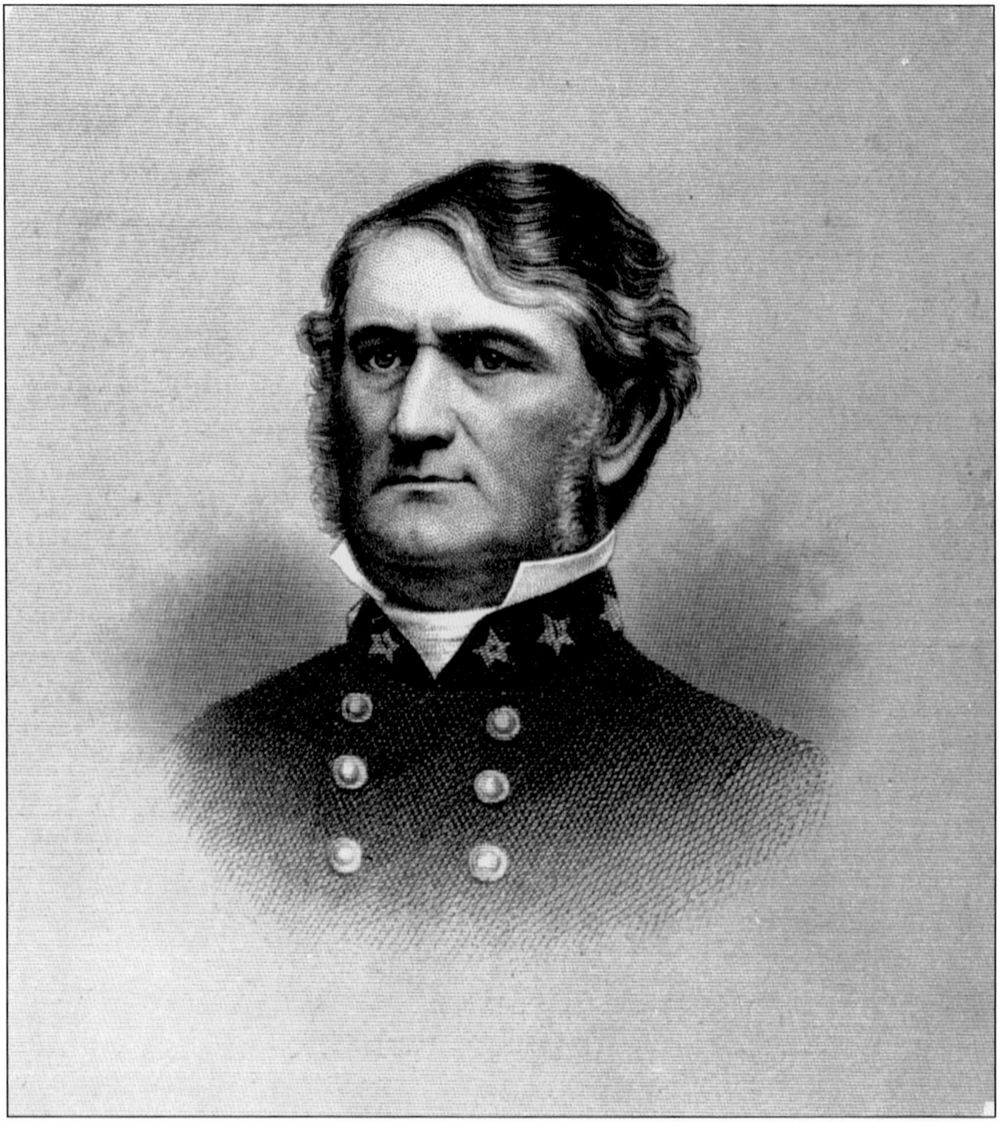

Bishop Leonidas Polk, Episcopal Bishop of Louisiana, conducted the first church services ever held in Shreveport on March 20, 1839. This is considered the founding date of St. Mark's Episcopal Church (now St. Mark's Cathedral), though in fact the present church was not formally organized until six years later. In late biographies of Polk it was stated that the Bishop met with resistance from ruffians who did not want the influence of religion to enter the rough river town of Shreveport. Contemporary newspaper and other accounts, however, give no indication of this and actually state the contrary. Polk, later a Confederate general, was killed at Pine Mountain, Georgia and is buried inside Christ Church Cathedral in New Orleans. He is seen here in his Confederate uniform.

Probably the city's first private school was the George Wyche Rives Academy, located at the northwest corner of Texas and Louisiana Streets in the 1840s. It was established by Prof. George Wyche Rives, a South Carolina native, who ran the school together with one other teacher named M.S. Paisely. Rives died in 1858, just ten days short of his 31st birthday.

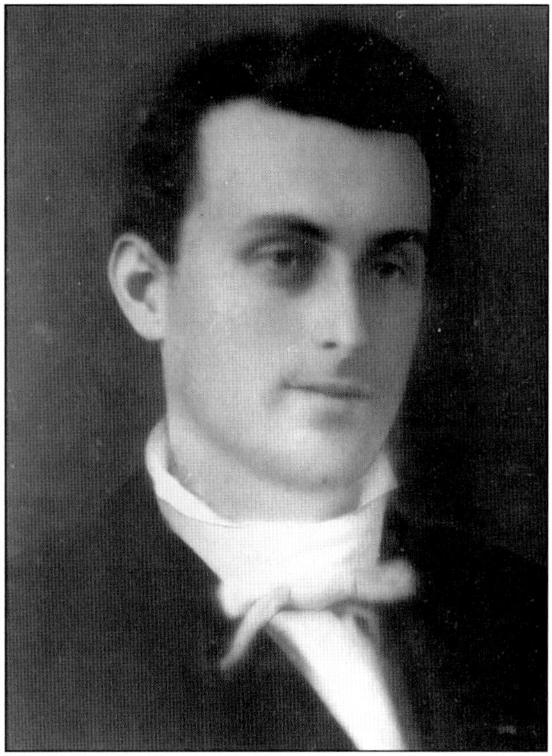

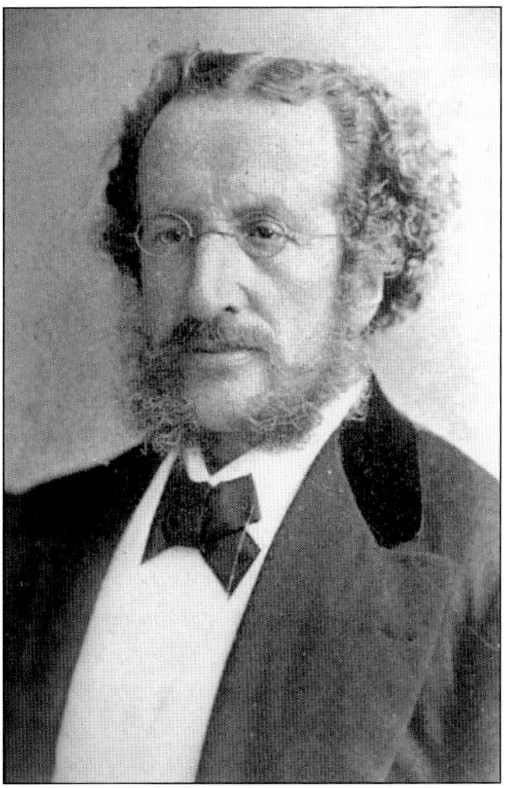

Rabbi Ferdinand Leopold Sarner, in addition to being leader of the Har El Synagogue (now B'nai Zion Temple), was headmaster of the German School, a grammar-through-high school established just prior to the Civil War and operated by the congregation during the 19th century. Classes were taught in both German and English and the school was well patronized by the large German population of Shreveport—Jews and Christians alike. It was located in the 300 block of Fannin Street.

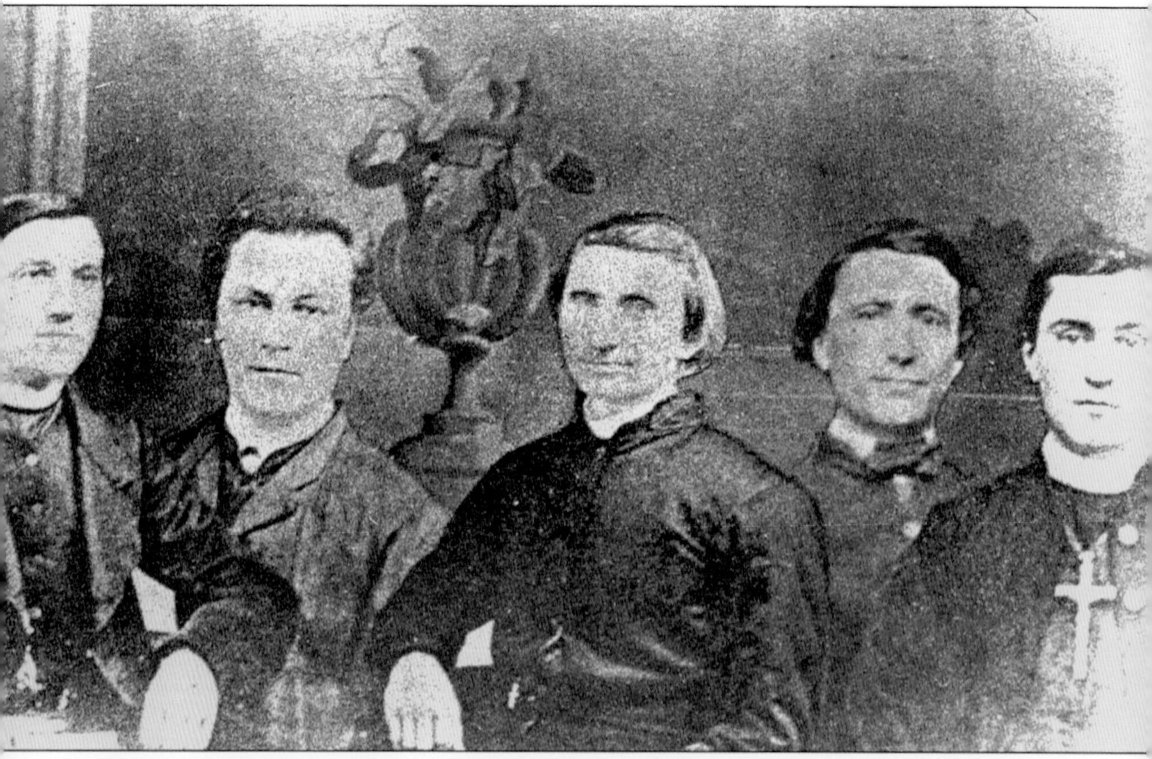

These are the martyrs of the great epidemic of 1873. Five local Catholic priests were among the approximately 1,000 victims (a quarter of the city's population at the time) of yellow fever in the epidemic of August to November 1873. Father Pierre, for whom Pierre Avenue is named, was the founding priest of Holy Trinity Parish. The parish ran a school and supported the convent schools of St. Mary and St. Vincent. The priests are memorialized in a garden beside Holy Trinity Church and in five stained glass windows within. From left to right they are the Reverends J.M.J. LeBiler (pastor to the nuns at St. Vincent's Convent), Louis Gergaud (parish priest of Monroe), Jean Pierre, Francois LeVezouet (parish priest from Natchitoches), and Isidore Queremais.

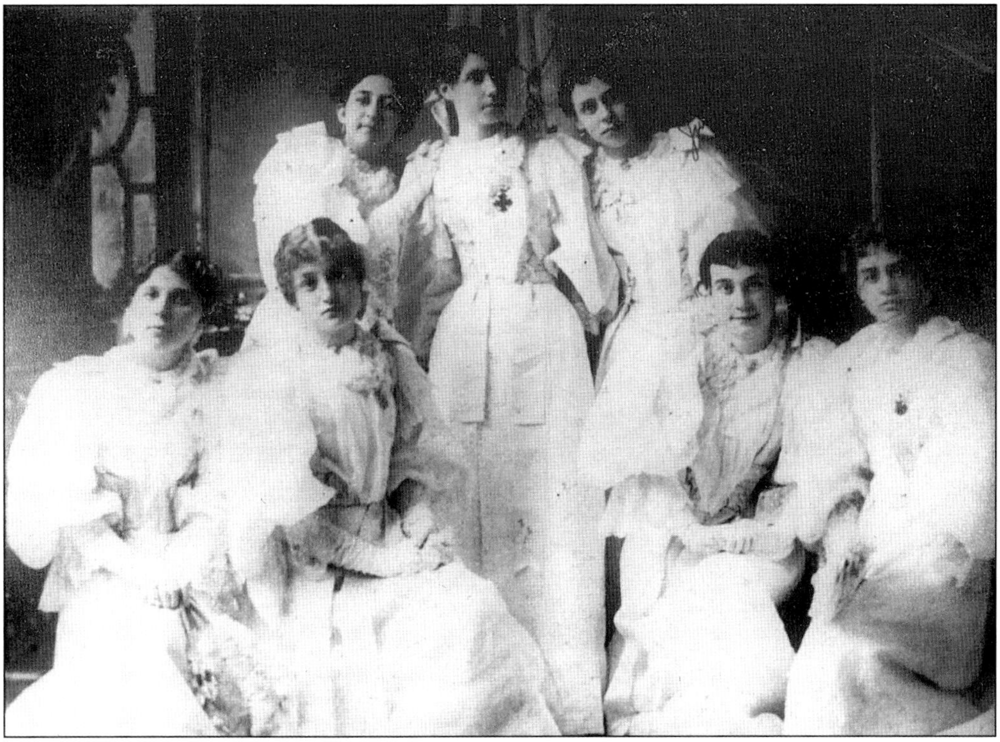

St. Vincent's Academy, a private girl's boarding school and later a day school, was founded by the nuns of the Order of the Daughters of the Cross in 1868. The academy was located south of Shreveport on what had formerly been the plantation of Col. LeRoy Moncure Nutt, "Fairfield Hill." Today the site is that of Mall St. Vincent and the area is densely urban. Above is a photo of the 1895 graduating class. Seen from left to right are May Prud'homme, Genie Burt, Julia Prud'homme, Ethel Dillon, Anna Price, Nina Chopin, and Annie March.

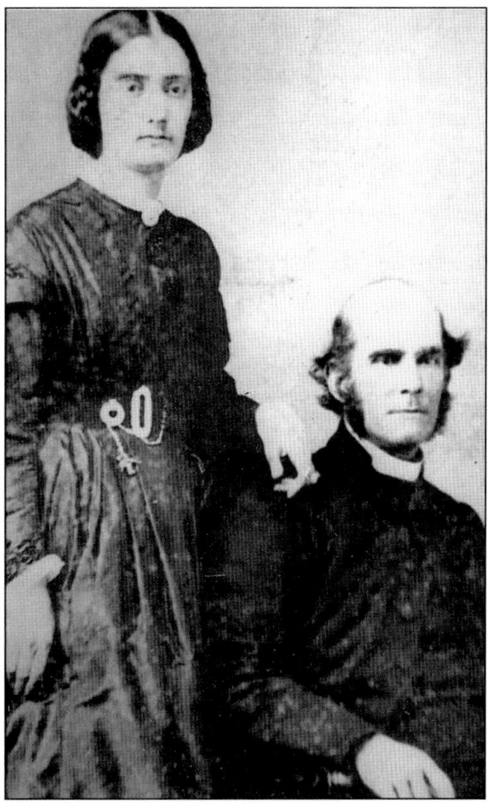

The Rev. William T.D. Dalzell was rector of St. Mark's Episcopal Church during the late 19th century and was a hero of the yellow fever epidemic of 1873, remaining in the stricken city to nurse the sick and comfort the dying, regardless of faith. Seen here with his wife, Estelle Logan Dalzell, about the time of the epidemic, Dr. Dalzell was a leading figure in the city's post–Civil War development. After his death in 1899, Dalzell Street in Highland was named for him.

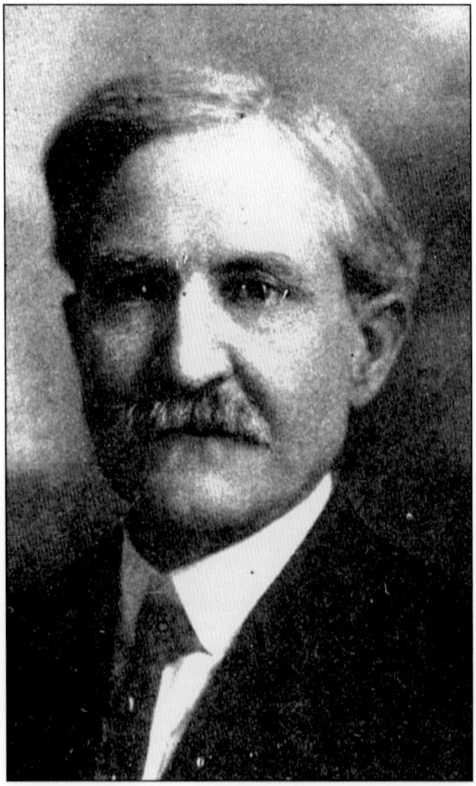

Prof. Clifton Ellis Byrd, a Virginia native, was a lawyer but left the bar for the educational profession, coming to Shreveport as a teacher and later helping to establish the Caddo Parish School Board and the Caddo public school system. For 34 years Professor Byrd's name was inextricably associated with local schools. Upon his death in 1926 the just-opened New Shreveport High School was renamed C.E. Byrd High. It remains one of the largest schools in the Shreveport area.

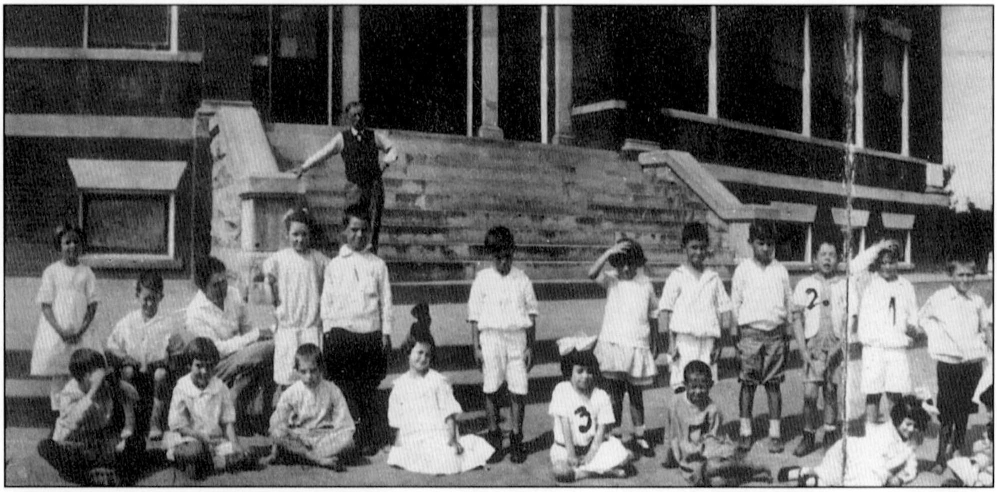

The Line Avenue School opened in 1905 at 1800 Line Avenue. Originally called the Texarkana Annex School, after the subdivision it was built in, the name was changed a few years after opening. Closed in the 1970s, the old Line Avenue School today is the main building of the Northwestern State University School of Nursing. Shown above is a class posed in Line Avenue in front of the school around 1912. Their teacher stands on the steps behind them.

Dr. Monroe Elmon Dodd (right), pastor of the First Baptist Church from 1912 to 1950, founded Dodd College (named by the church in his honor) in 1925. A private girls' junior college, it closed in 1942. Below is a graduating class from Dodd posed on the steps of Shreveport Hall around 1940; Dr. Dodd stands at front on the left. Today the Dodd College campus is the site of the First Baptist Church and Shreveport Hall is now known as Dodd Hall in memory of both the college and its founder.

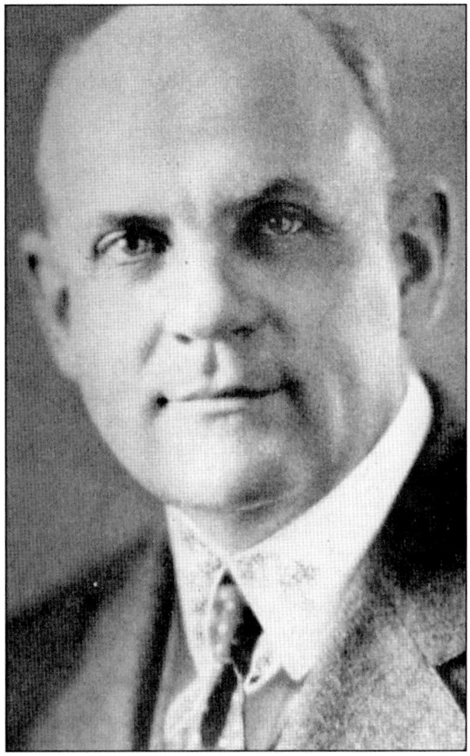

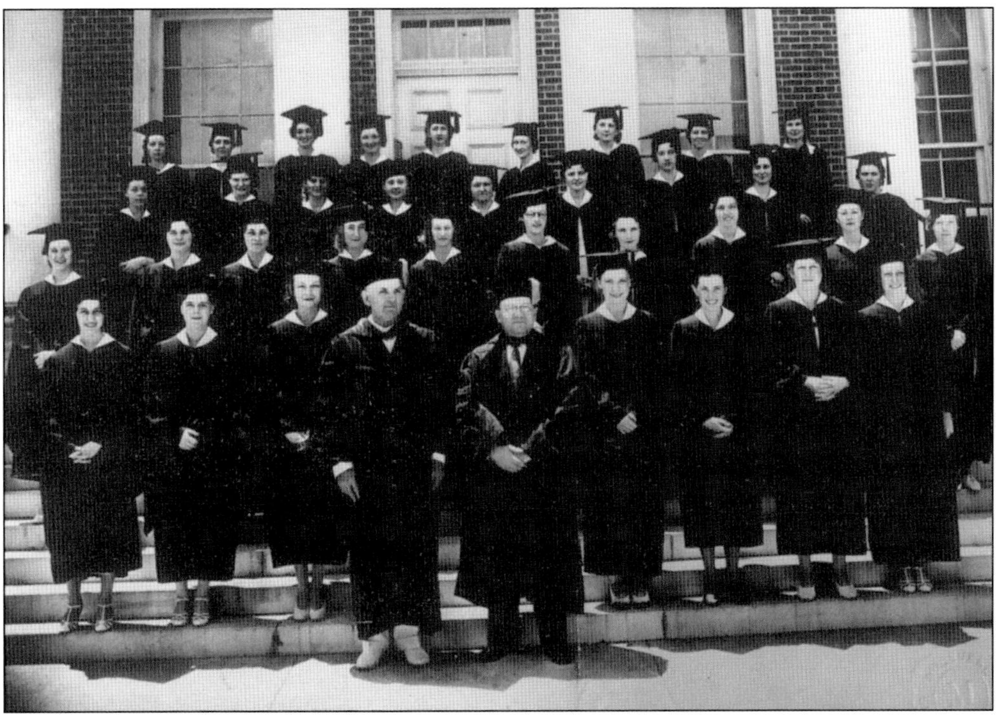

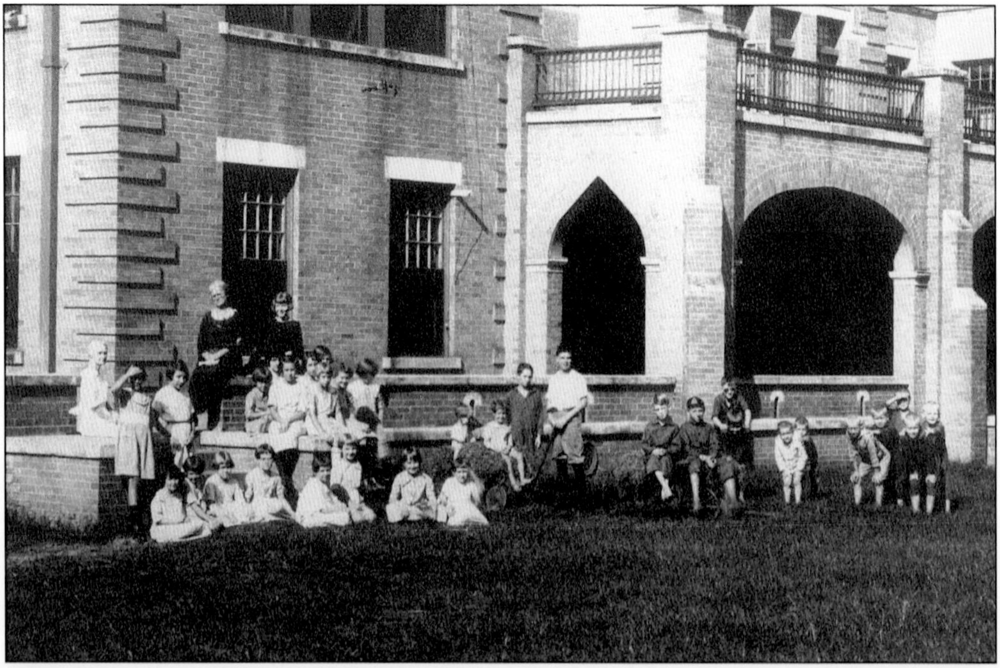

(Above) Resident children and staff of the Genevieve Orphanage gather in front of the main building at Olive and Elizabeth Streets around 1915. The orphanage was founded in 1890, principally by Dr. W.S. Penick, pastor of the First Baptist Church, and Palestine Cole Jacobs, widow of banker Ed Jacobs. It was named in memory of Reverend Penick's little daughter, Genevieve, who died accidentally at age six in 1889. (Below) The children's Sunday School class in the old wooden "tabernacle" of Broadmoor Baptist Church on Youree Drive, seen around 1930.

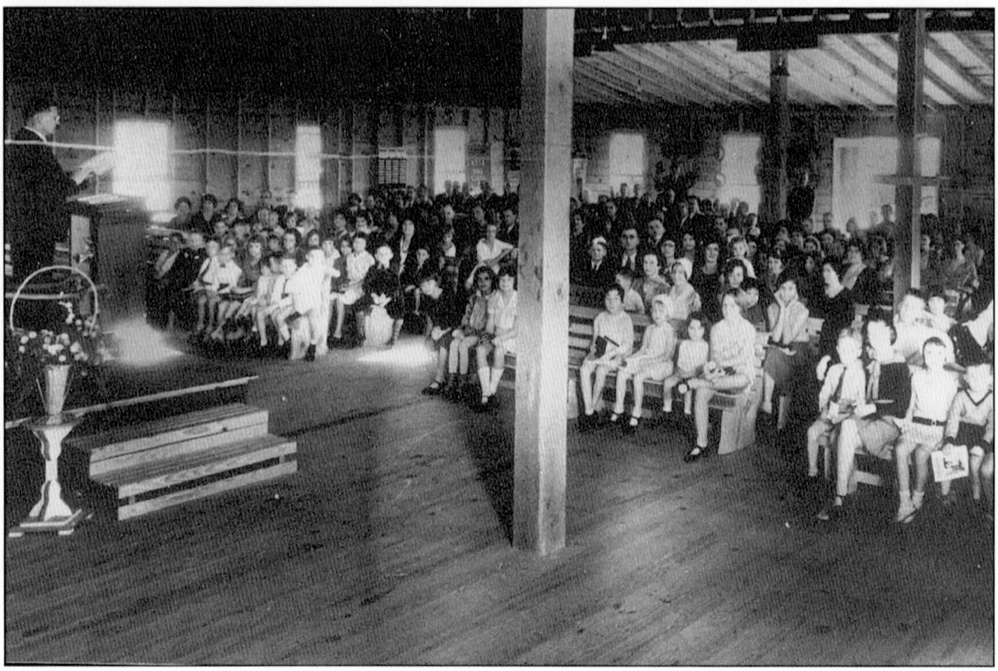

Early evangelist Billy Sunday visited Shreveport during the 1920s, attracting huge crowds to his revivals, which took place at the corner of Grand Avenue and Milam Street. Late in the 1920s the Municipal Auditorium was built on that same site. Sunday was a nationally popular religious personality and was friends with local pastor and radio evangelist M.E. Dodd.

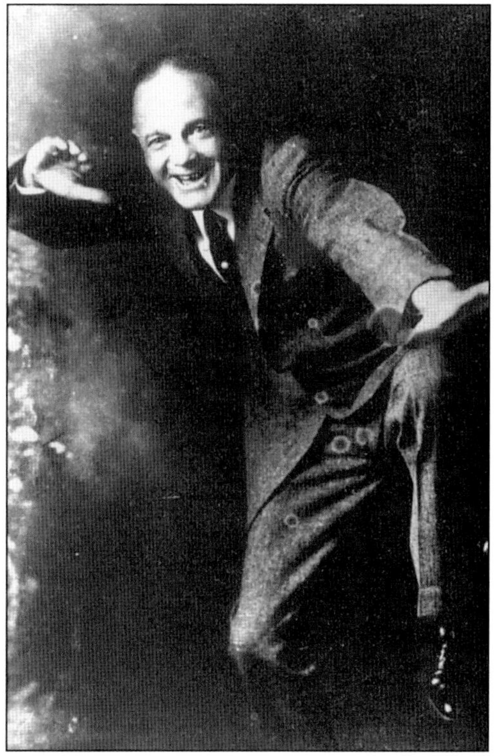

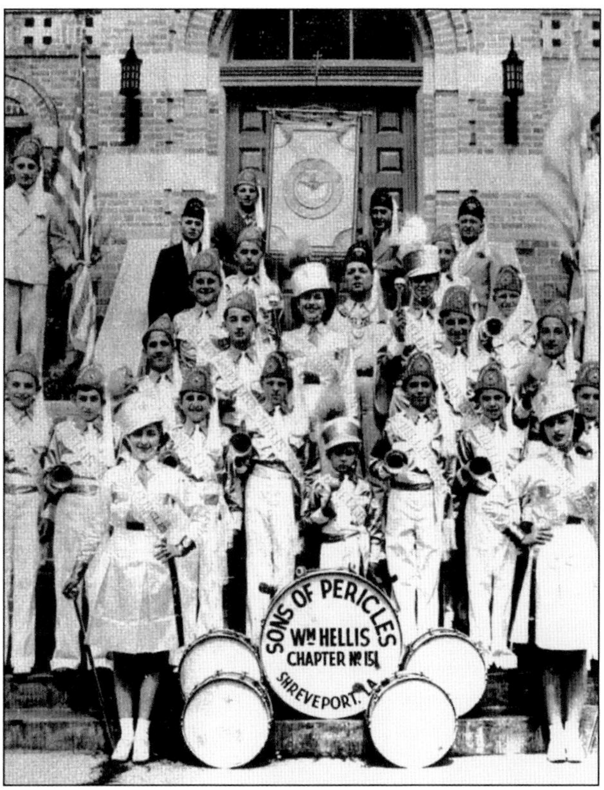

The local chapter of the Sons of Pericles, a Greek fraternal society, gathers on the steps of St. George's Greek Orthodox Church on Creswell Avenue in Highland around 1940.

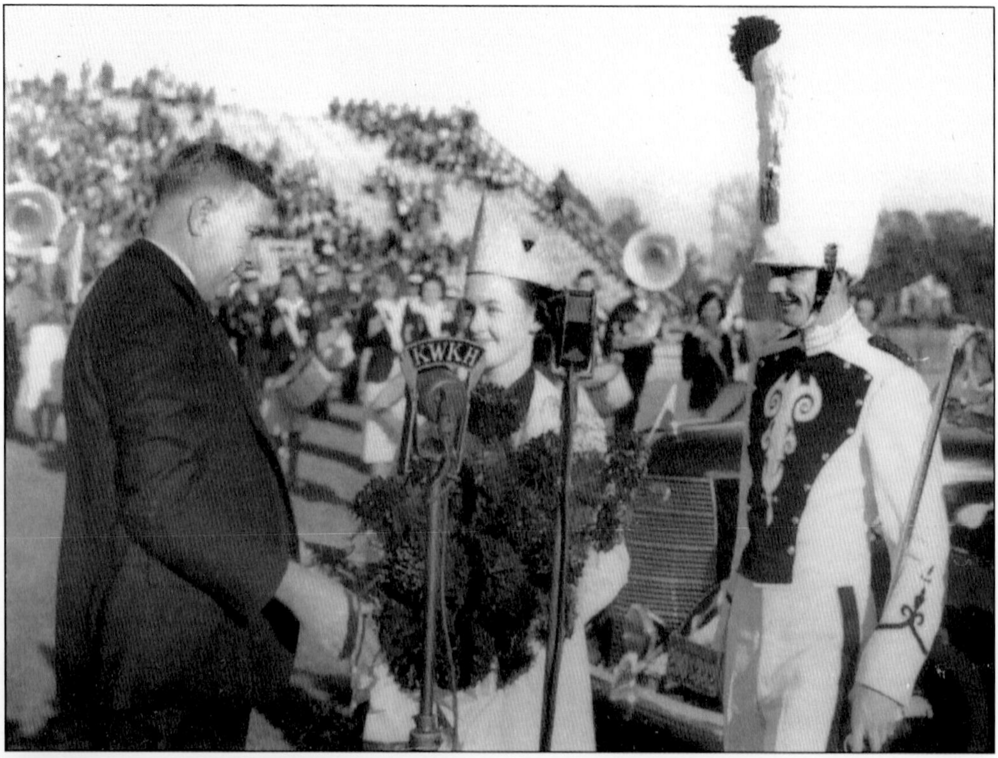

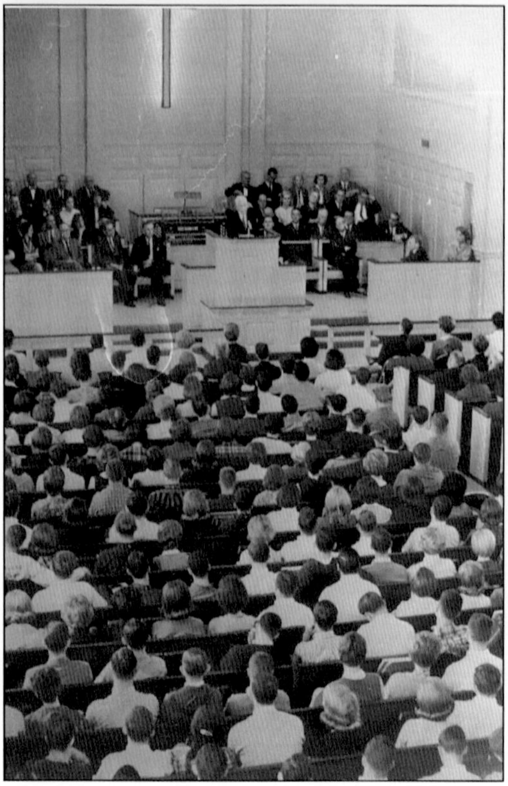

Centenary College of Louisiana, founded in 1825, located its campus at Shreveport in 1908 and has been a major part of the city's life since. At top is a photo from the school's 1939 homecoming football game. President Pierce Cline (left) crowns the May Queen, Mary Agnes Railsback (center). At bottom, students gather for a convocation in Brown Chapel in the early 1960s.

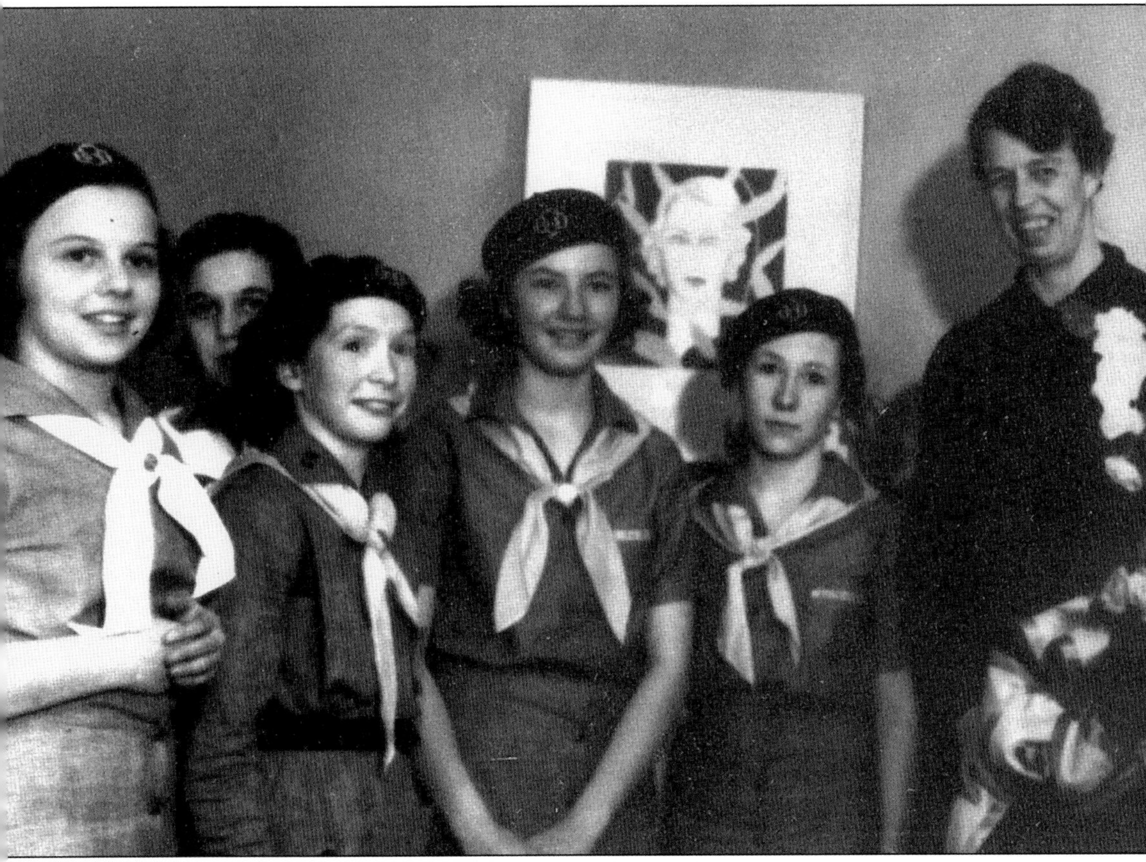

First Lady Eleanor Roosevelt visited Shreveport on March 10, 1937, delivering two addresses at the Municipal Auditorium and meeting with various local dignitaries. She is seen here with five Girl Scouts who presented her with a bouquet of roses in honor of her visit.

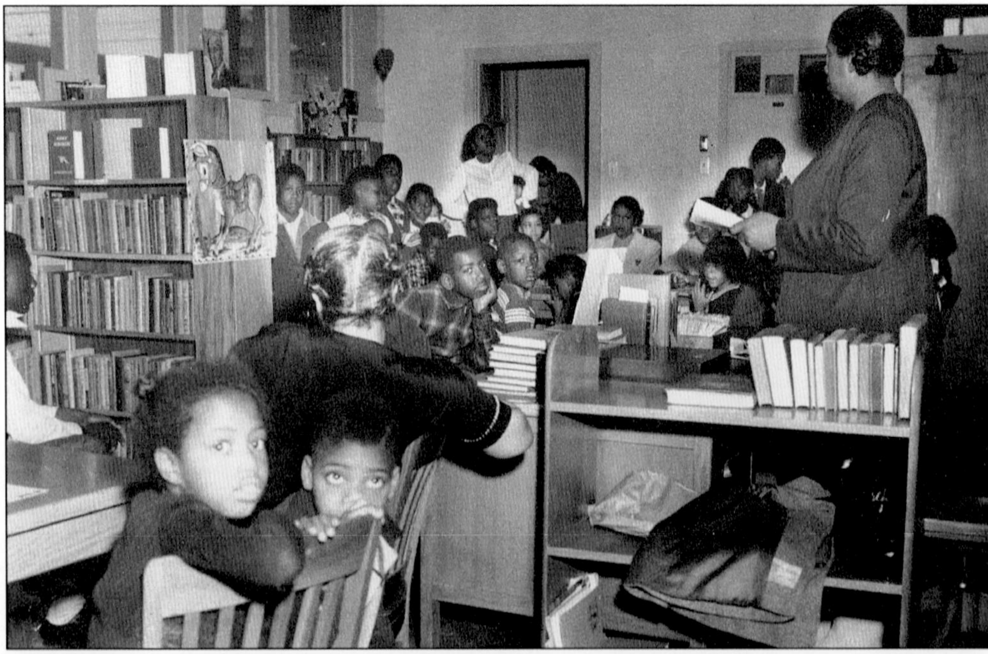

Storytelling at the newly opened Lakeside branch of the Shreve Memorial Library took place in February 1953. Muriel Bolton Boyd, right, talks to the children attending. The Lakeside Library, located on Milam and Elder Streets, was the first branch opened in a black neighborhood.

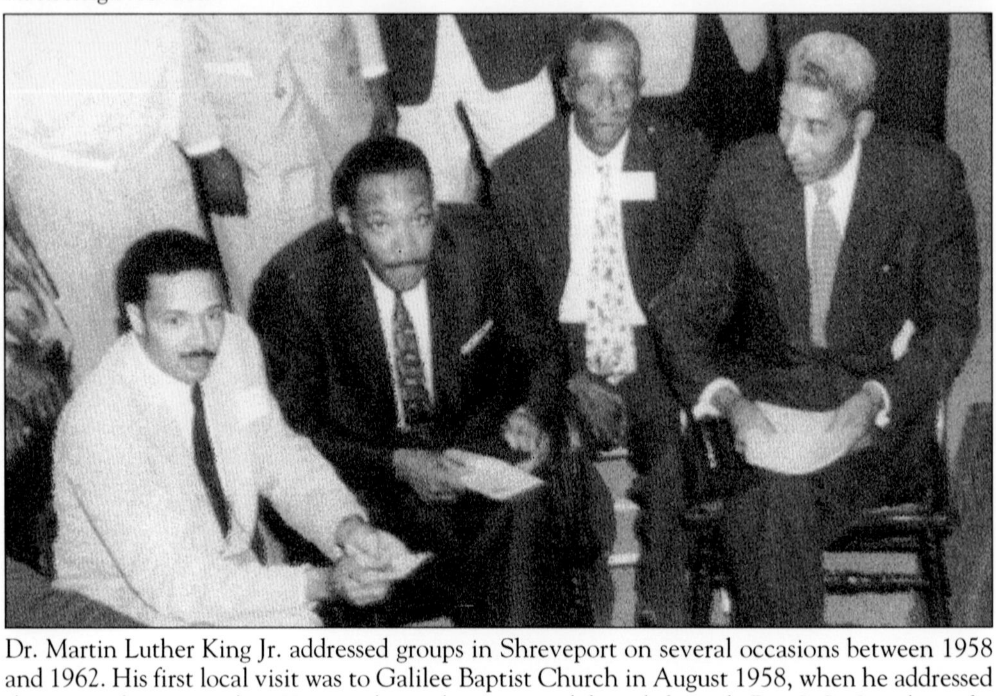

Dr. Martin Luther King Jr. addressed groups in Shreveport on several occasions between 1958 and 1962. His first local visit was to Galilee Baptist Church in August 1958, when he addressed the issue of voting rights. King is shown here, second from left, with Dr. C.O. Simpkins, far left, and deacons of the Galilee Baptist Church (see page 35). The role of the church in the educational and political life of the black community cannot be overstated.

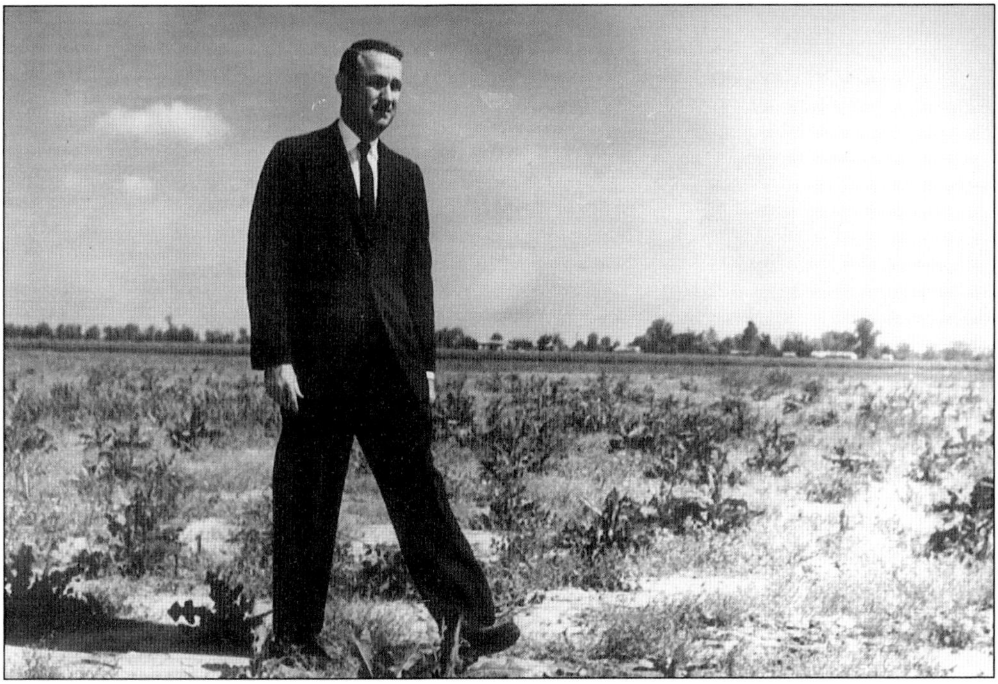

Dr. Donald E. Shipp, LSU dean, walks on a field at Dogwood Plantation on the southeast edge of Shreveport in 1964. Shortly thereafter ground would be broken for the campus of LSU-Shreveport on the site. Dr. Shipp would be the new school's first chancellor.

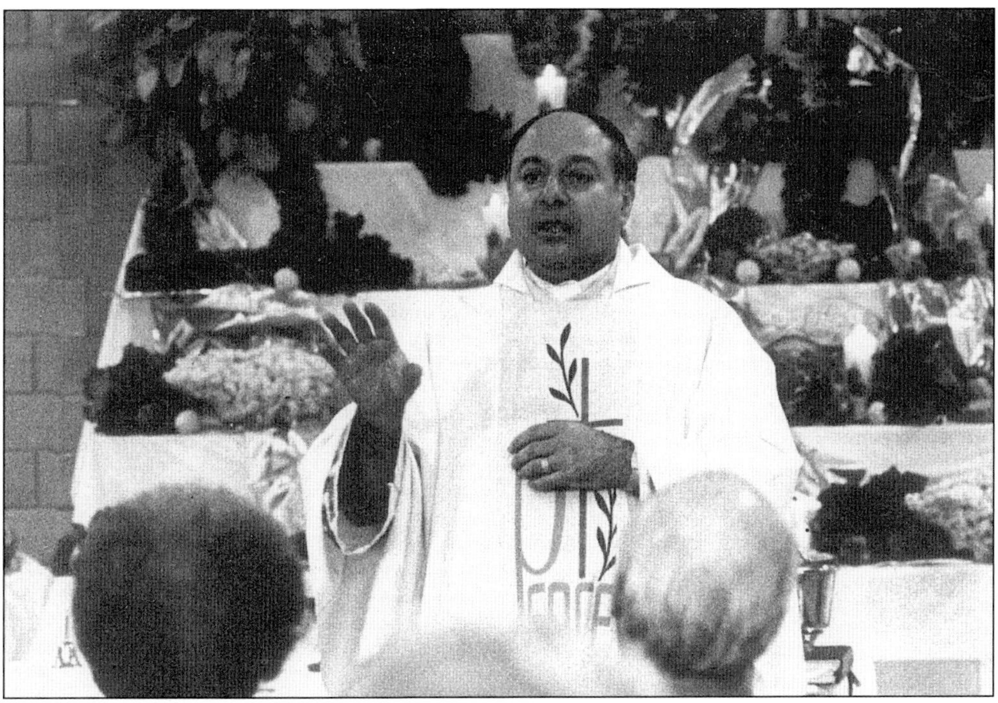

Monsignor Earl Provenza celebrates a Mass at St. John Berchmans Cathedral on Jordan Street to celebrate the St. Joseph altar in 1992.

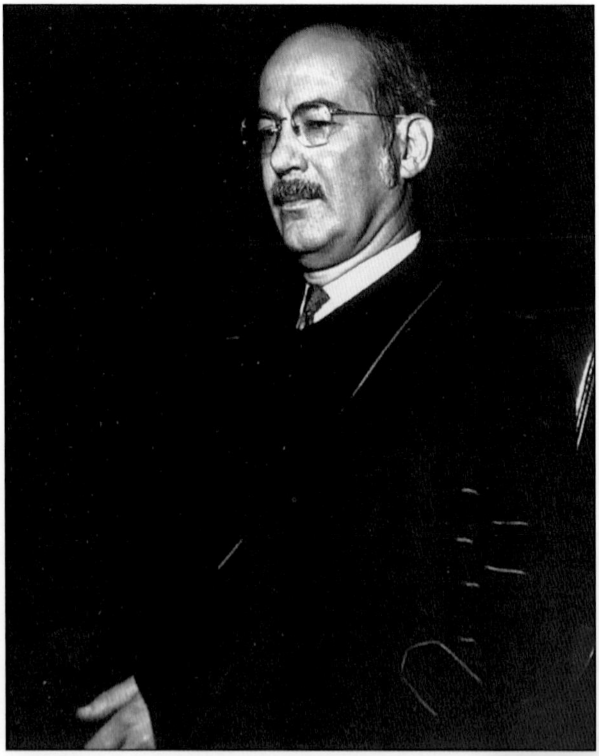

(Left) One of Shreveport's popular and influential 20th-century clergymen was Rabbi David Lefkowitz Jr. Rabbi Lefkowitz came to Shreveport's B'nai Zion Temple in 1940 and served the congregation until his retirement in 1973. He taught at Centenary College and LSUS, was a leader in the American Legion, and was involved in many civic organizations. (Below) Rabbi Lefkowitz's successor, Rabbi Richard Zionts, who led the temple until 1989, continued in his predecessor's tradition of being a community leader and educator. Both did much to promote an ecumenical understanding between faiths locally.

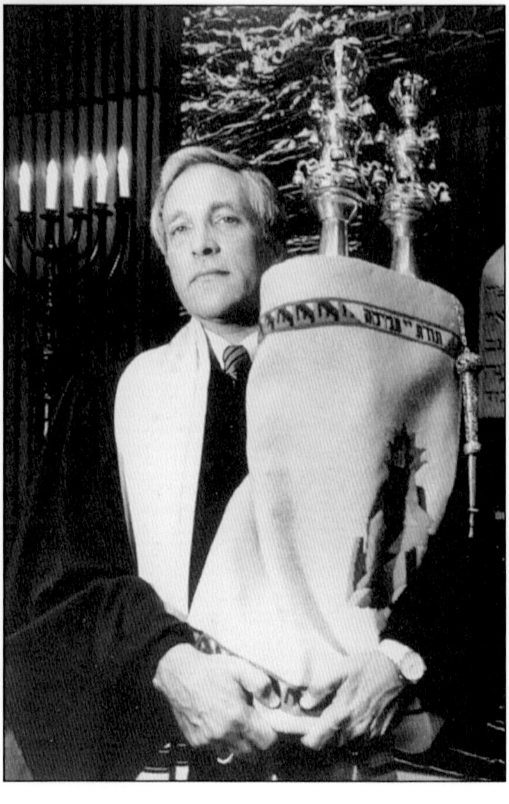

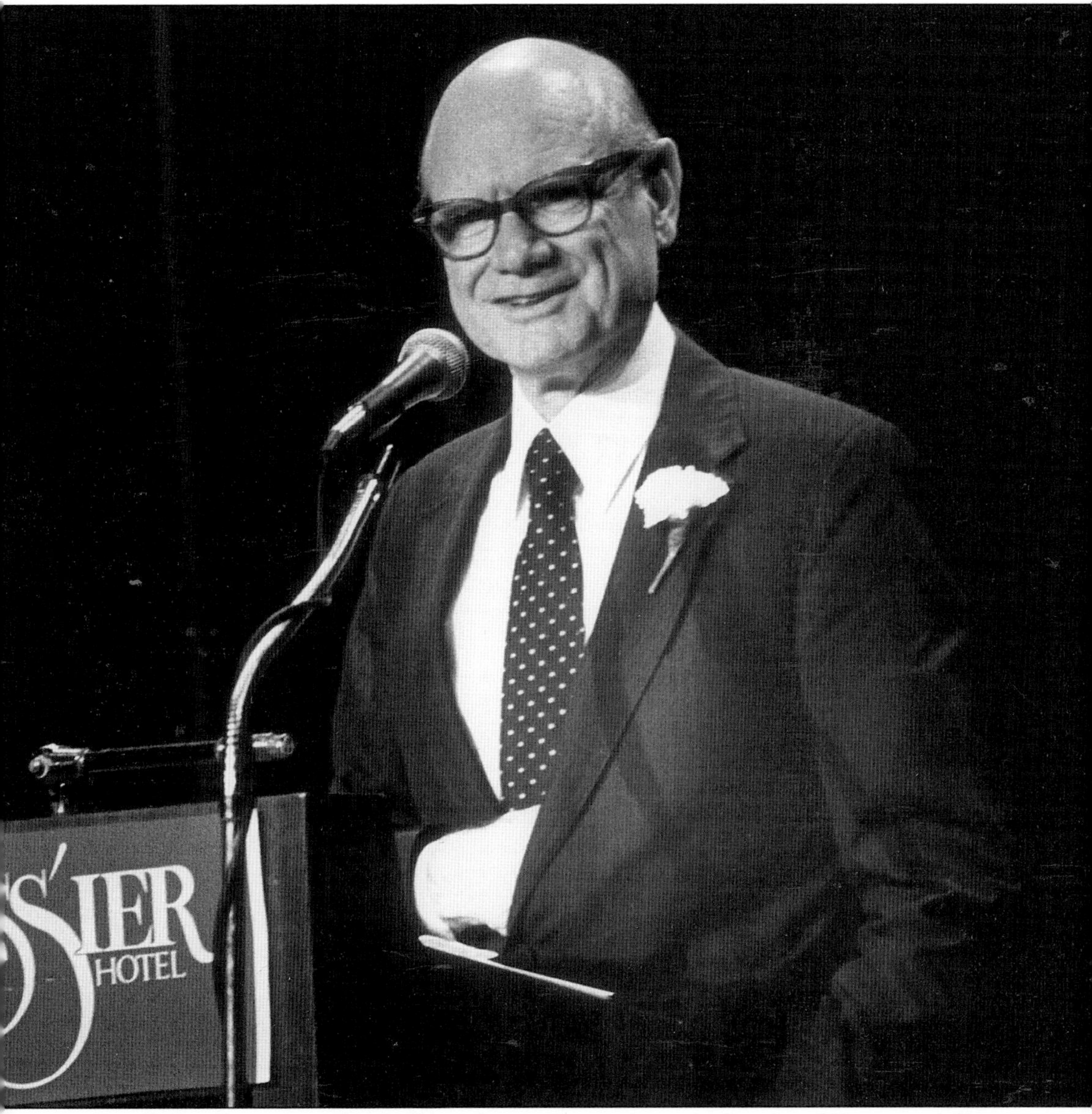

Dr. D.L. Dykes, the immensely popular and sometimes controversial pastor of Shreveport's First United Methodist Church, was active in the overall community and was known as a civic and educational leader as well as a religious leader. He served as pastor from 1955 to 1984, and it was during Dr. Dykes's tenure that First Methodist established the Alternate Views television network (AVN), which would grow into a national independent television network. Here he addresses a gathering at Bossier City's LeBoss'ier Hotel in October 1983.

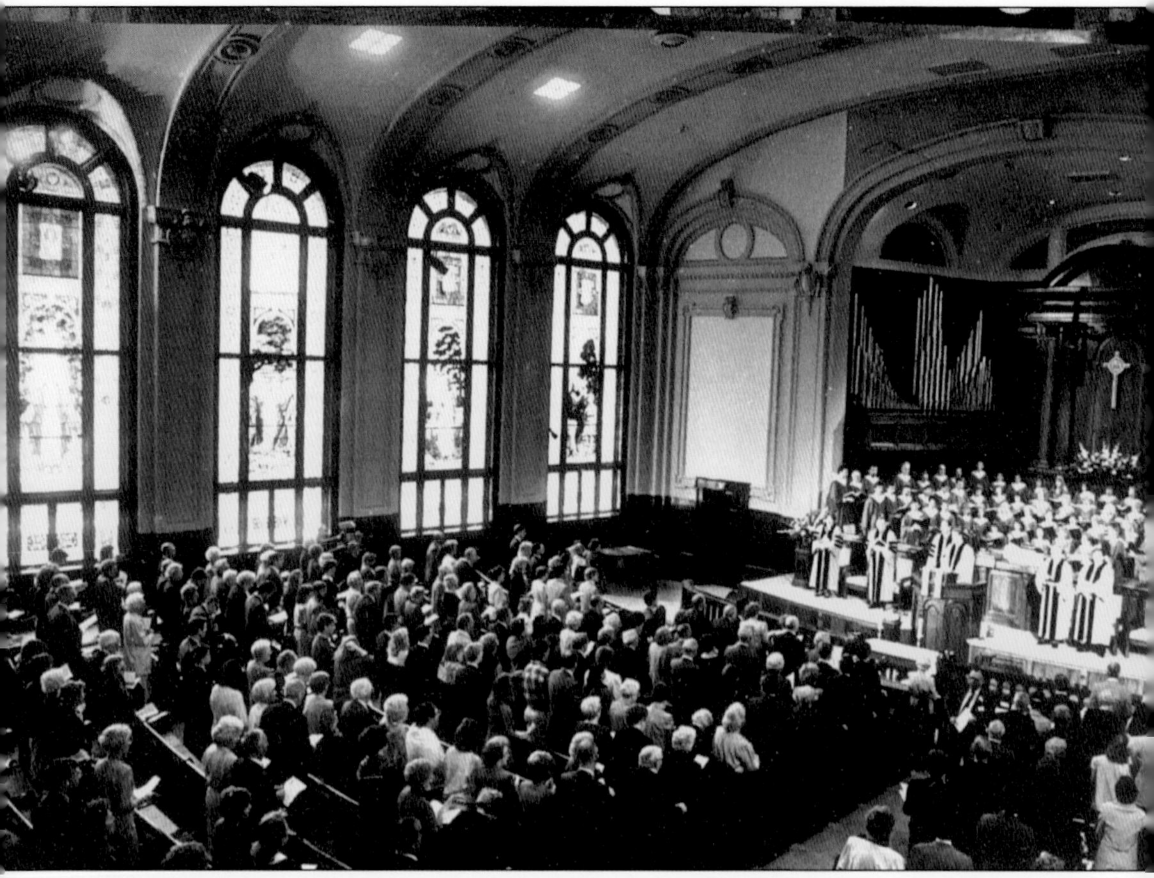

A service is seen at the historic First United Methodist Church, which was founded in 1845. The present church was built in 1913. Religion has always been a cornerstone of Shreveport's social and educational life. Churches and religious groups were responsible for the earliest schools in the area and remain responsible for most of the area's private schools, including St. Mark's Day School, St. John's Cathedral School and Loyola High School, Evangel Academy, St. Pius X School, St. Paul's Day School, and Centenary College, to name a few. Religion has also played a pivotal role in the city's growth and development over the past century and two-thirds, influencing its leadership and enhancing the lives of its citizens.

Three

People, Daily Life, and Society

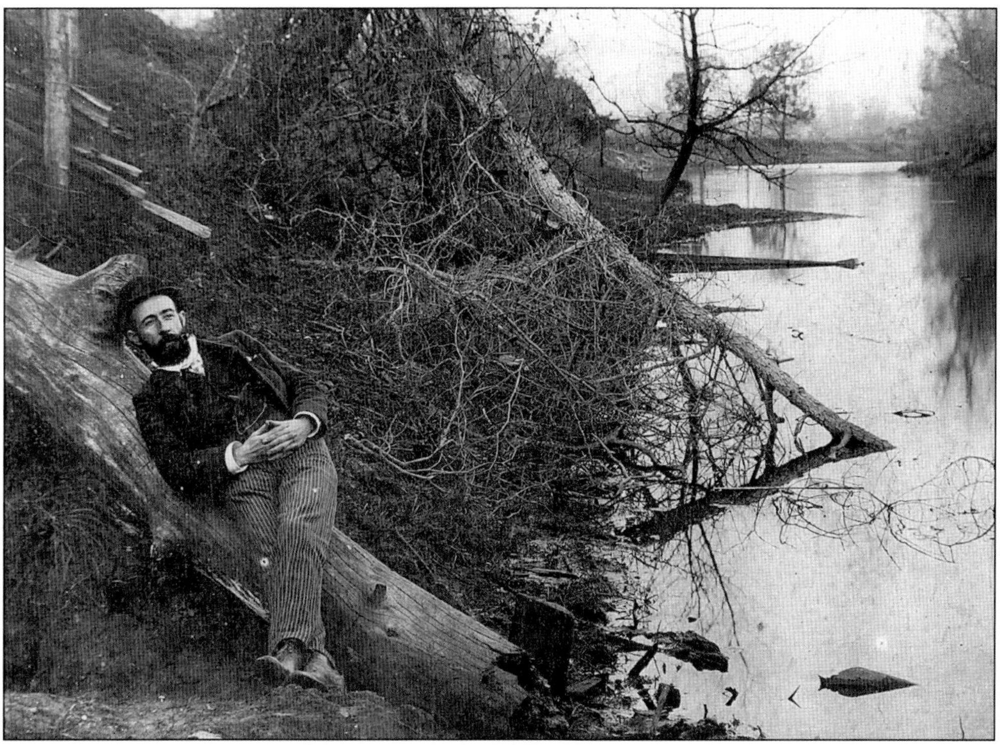

This 1896 photo depicts a man relaxing on the banks of Sand Beach Bayou, then south of Shreveport but today well within the city limits. The photo was made on a camera club outing. Note the street clothes that were worn on the trip to the country; this was commonplace in the Victorian era.

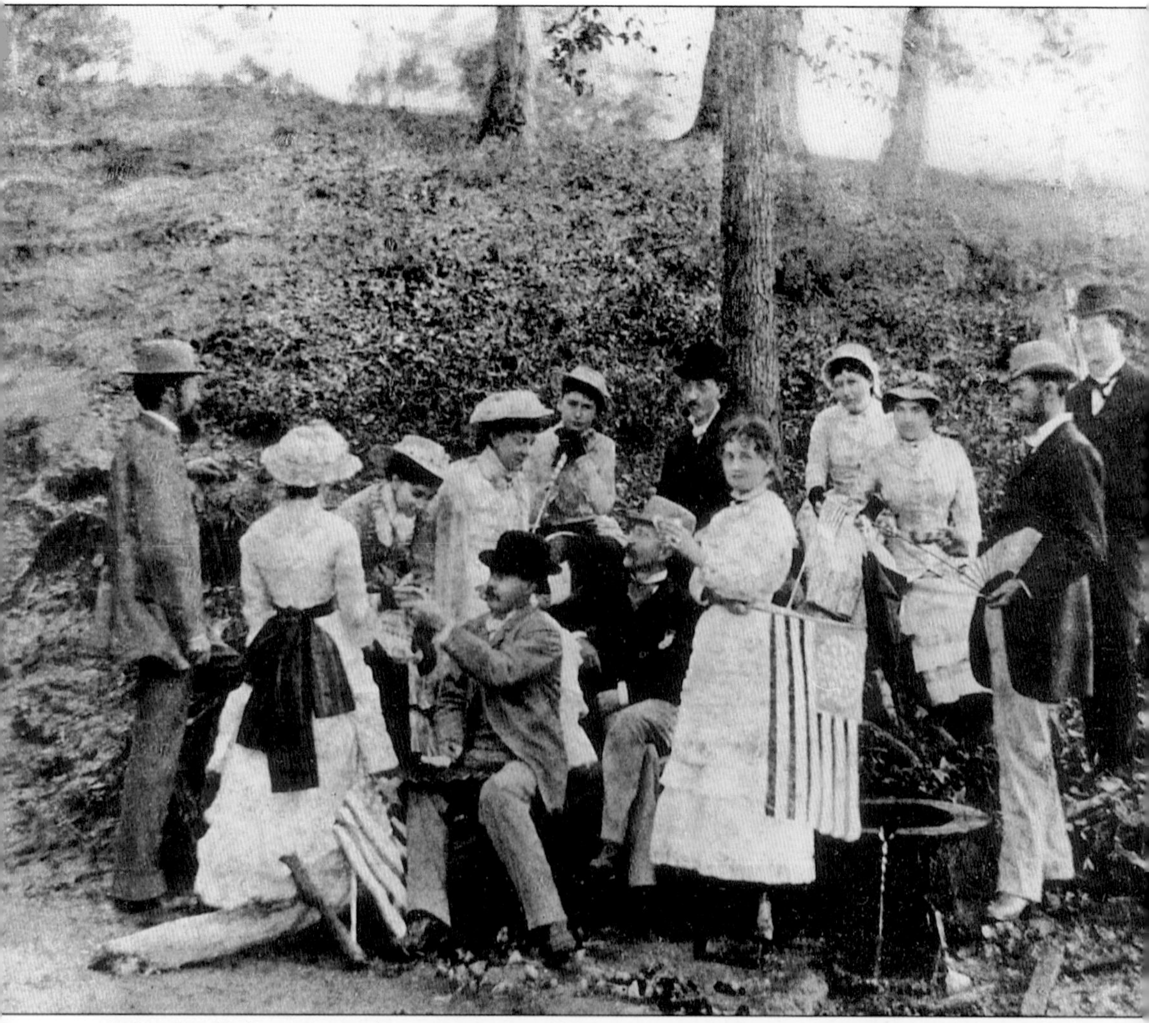

A fourth of July picnic in the country near Shreveport took place about 1890. Note the flags of different sizes and the arrangement of stars on the large flag held by the woman at center. The man second from right holds a patriotic, flag-themed fan. Such picnics were popular events in that era and were usually day-long occasions.

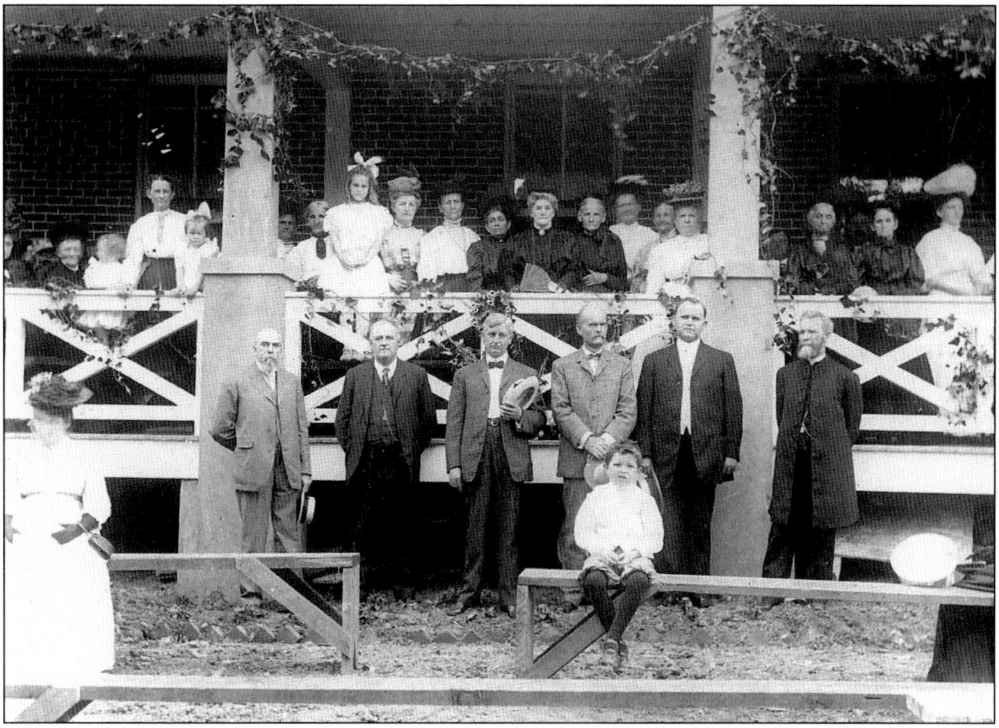

Trustees and residents of the Home for the Aged, along with their families, pose on the porch of the institution's original Logan Street location in the late 1890s. The Home for the Aged or the "Old Ladies' Home" began as the "Home for the Homeless" and later became the Glen Oaks Home. Today it still exists as the Glen Retirement System.

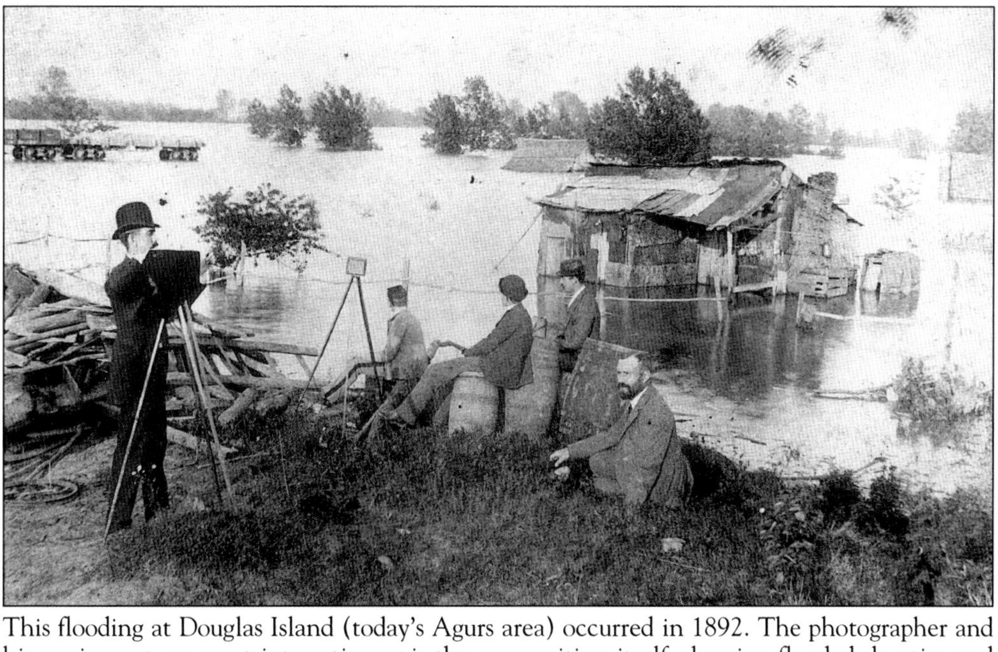

This flooding at Douglas Island (today's Agurs area) occurred in 1892. The photographer and his equipment are most interesting as is the composition itself, showing flooded shanties and stranded rail cars (above the photographer at left).

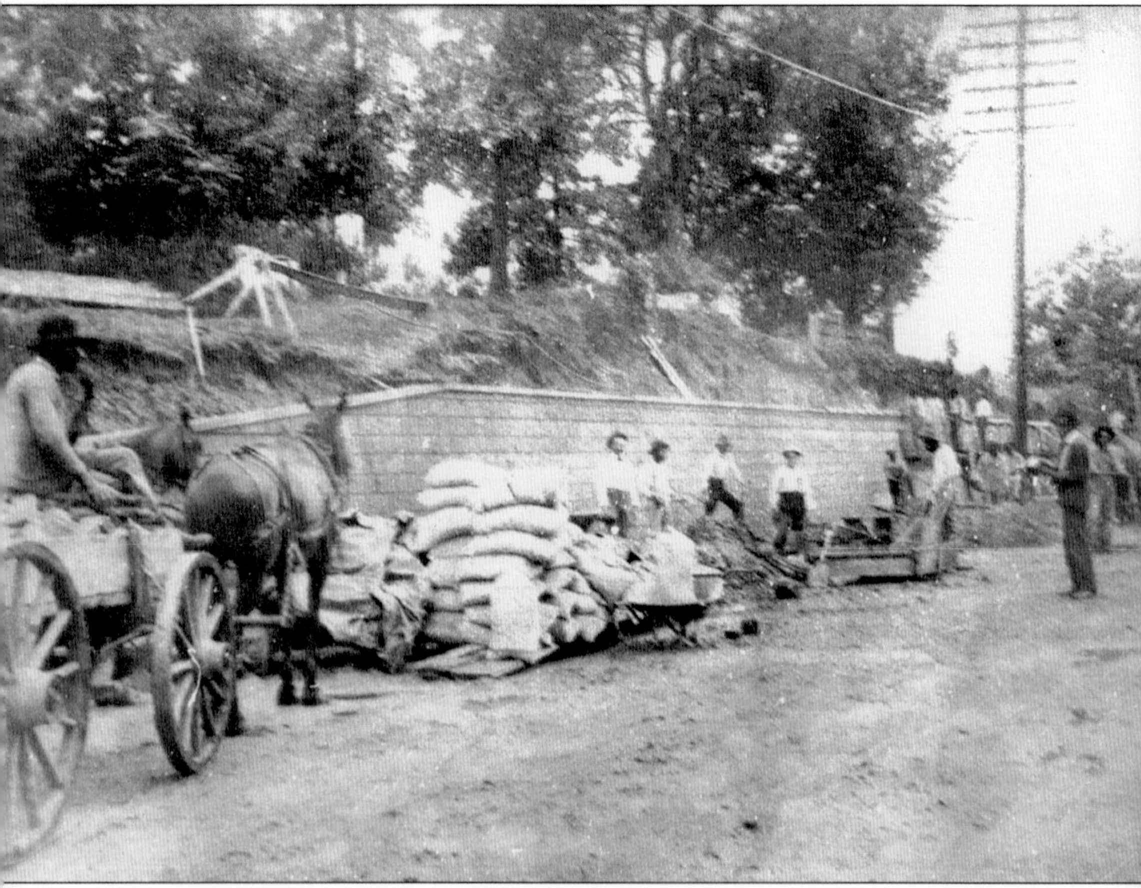

Workmen build the retaining wall of Oakland Cemetery along Sprague Street near Christian Street in 1905. Most were African-American. These walls are still in place today.

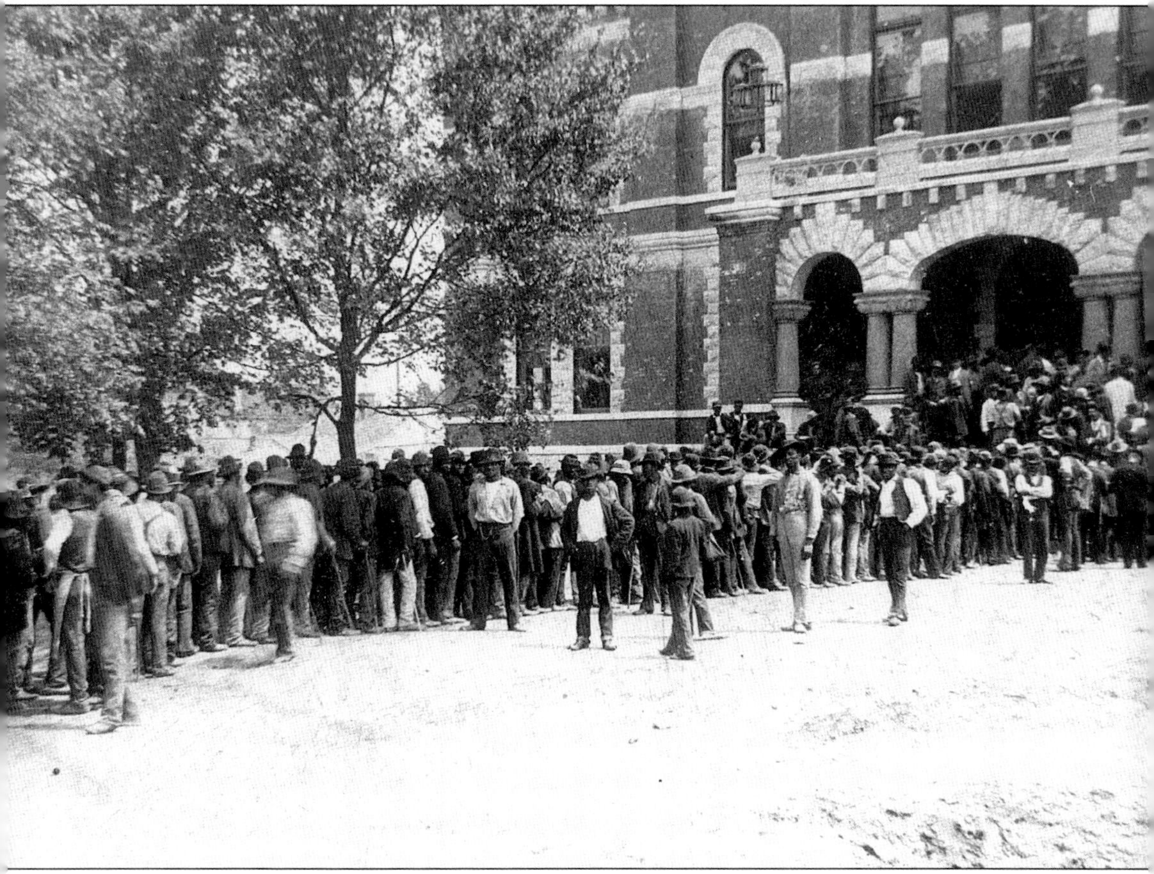

Prior to the disenfranchisement of black voters in 1898, African-American men turned out in droves to exercise their right to cast a ballot. The image above shows crowds at the Caddo Parish Courthouse on Texas Street on election day in 1896.

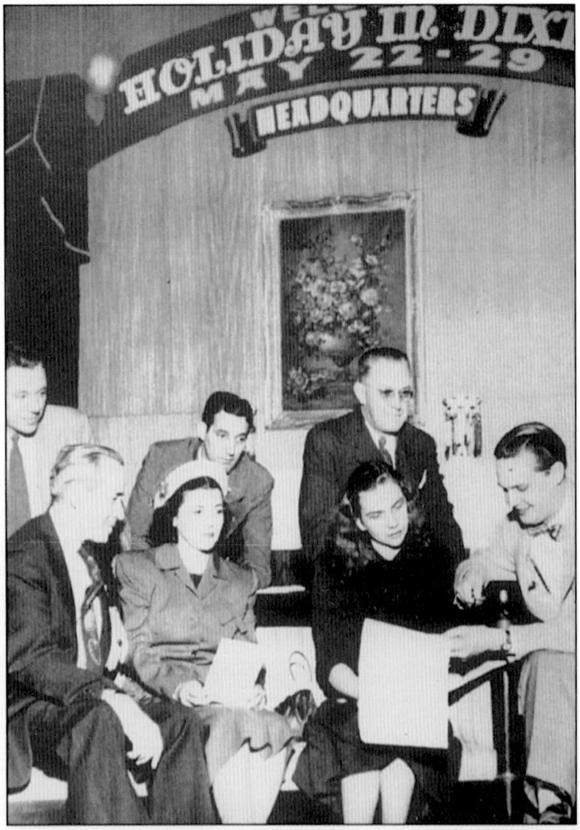

The first Holiday in Dixie, an annual Shreveport springtime festival commemorating the Louisiana Purchase, was held in 1949. Organizers of the original event are shown meeting at the Washington-Youree Hotel. From left to right are Dr. R.B. DeLee, Amos Lee Armstrong, Mrs. Carl L. Stewart, Frank Fulco, Frank W. Bruner, Mrs. R.W. Norton Jr., and Paul Hagen.

A reception for the 25th anniversary of the Shreve Memorial Library took place on December 5, 1948. Standing in the original library (now the Chamber of Commerce Plaza) are, from left to right, George Meadows (chairman), Mrs. J.D. Hanks (librarian), John McWilliams Ford (former mayor), Lois White Henderson (former librarian), F. Leonard Hargrove (board member), Essae M. Culver (state librarian), J. C. Hamilton (board president), Clyde E. Fant (mayor), and Bessie Vaughn (librarian).

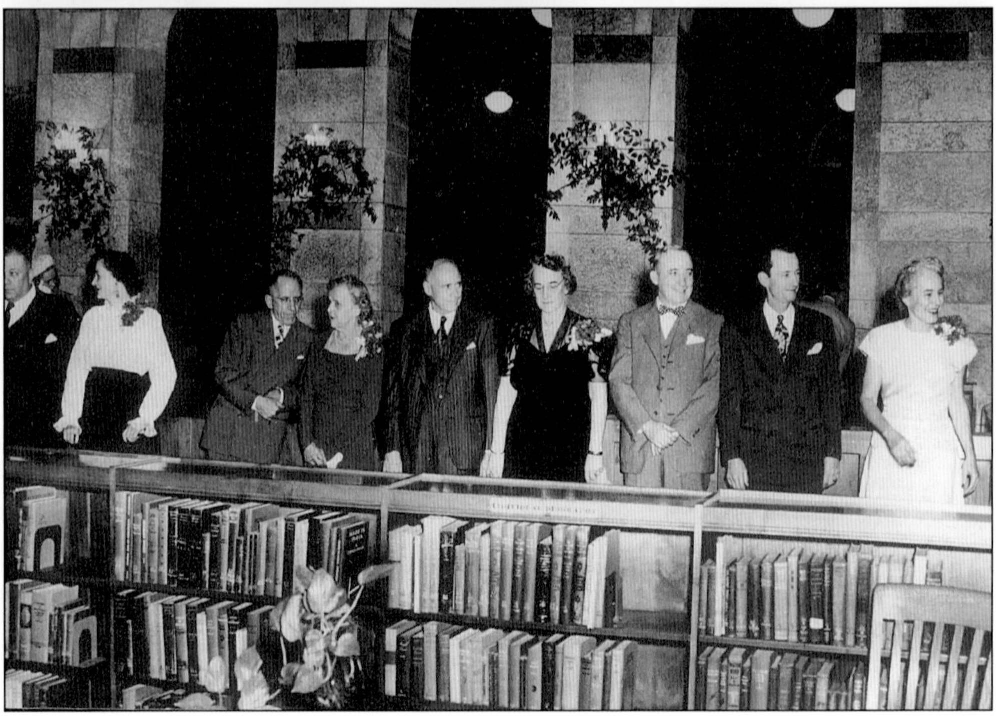

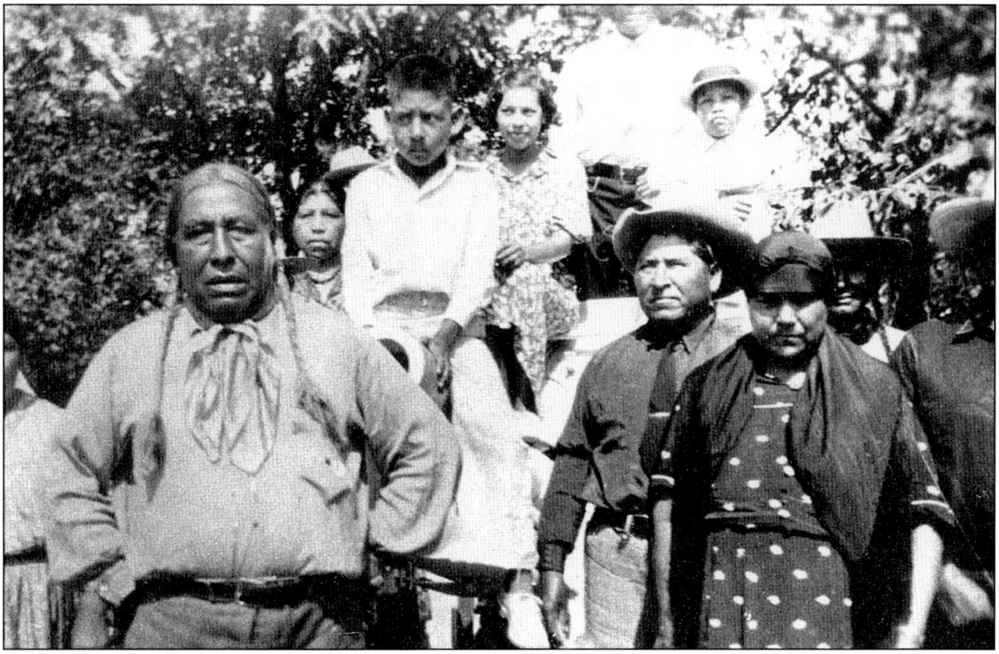

During the Shreveport Centennial Festival of 1935, which commemorated the Caddo Indian Treaty of 1835, many Caddo Indians whose ancestors had left the Shreveport area for Oklahoma following the treaty's ratification were invited back to visit. Here a group gathers downtown during ceremonies honoring them.

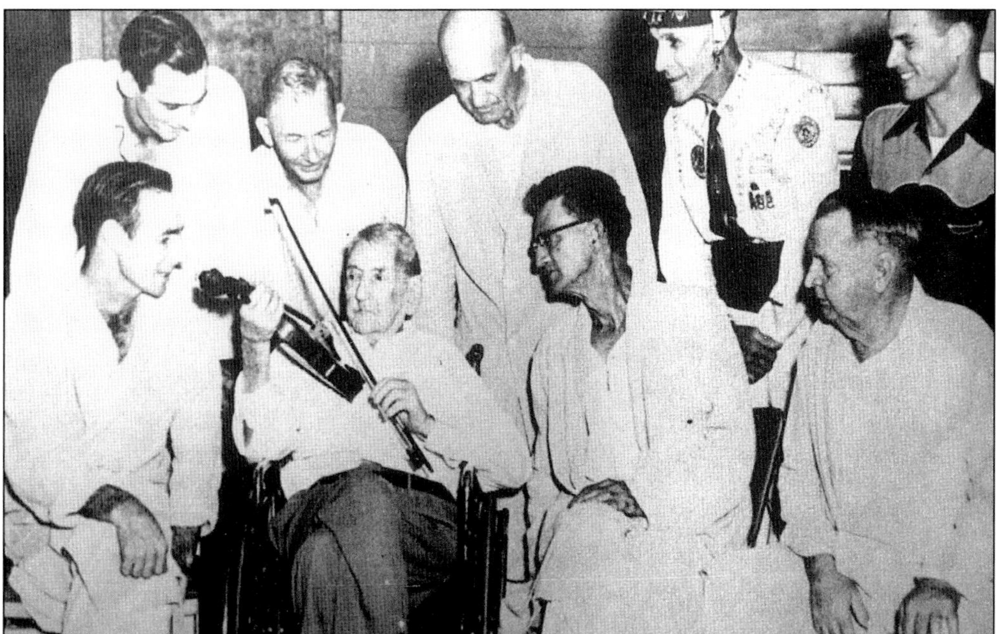

Three of the last surviving Confederate veterans in the world resided in Shreveport and are buried here. Here, the last of the group, William D. Townsend, entertains other patients at the Veterans Administration Hospital in 1952. Townsend, a native of nearby Vienna, in Lincoln Parish, died in 1953 at the age of 107.

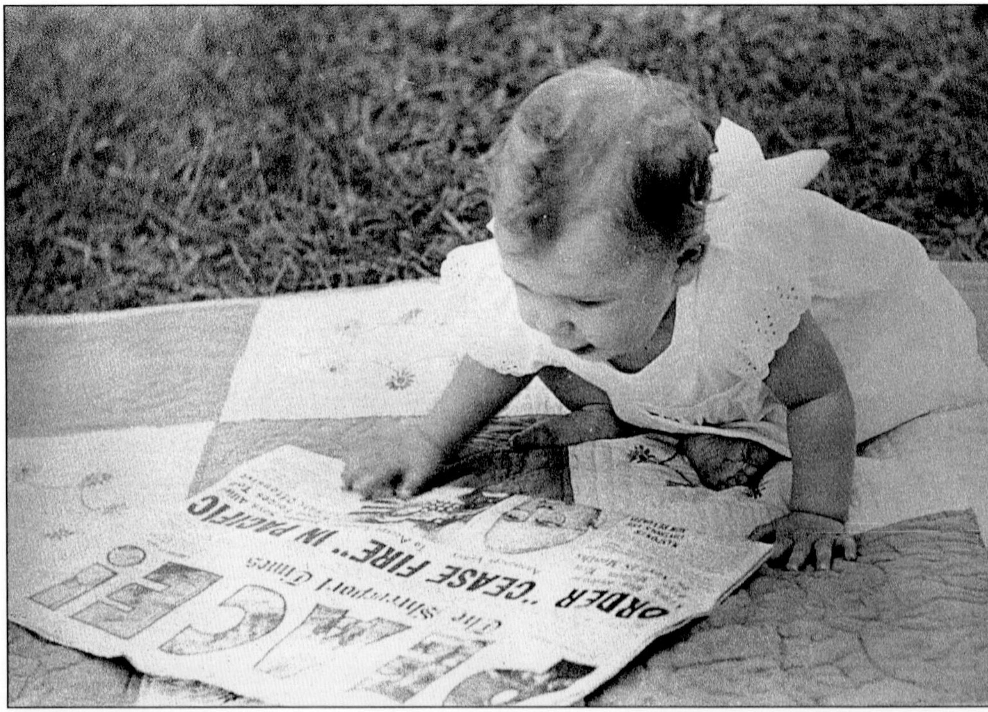

An infant seems to ponder the significance of the August 1945 *Shreveport Times* issue declaring the end of World War II. Fifteen thousand Shreveporters served in the military during the war and another sixteen thousand served in civil defense.

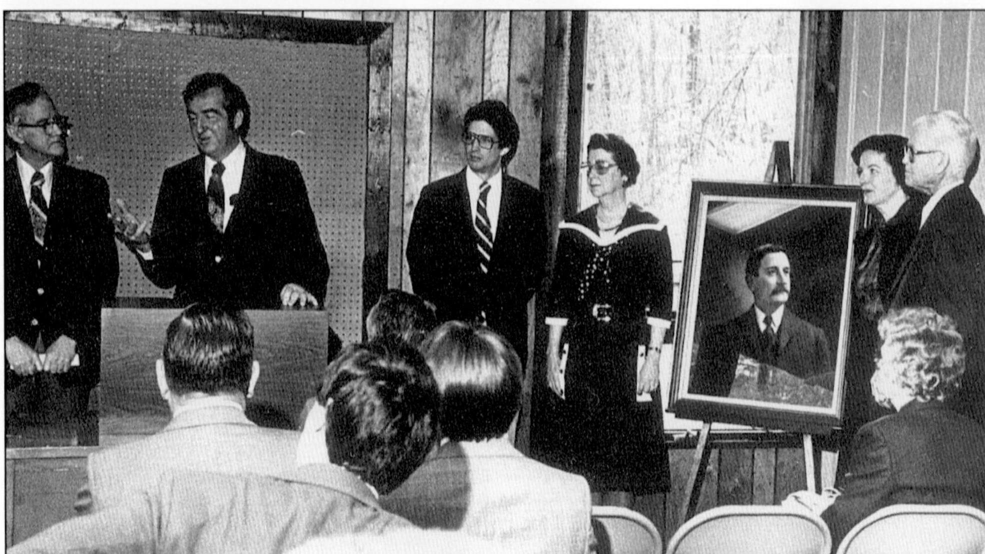

Participating in the dedication of the Walter B. Jacobs Nature Park, on the north side of Shreveport near Blanchard, are (from left to right) Bill Cockrell (Caddo Police Jury president), Joe Lawler (Caddo Police Jury vice president), Walter Jacobs Smith, Elise Lloyd Allison, Martha Harbison, and Horace Downs (police juror). Between Mrs. Allison and Mrs. Harbison is a portrait of Walter Jacobs Sr., president of First National Bank, who died in 1904 and for whom the park is named.

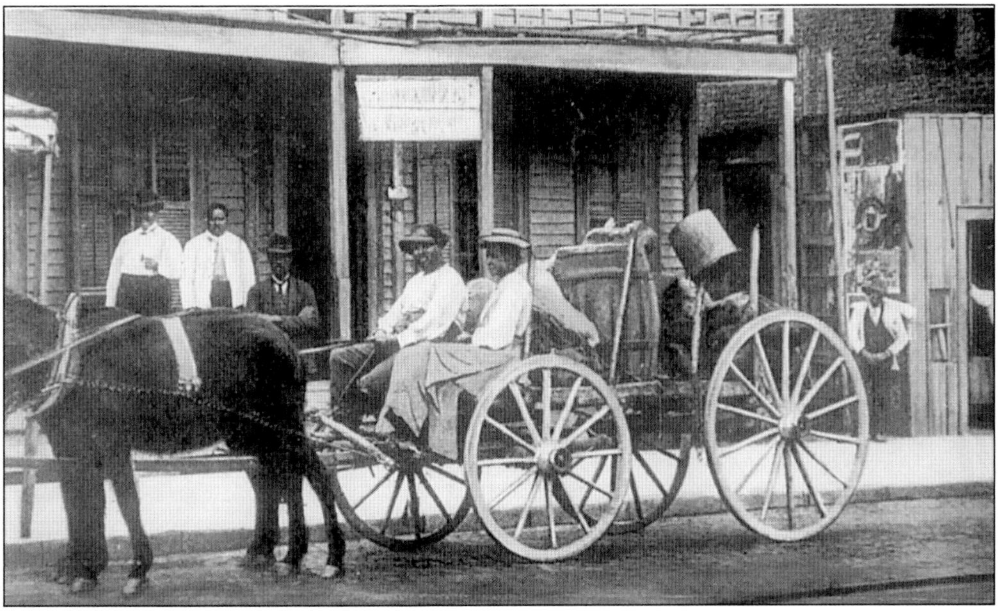

A scene on Common Street is captured around 1900.

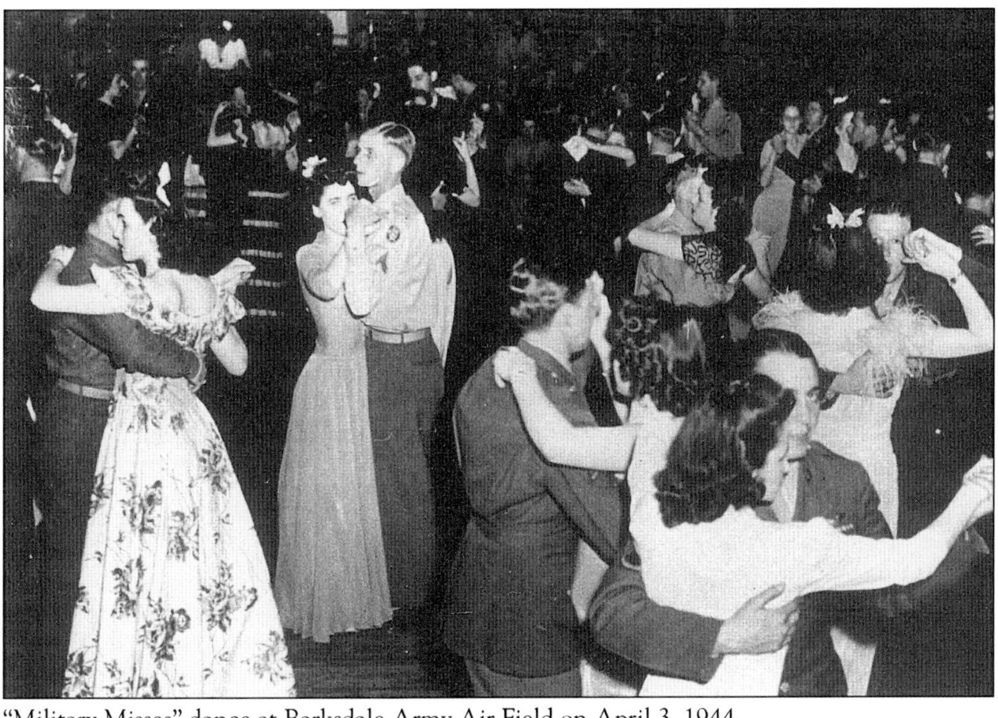

"Military Misses" dance at Barksdale Army Air Field on April 3, 1944.

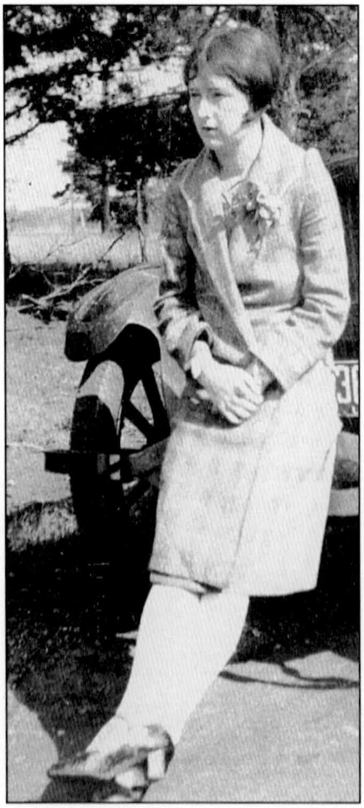

From 1903 through 1917 Shreveport sanctioned a legal red light district in the Bottoms area near downtown. After its official closure the city continued to tolerate its presence until World War II. At one point it was the second largest red light district in the state and the largest, per-capita, in the nation. Here "Lucille," a resident of the district, was photographed by a client around 1920. Her appearance gives no indication of her profession, which was shared by hundreds of other girls and women in "the district."

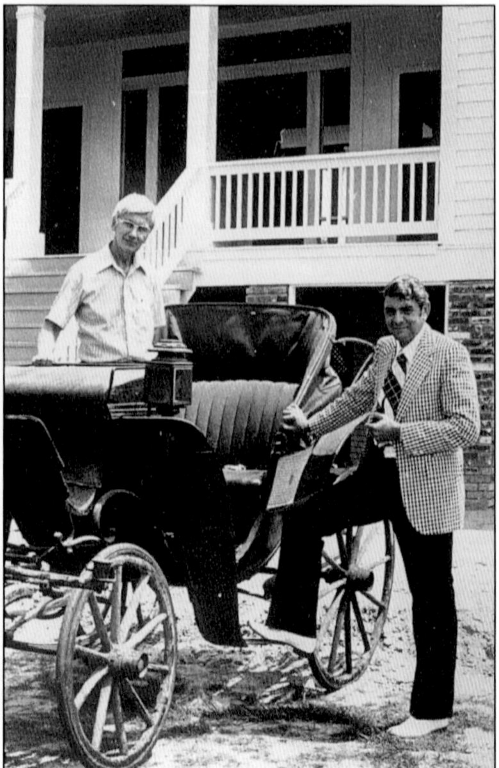

Goodloe R. Stuck (left) chronicled the history of Shreveport's red light district in his popular book *Shreveport Madam*. He was also a pioneer preservationist and regional historian. Here he is seen at the Pioneer Heritage Center at LSUS with history professor and fellow preservationist Dr. John Hall in the late 1970s.

(Above) During the early years of Holiday in Dixie the "Goodwill Ambassadors" traveled the Ark-La-Tex region to promote the festival in nearby towns. Here Ambassador Irving Selber of Shreveport's Selber Bros. Department store is "arrested" by a Kilgore College Rangerette in Kilgore, Texas in 1952. (Below) Kilgore Rangerettes are seen on Milam Street in downtown Shreveport during the 1950 Holiday in Dixie parade.

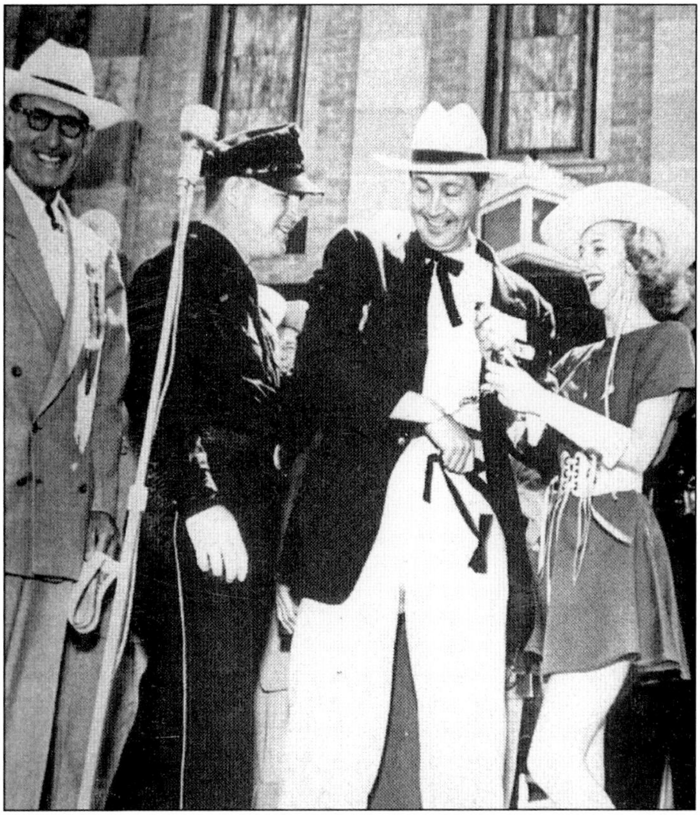

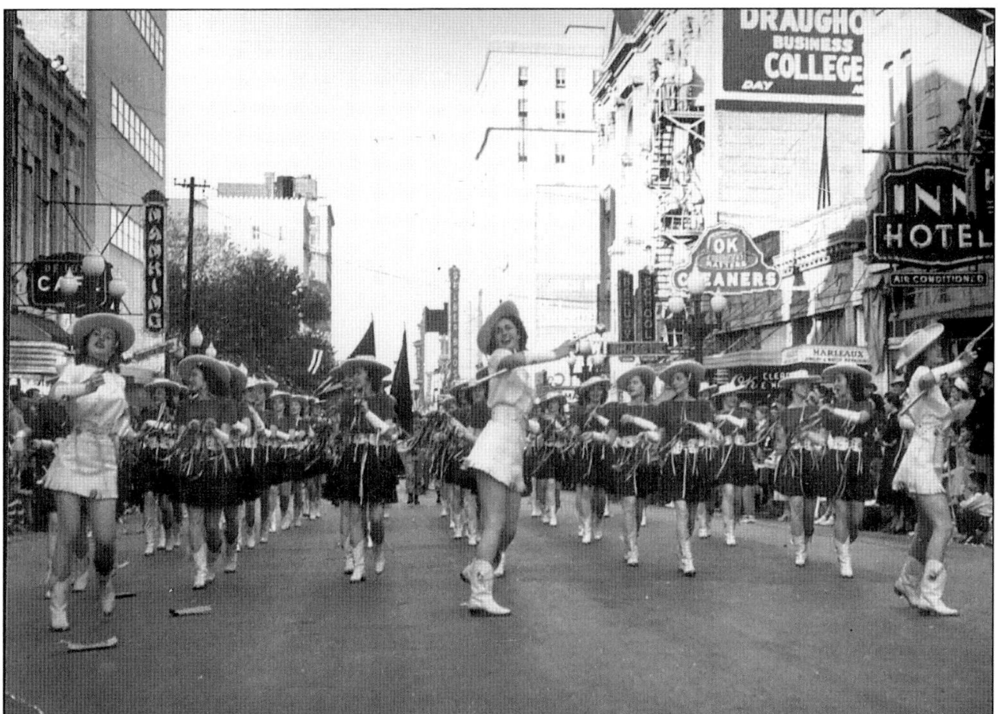

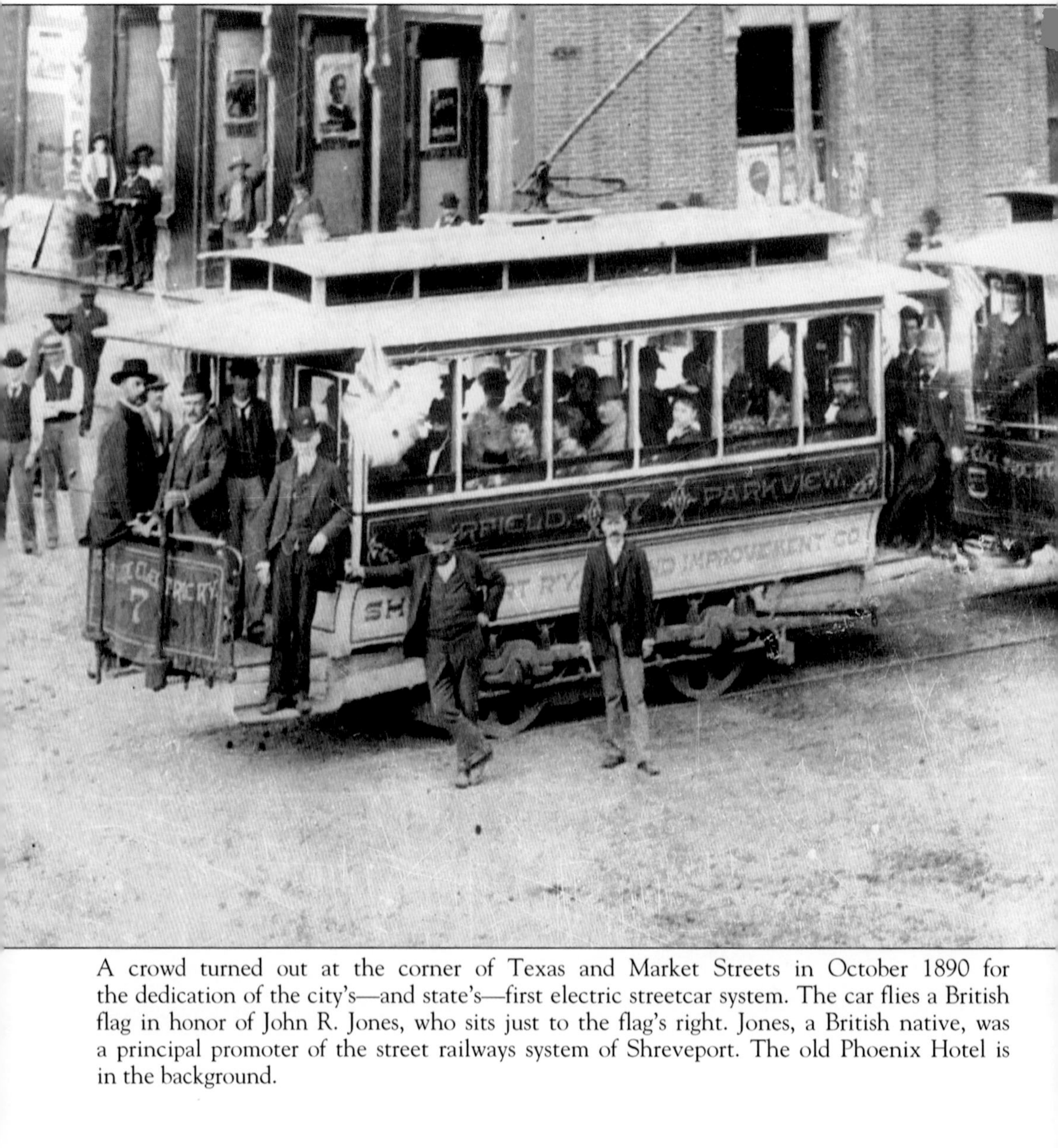

A crowd turned out at the corner of Texas and Market Streets in October 1890 for the dedication of the city's—and state's—first electric streetcar system. The car flies a British flag in honor of John R. Jones, who sits just to the flag's right. Jones, a British native, was a principal promoter of the street railways system of Shreveport. The old Phoenix Hotel is in the background.

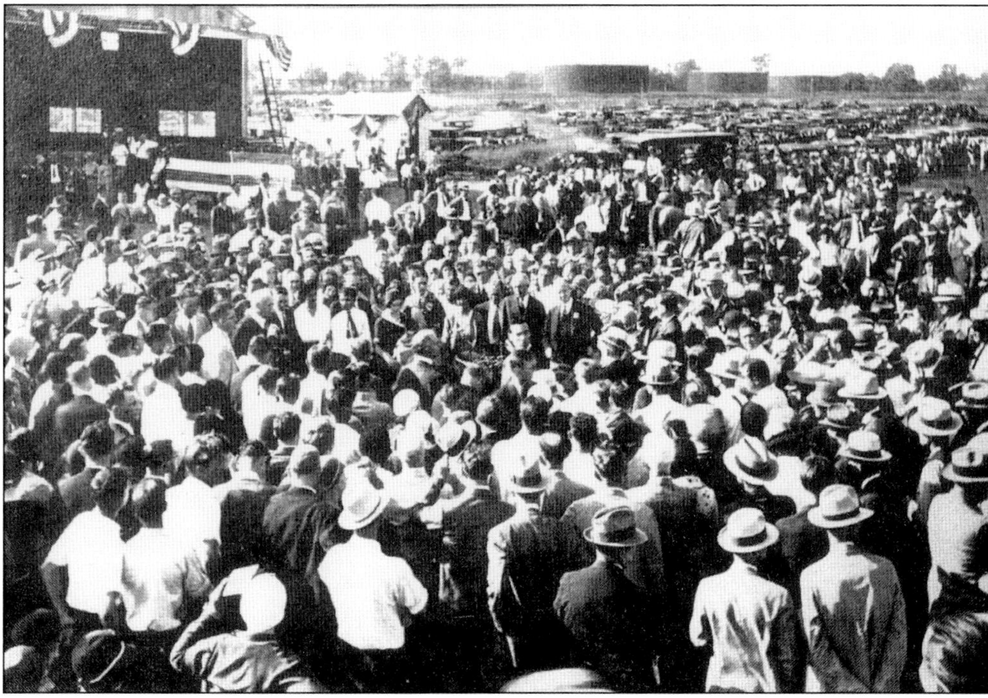

Shreveport's air fields have always been appropriate venues for large gatherings, from the inauguration of airmail service to and from Shreveport at the Texaco Riverside Airport on Anderson Island on October 15, 1930 (above) to presidential visits such as that of President Ford in April 1976 (below).

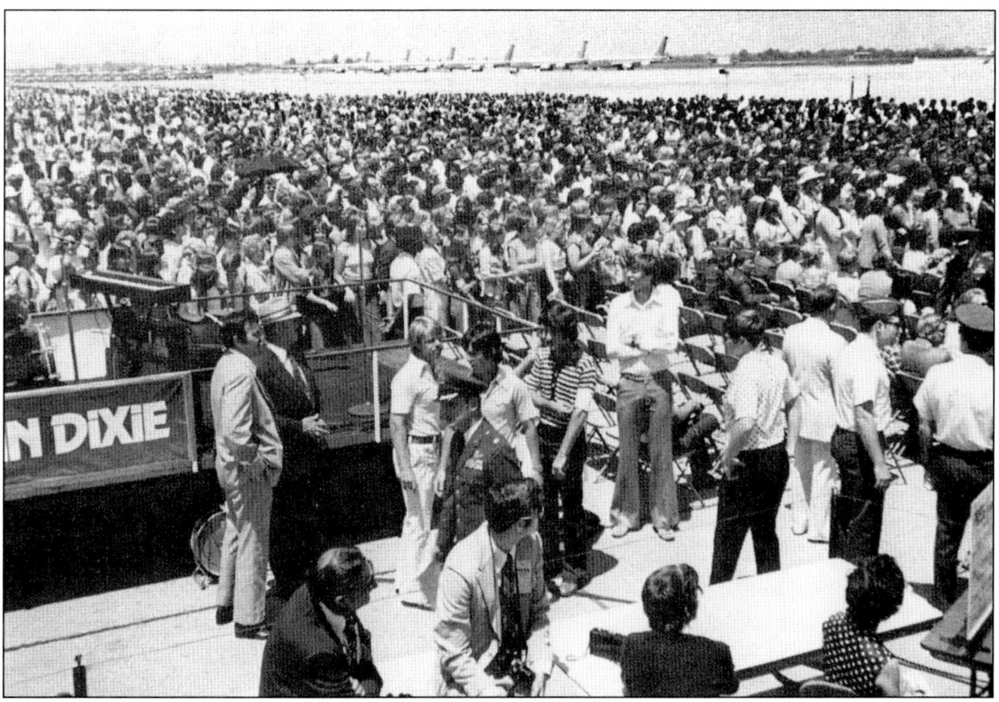

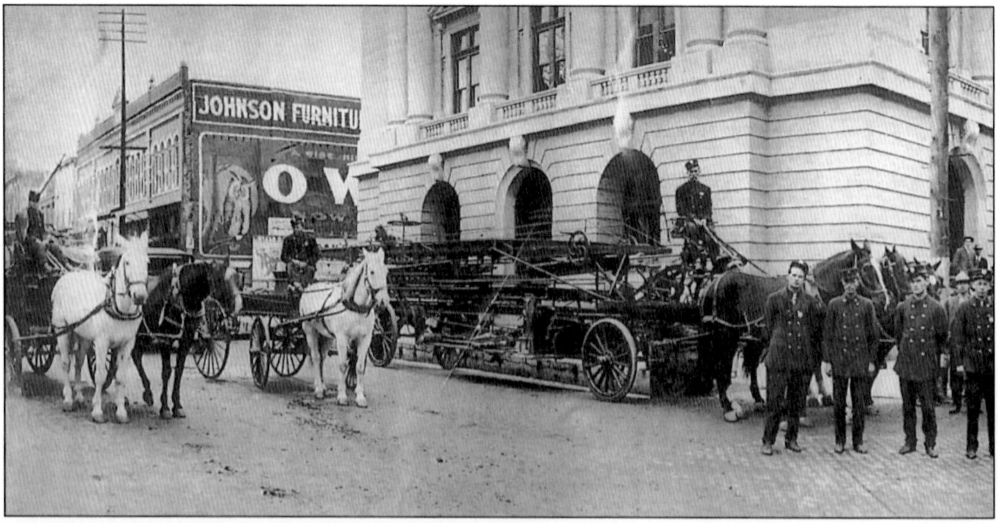

Members of the Shreveport Fire Department gather in front of city hall on Milam Street about 1910. The old Central Fire Station was directly across the street from the building with the Johnson Furniture sign.

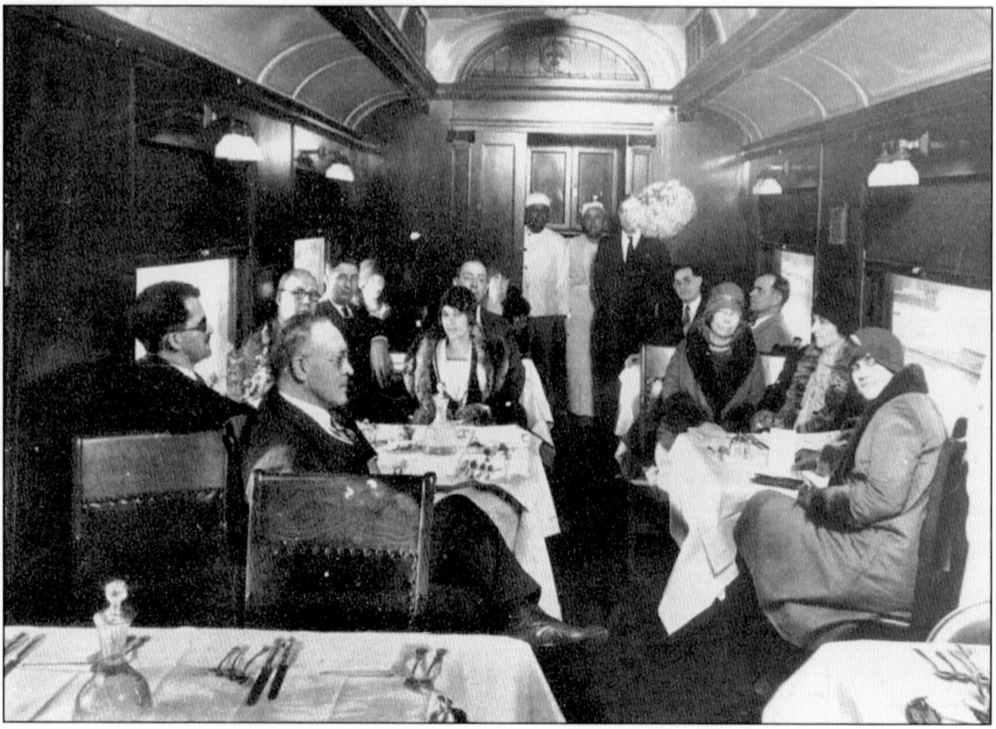

Passengers prepare to have dinner aboard the inaugural run of the Louisiana & Arkansas Railroad's *Shreveporter* in December of 1928.

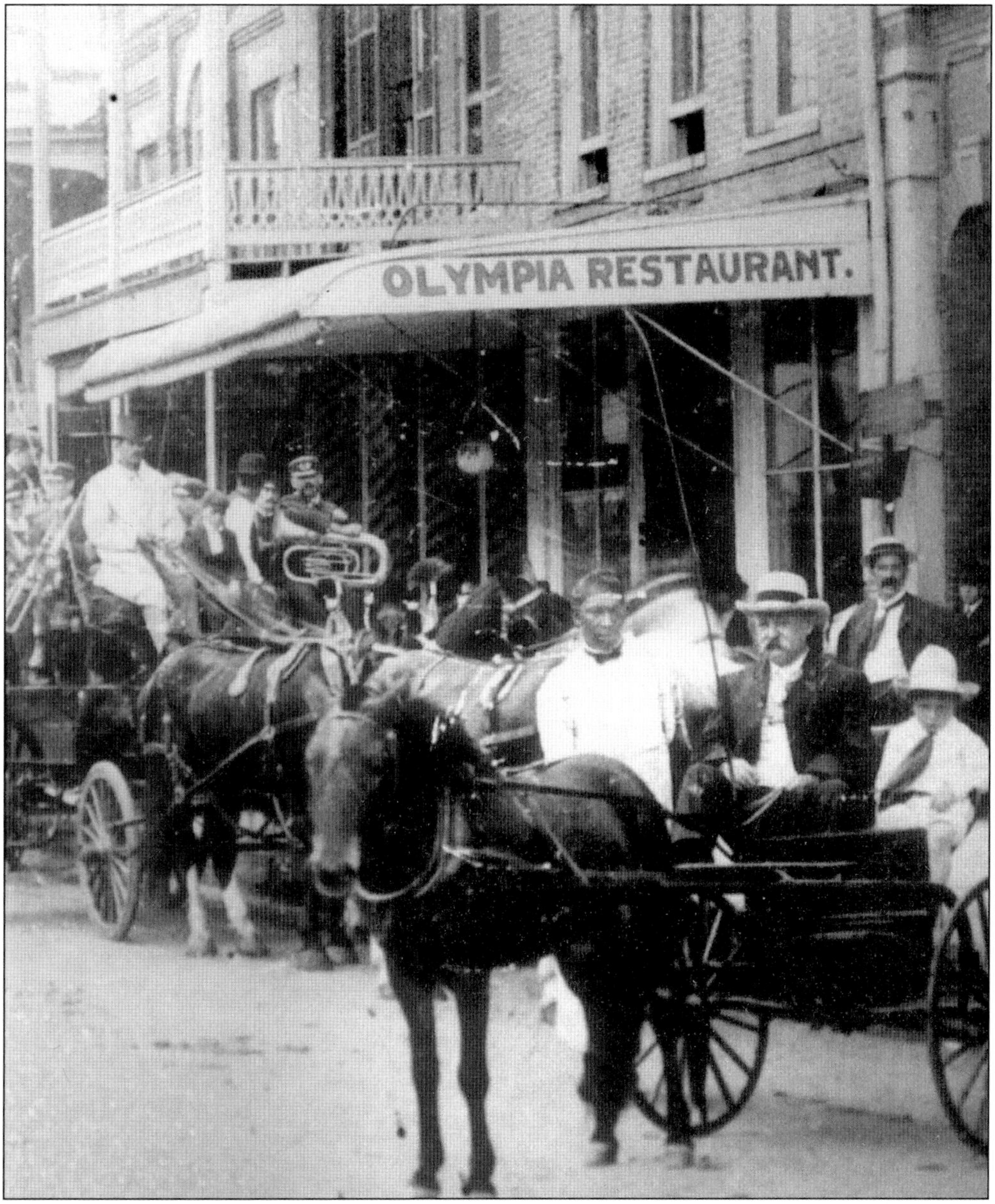

Participants in the band of an 1890s Mardi Gras parade wait on Market Street outside the Olympia Restaurant, a 19th-century Shreveport institution (predecessor to the old Columbia Restaurant) while Rex and his entourage dine within. From the 1860s through the 1920s Mardi Gras was a major Shreveport event. It was revived again in the 1980s.

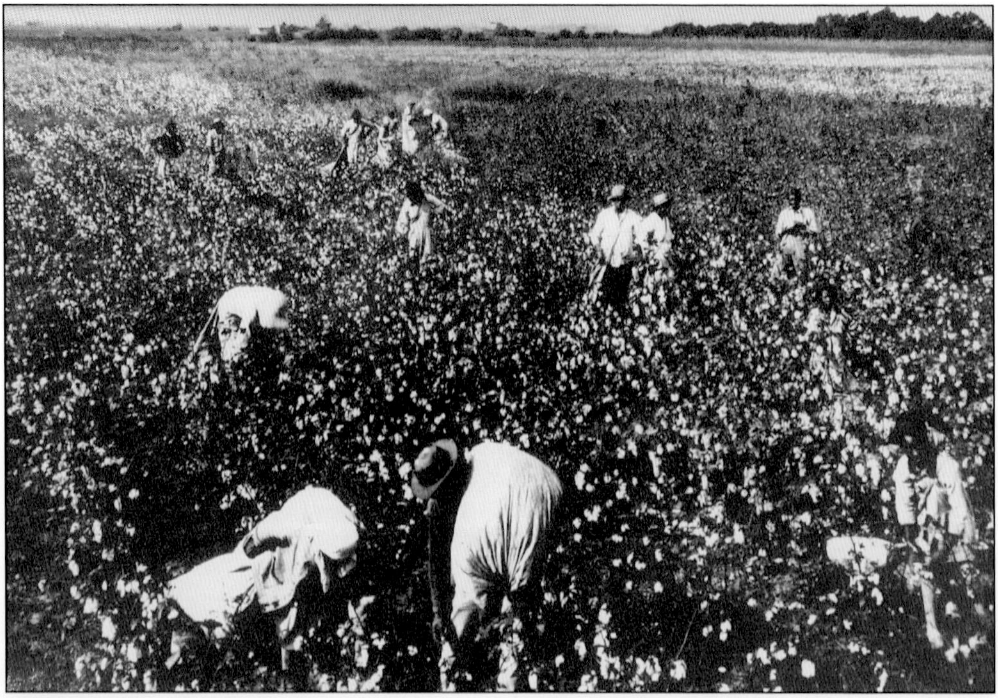

(Above) A late 19th-century view depicts cotton picking in the fields just south of Shreveport. Once cotton was the center of the area's economy and vast cotton plantations surrounded the city. Today many of Shreveport's and Bossier's modern subdivisions are built on land which was formerly cultivated in cotton. (Below) A Chamber of Commerce publicity shot of a planter's daughter, Margaret Moore, and helper is from the early 1930s.

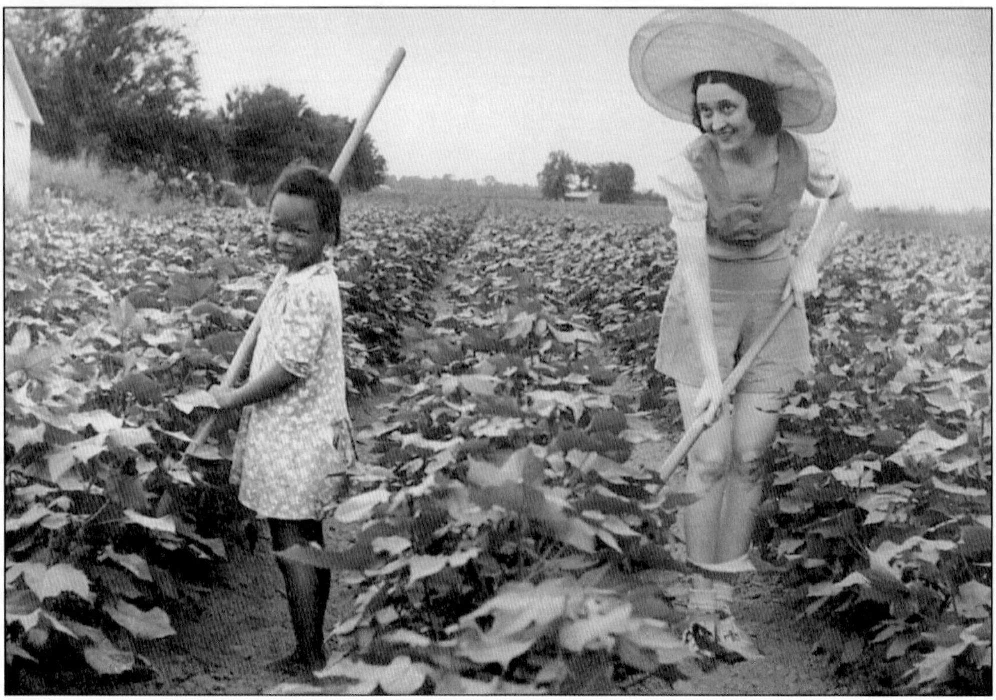

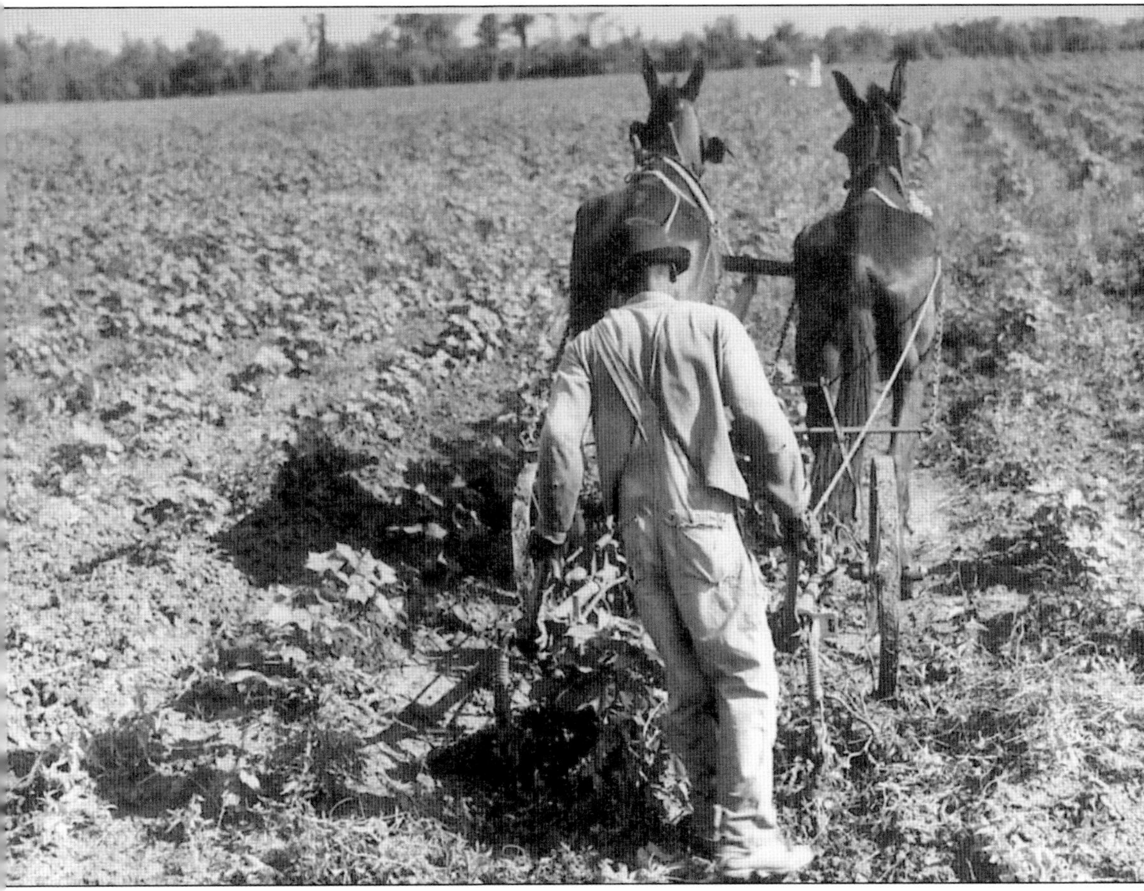

A sharecropper cultivates cotton with a mule-operated plow in the Shreveport vicinity in June 1931. As late as the 1930s much agricultural work was still done in a primitive fashion, hardly more advanced than a century before.

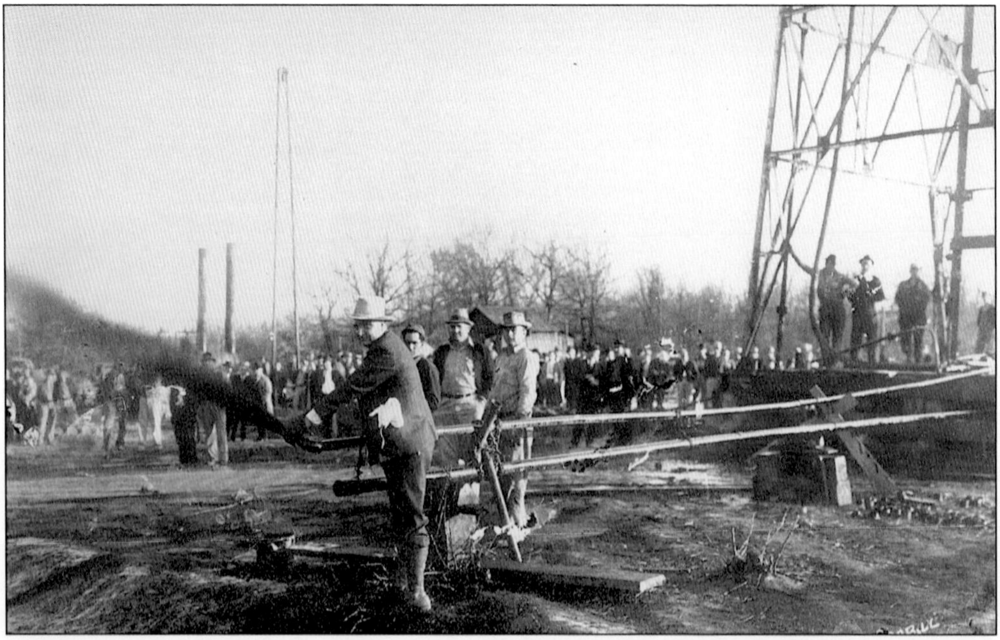

Early in the 20th century, oil replaced cotton as the premier commodity of the Shreveport area's economy. Many fortunes were made in the oilfields of Caddo and nearby parishes, including, at least in part, those of Howard Hughes and H.L. Hunt. At top, pioneer Shreveporter Reb Oakes is pictured with a well that proved productive. Below, the drilling of a well north of Shreveport is depicted around 1910. Third from the left is driller Alex Rice, later one of Shreveport's most prominent and successful oil operators.

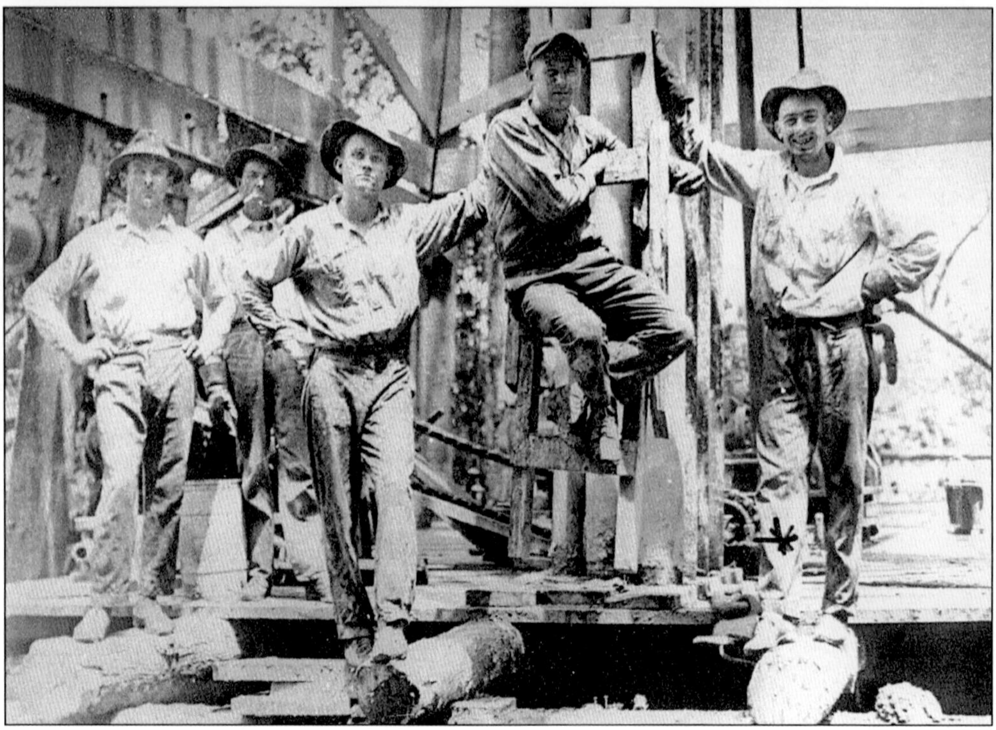

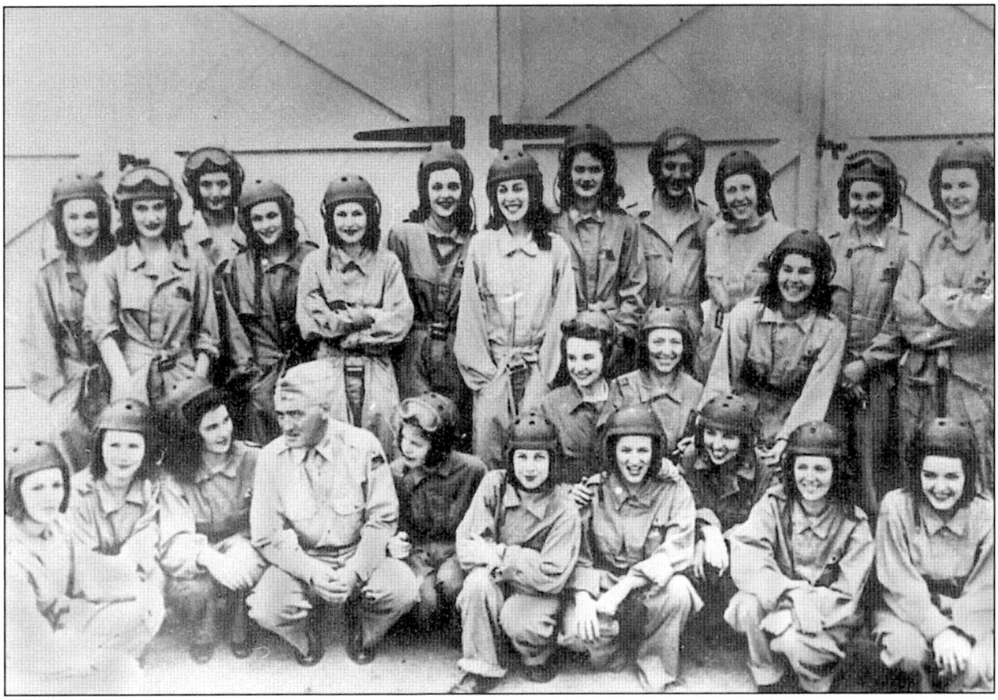

Members of the Women's Army Corp at Barksdale Army Air Field are pictured during World War II.

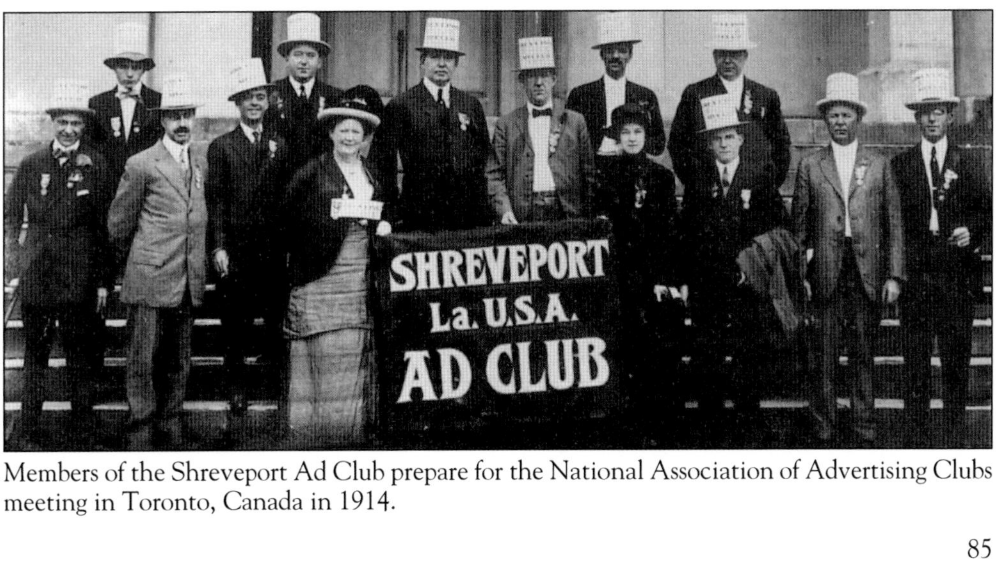

Members of the Shreveport Ad Club prepare for the National Association of Advertising Clubs meeting in Toronto, Canada in 1914.

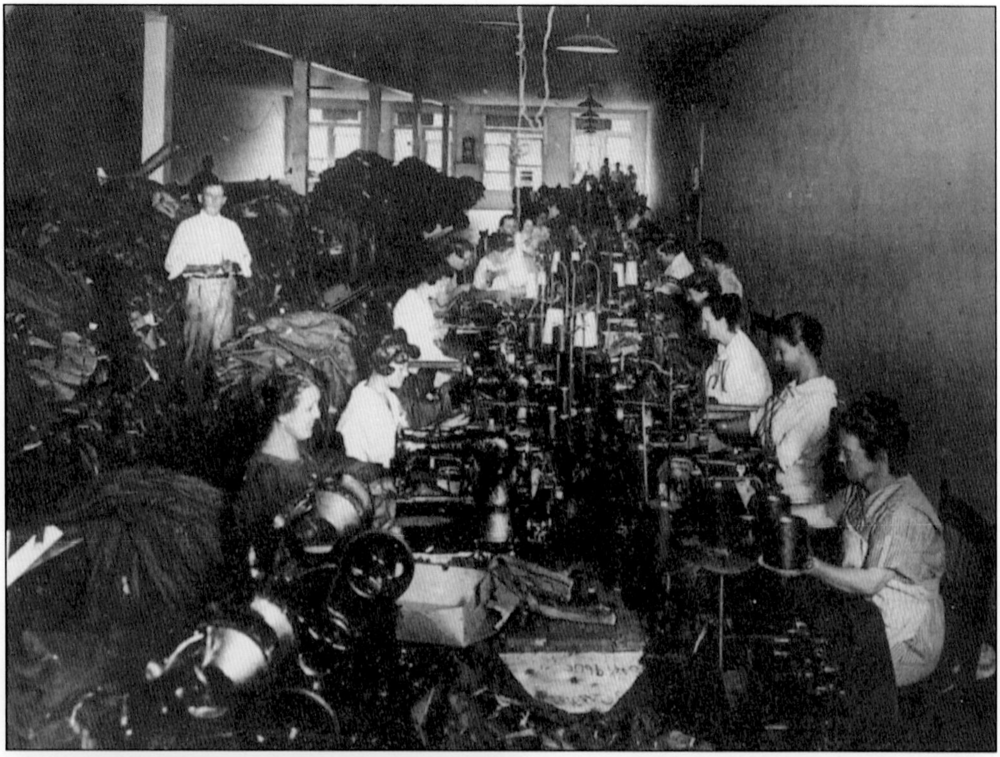

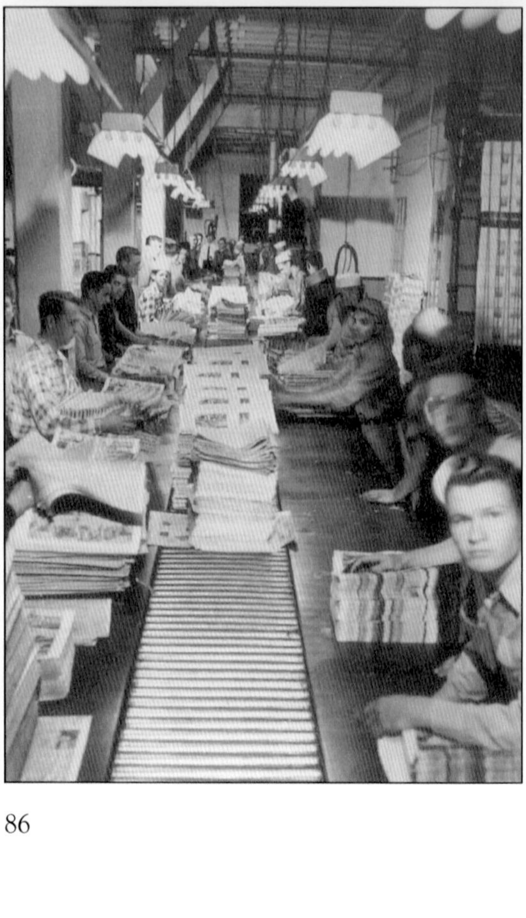

(Above) The sewing department of the Long-Hargrove Manufacturing Company in Shreveport is the subject of this 1910 photo. (Below) The assembling and bundling of newspapers is taking place at the *Shreveport Times* Marshall Street production plant in the 1940s.

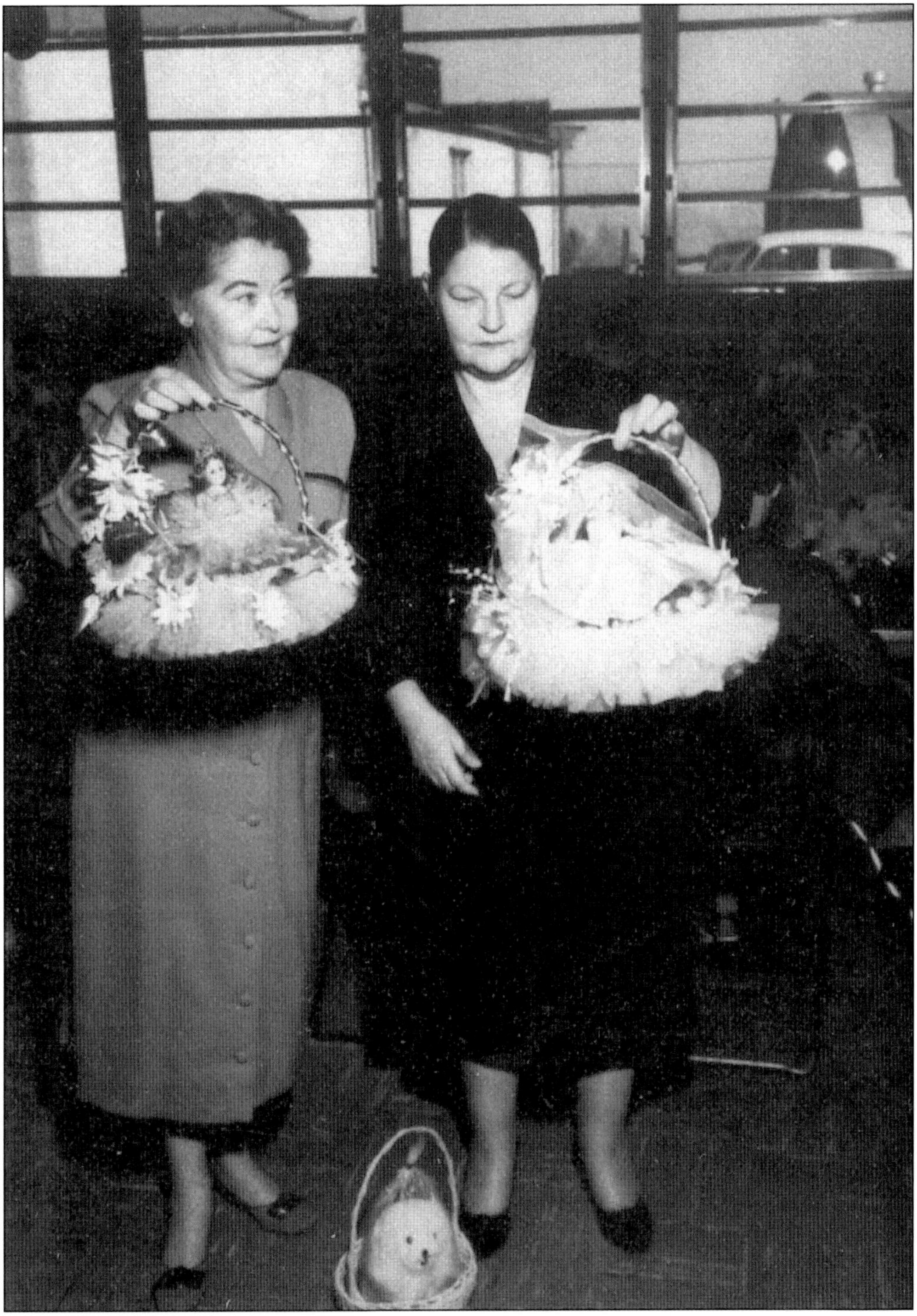

Two "Easter Basket Ladies," Lady J. Tanner and Katherine F. Piper, display their creations in the 1950s. The Easter Basket Ladies were a volunteer group organized in 1950 to make special decorative gift baskets using core baskets made by the blind. The gift baskets, each unique and having a different theme, were sold to raise money for the Shreveport Association for the Blind.

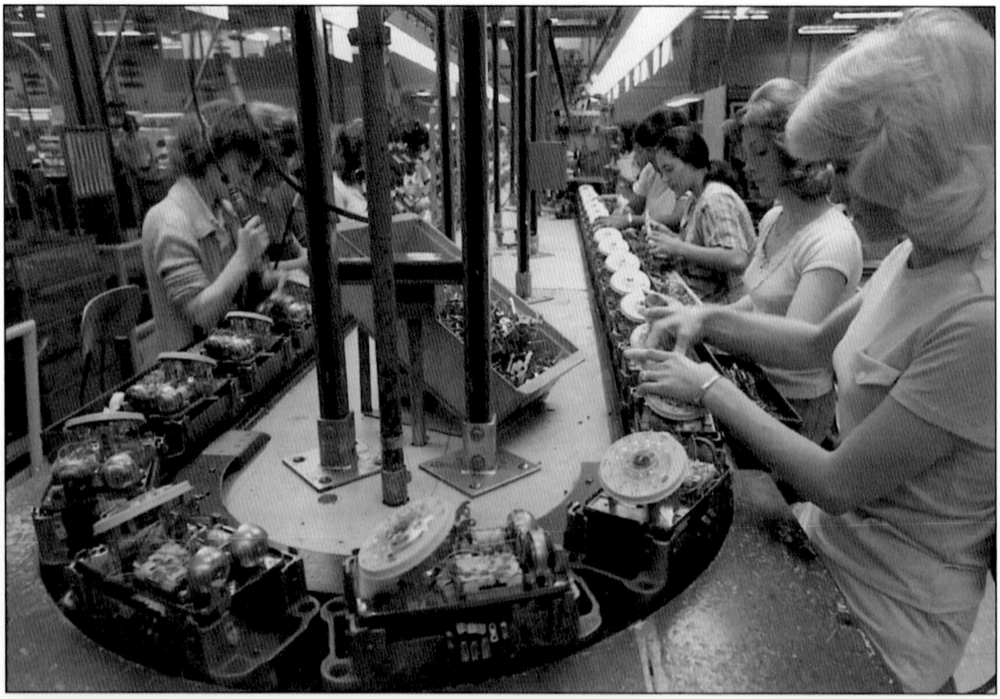

(Above) Telephones are assembled at the Western Electric Plant on Mansfield Road in 1977. Shreveport was once the center of telephone production in the United States. (Below) A downtown office interior is pictured about 1915. Note the presence of a pot-bellied stove in front of the window and behind the desks. Note also the roll-top desk at left center.

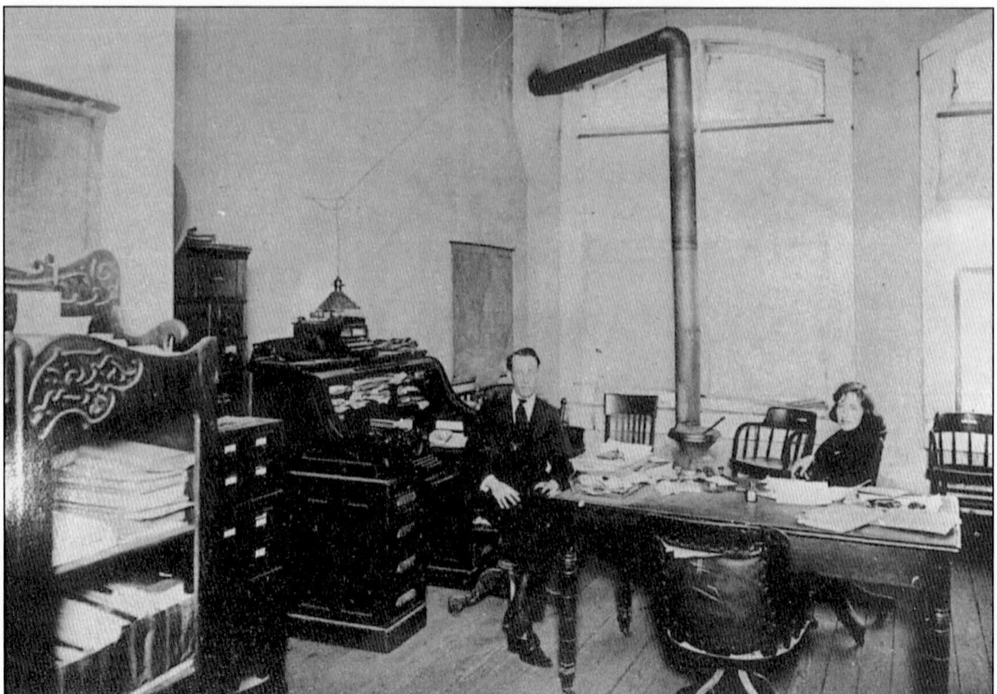

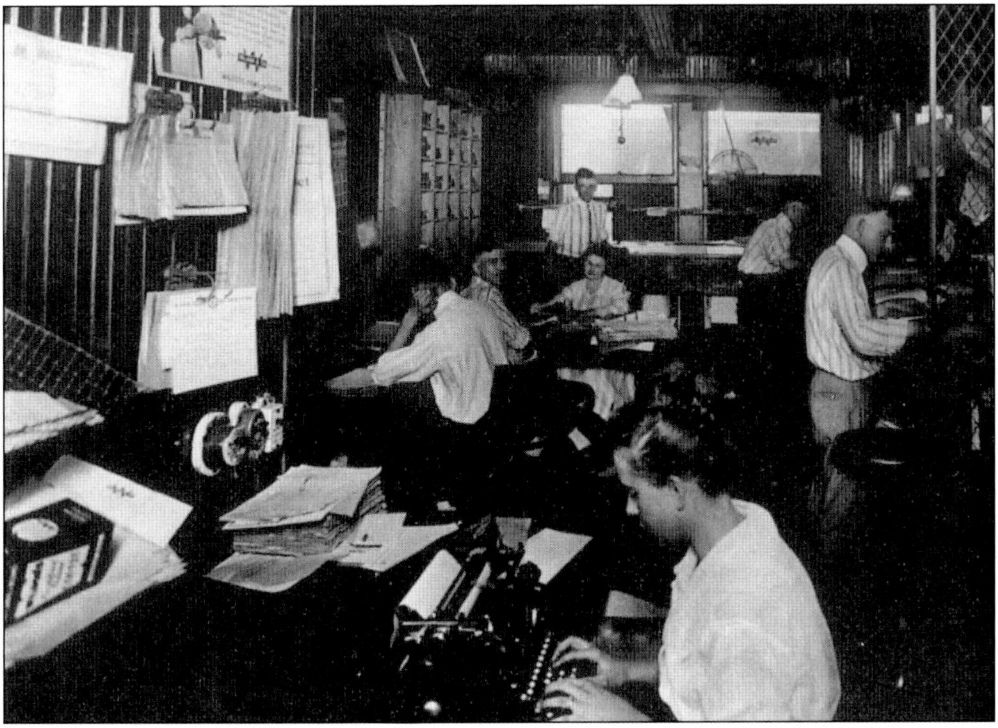

(Above) The accounting department of the Wilson Meat Packing Company's Shreveport plant poses for a photograph around 1915. (Below) Robert L. Jackson and another employee of the Excelsior Laundry Company, together with their horse Reff, pose for the camera on Fairfield Avenue in 1912.

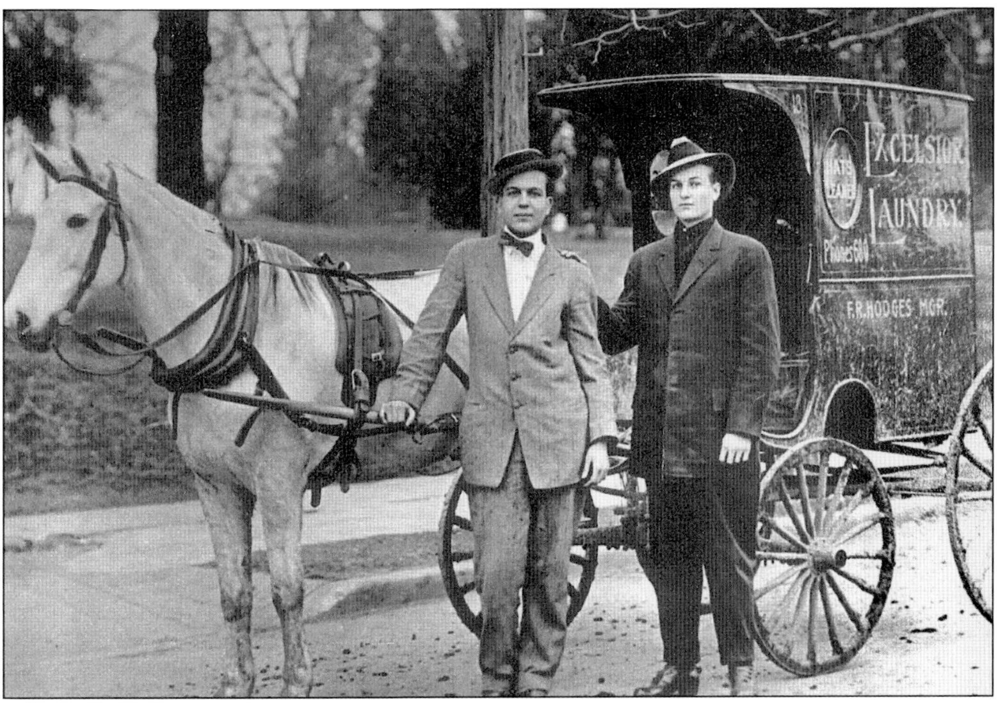

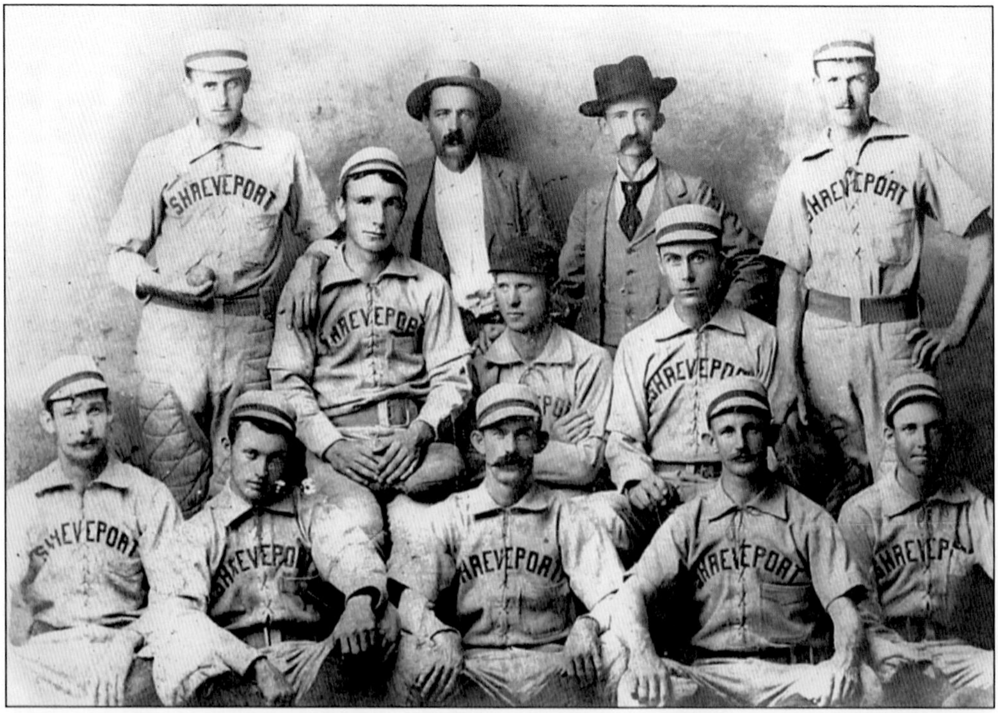

The first team sport supported by the city of Shreveport was baseball; it remains popular today. At top is a photo of the first Shreveport baseball team—the O.K. Club of 1885. By 1900 it had evolved into a professional Southern League team. Below is a local amateur team, the Hirsch-Lehman Wampus Cats, in 1917.

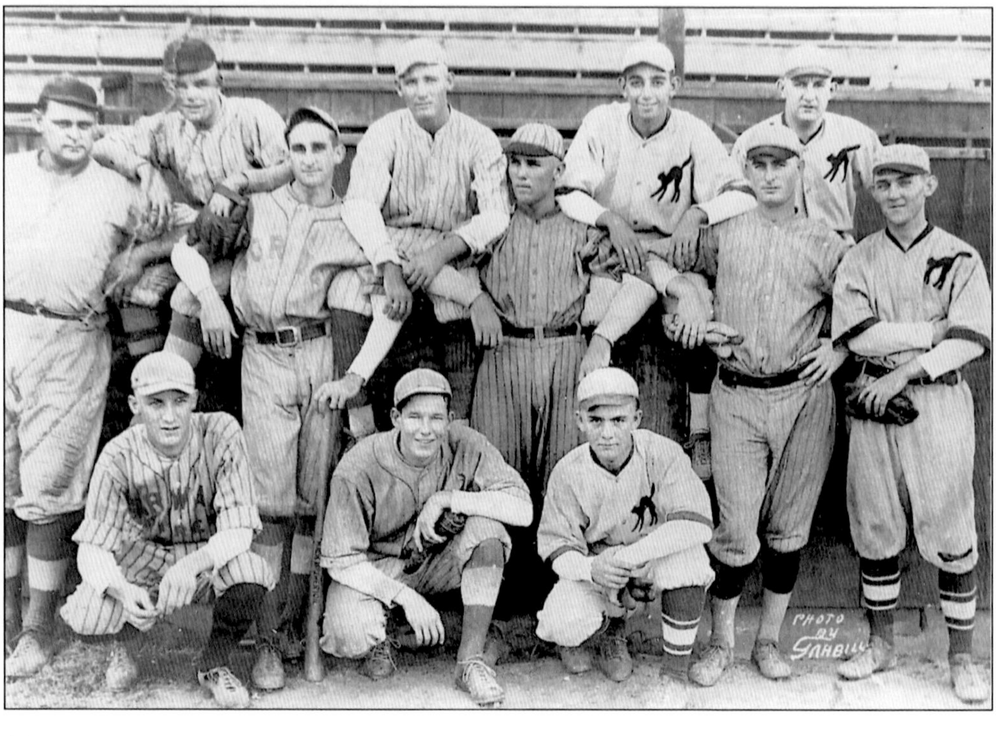

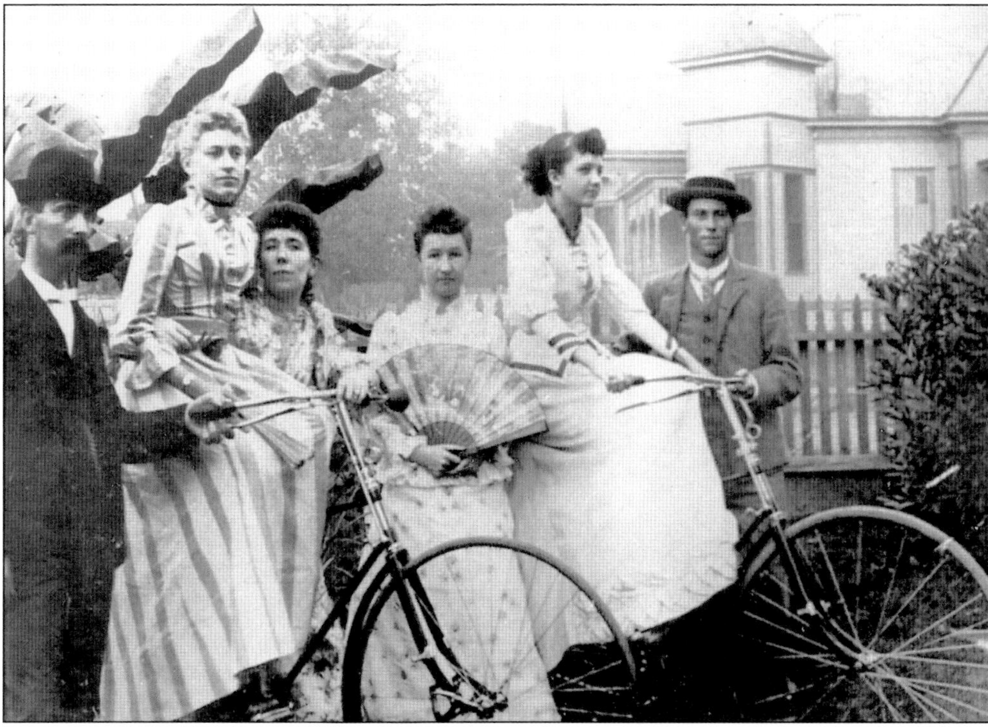

A group of young cyclists pose in front of the Jordan Street home of William J. Bayersdorfer, one-time president of First National Bank, around 1900.

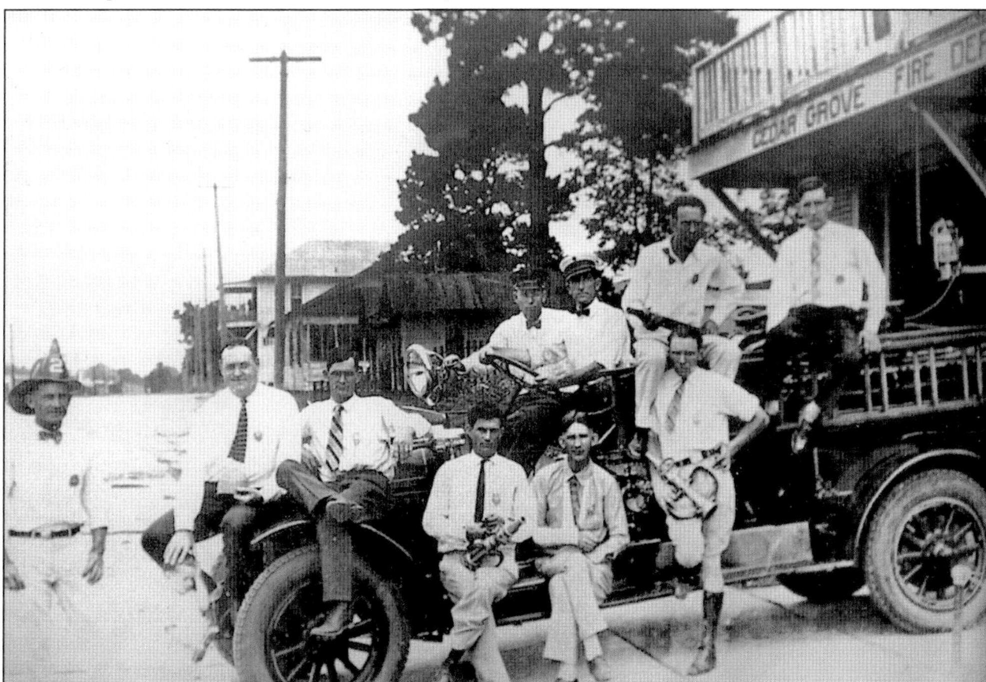

Members of the Cedar Grove Fire Department are pictured in front of their firehouse on East 70th Street in the early 1920s.

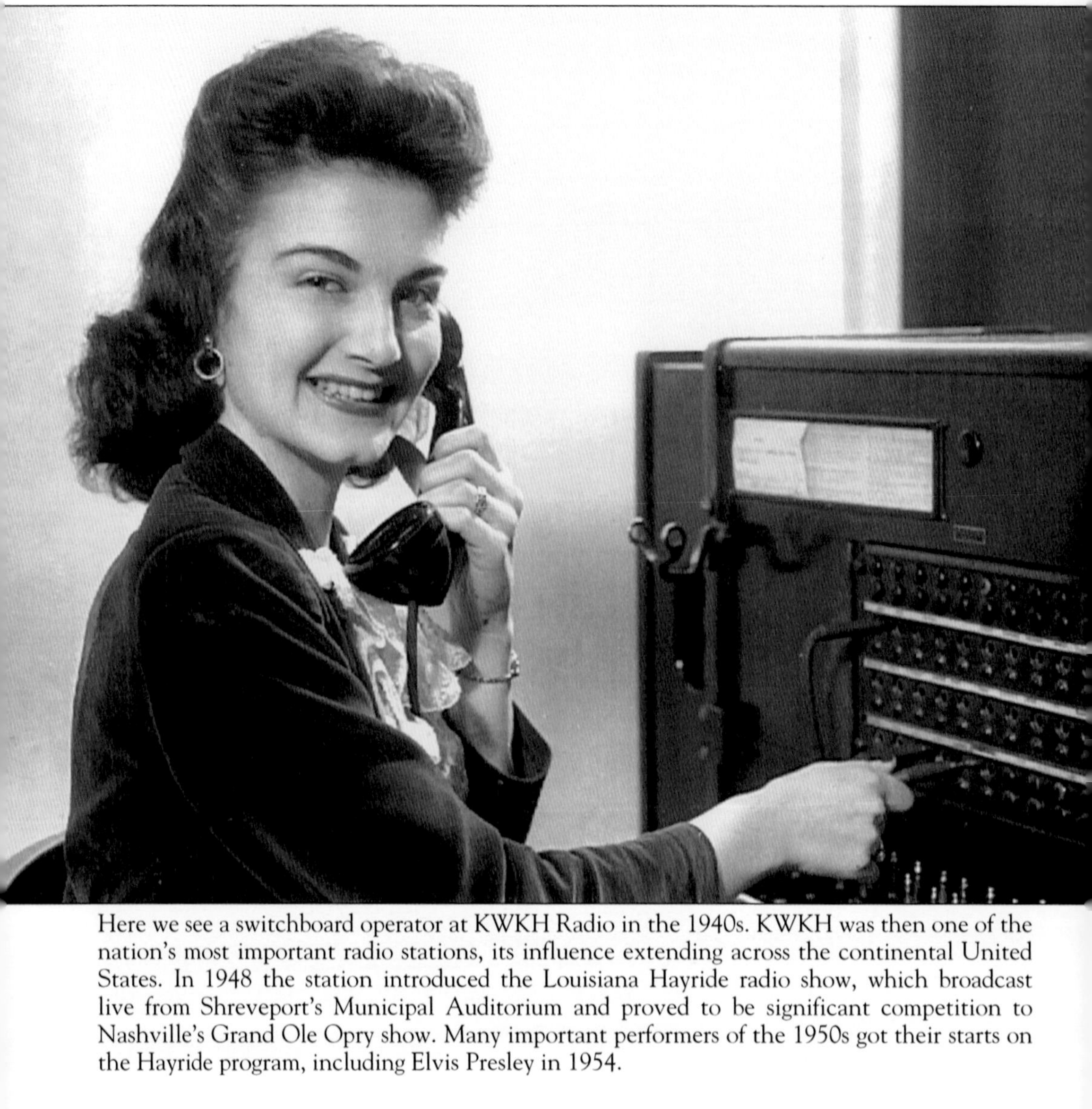

Here we see a switchboard operator at KWKH Radio in the 1940s. KWKH was then one of the nation's most important radio stations, its influence extending across the continental United States. In 1948 the station introduced the Louisiana Hayride radio show, which broadcast live from Shreveport's Municipal Auditorium and proved to be significant competition to Nashville's Grand Ole Opry show. Many important performers of the 1950s got their starts on the Hayride program, including Elvis Presley in 1954.

Local actors Henry Clements and Katherine Brash Jeter rehearse their lines in a play for the Shreveport Little Theatre in 1963. Kay Jeter is a noted local historian and attorney and for a time in the 1980s was a state district court judge.

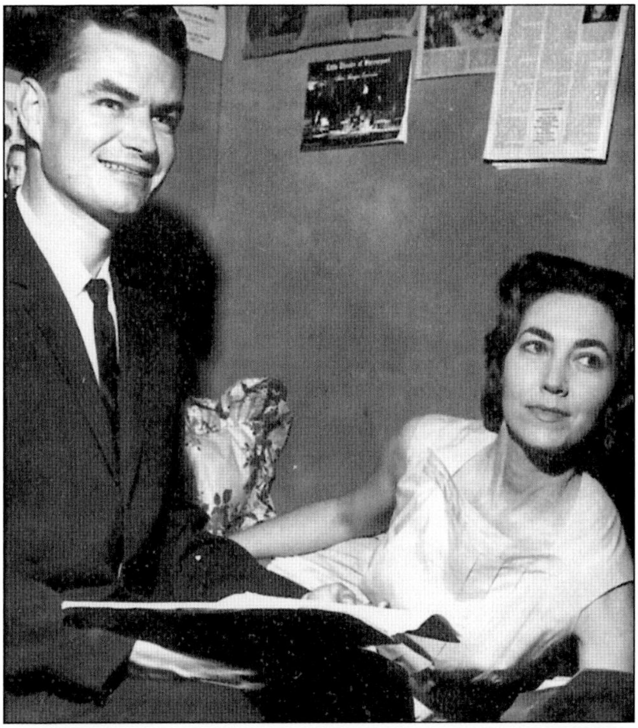

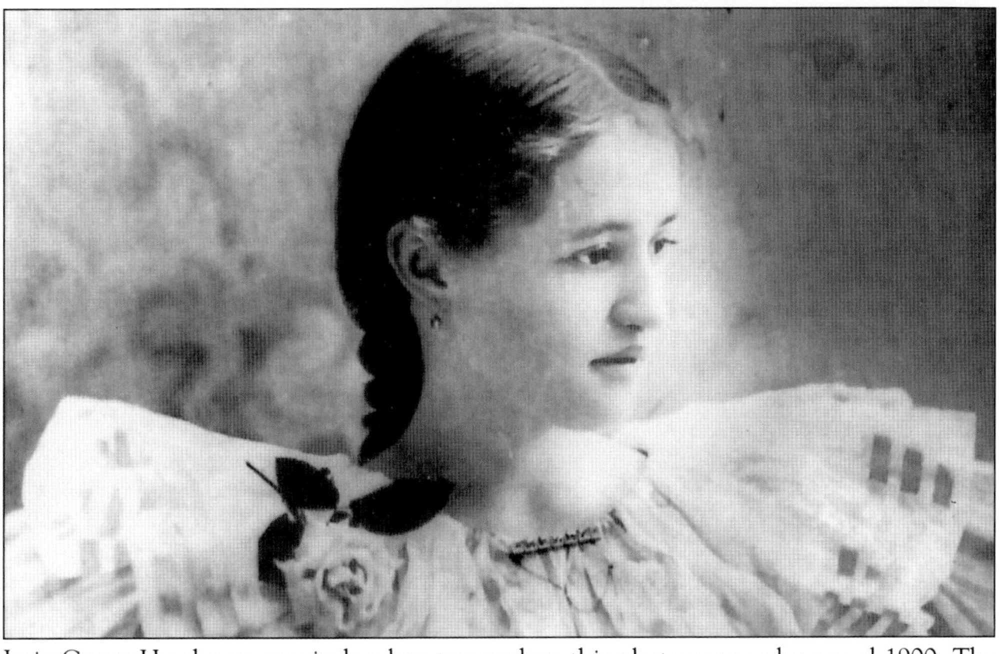

Josie Carter Henderson was in her late teens when this photo was made around 1900. The wife of flamboyant radio personality and business leader William Kennon Henderson and the daughter of flamboyant local showman and businessman Leon Marks Carter, Josie made a name for herself with political activism. She was a delegate to the Republican National Convention of 1932, an era in which few Louisianans and even fewer Shreveporters were registered Republicans. She died in 1945.

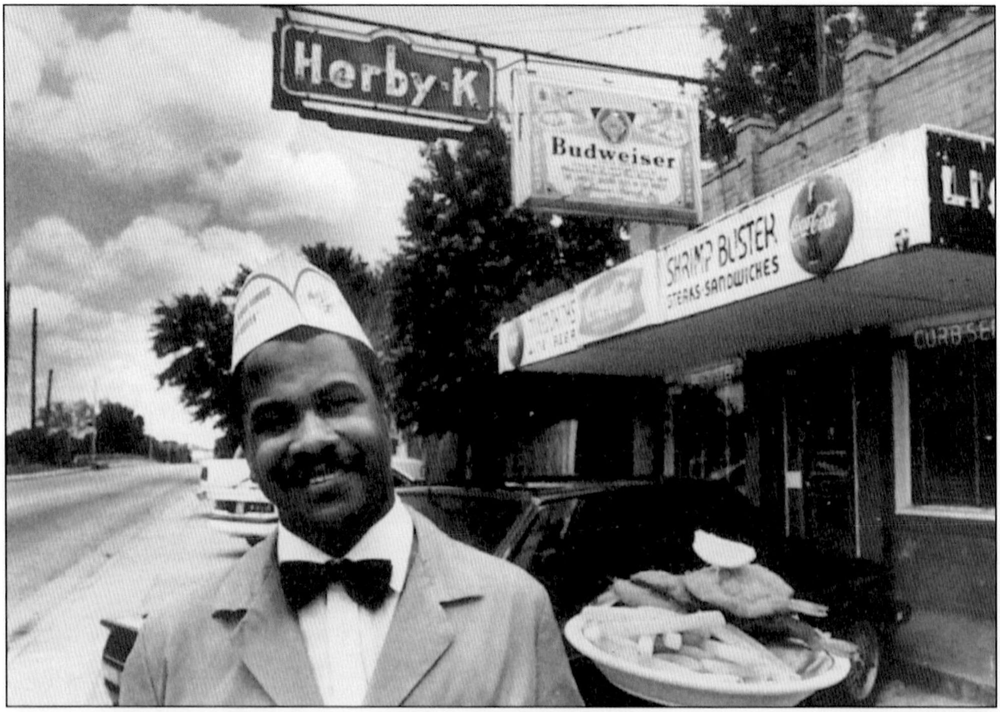

(Above) The late Jimmy Jenkins displays the famous "shrimp buster," the house specialty of Herby K's Restaurant on Pierre Avenue. Both the restaurant and Jimmy were longtime Shreveport institutions. Herby K's is still in operation. (Below) Another longtime Shreveport institution was Abe Ritman and his Abe's Sea & Sirloin restaurant on Marshall Street.

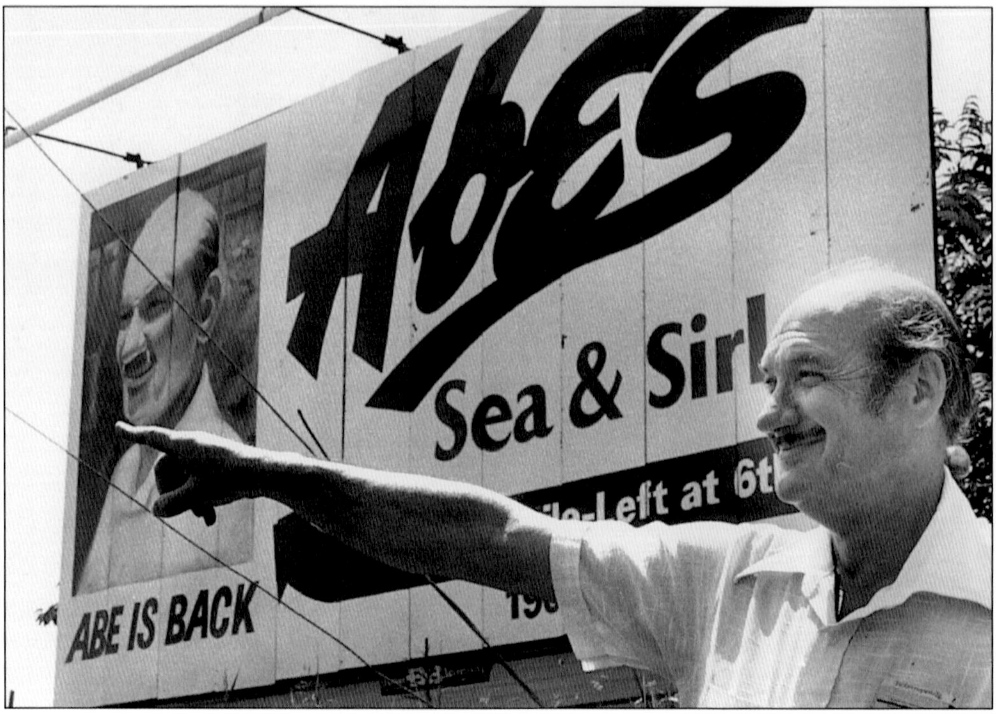

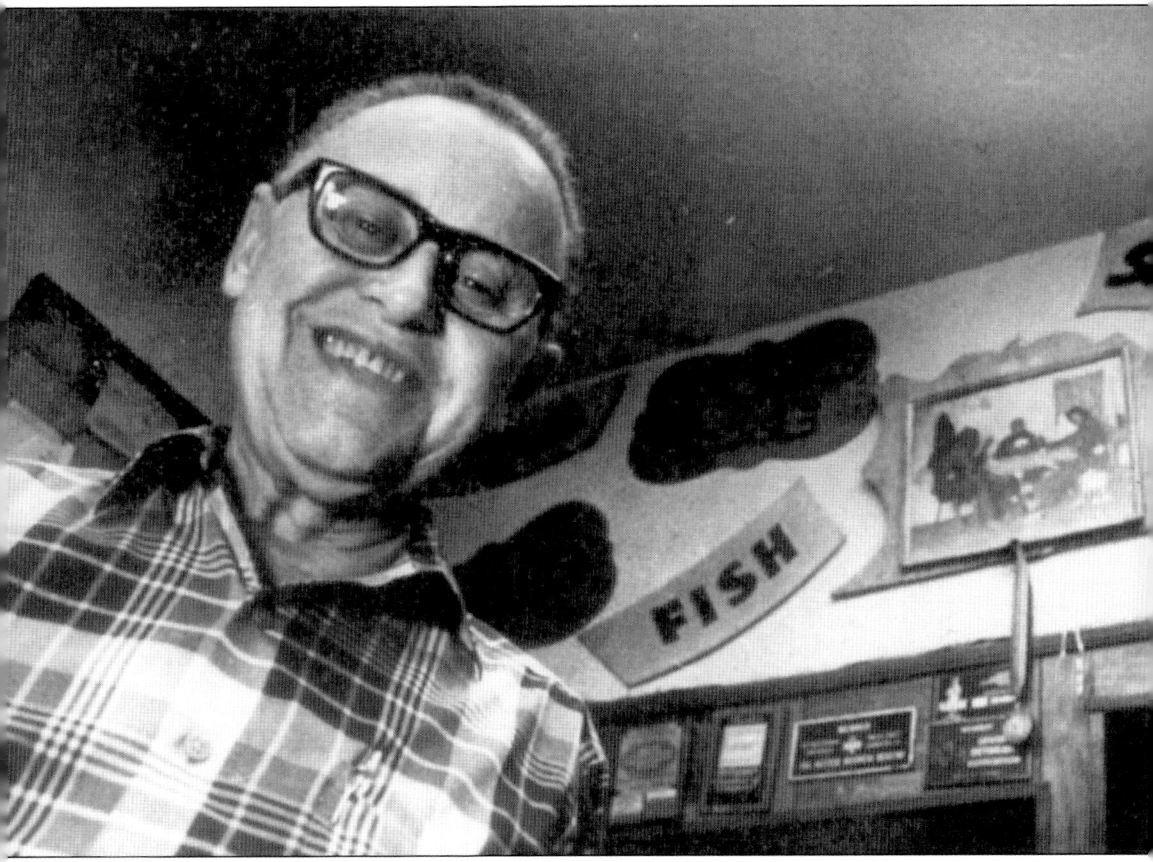

Pete Harris, longtime proprietor of Freeman and Harris Café on Western Avenue, was the nephew of the restaurant's founders. Established in 1921, Freeman and Harris was the oldest continuously operating family-owned, African-American-owned restaurant in the nation at the time of Harris's death in 1992. It was also the first restaurant in the city to be integrated when Harris began allowing white customers in the early 1950s. Pete Harris Café on Milam Street is the successor to Freeman and Harris and retains the old restaurant's menu. Western Avenue is now Pete Harris Drive.

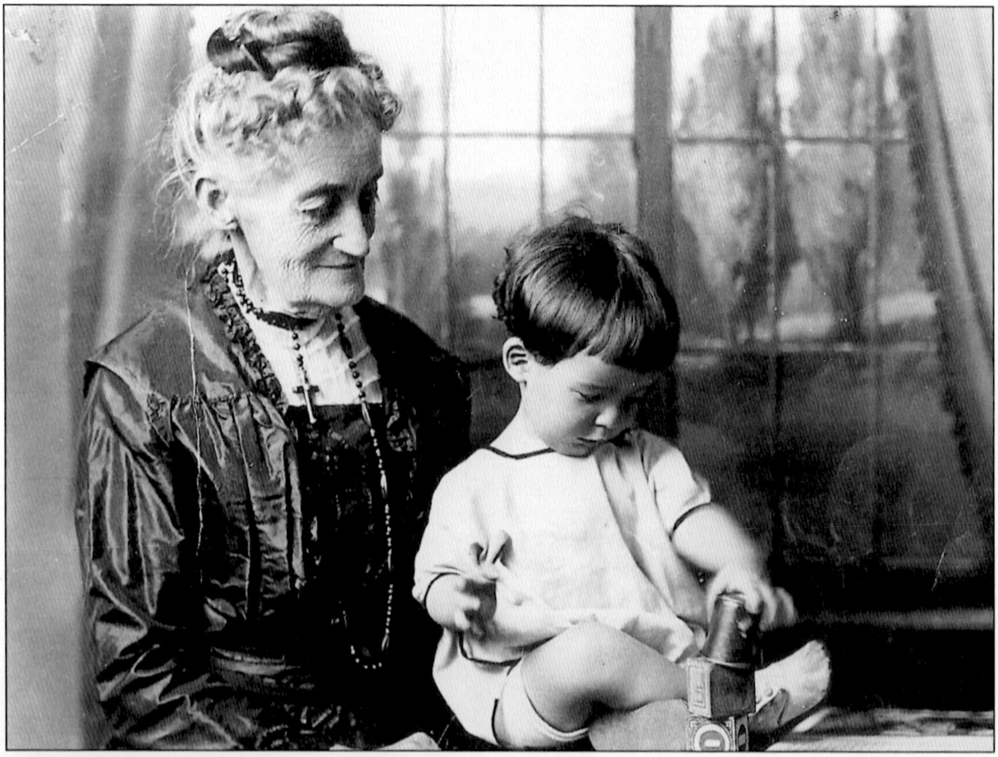

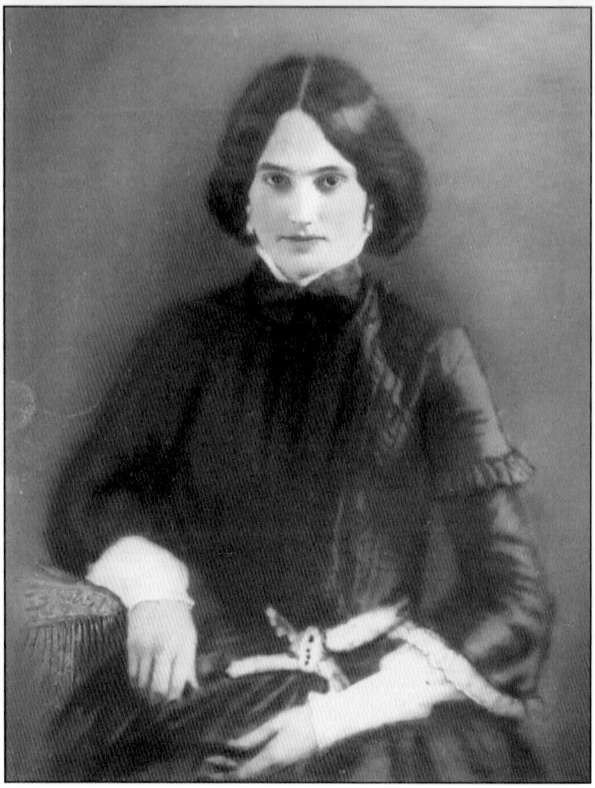

(Above) Julia Sparke Rule was Shreveport's first society columnist, writing under the pseudonym "Pansy" in the *Shreveport Times* during the late 19th and early 20th centuries. She is pictured with her granddaughter around 1920. (Left) Mary Elizabeth Carter Rives was a local socialite of the 19th century. She came to Shreveport with her husband George Wyche Rives (see page 53), founder of the city's first private school but was widowed at the age of 28. She died in 1900 at the age of 71.

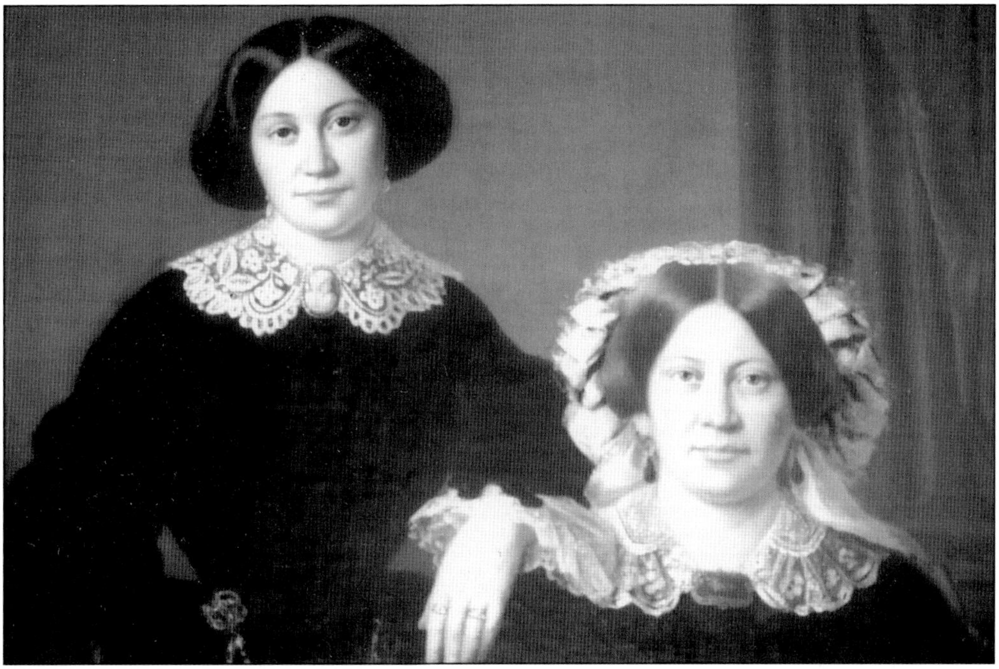

(Above) Paulina deGraffenried Pickett (right) and her daughter Sallie Pickett Cummings were leaders of local society prior to the Civil War. Paulina's husband, James Belton Pickett, was a co-founder of the city with Shreve (Pickett Street is named for him). Sallie was the wife of planter Robert Campbell Cummings, originally of New Orleans. Their multiple plantations were the scenes of many fabulous parties during the antebellum era. Sallie died in 1854, her mother in 1899. (Below) A group of well-to-do young ladies of Shreveport assembled and posed at a photographer's studio around 1875.

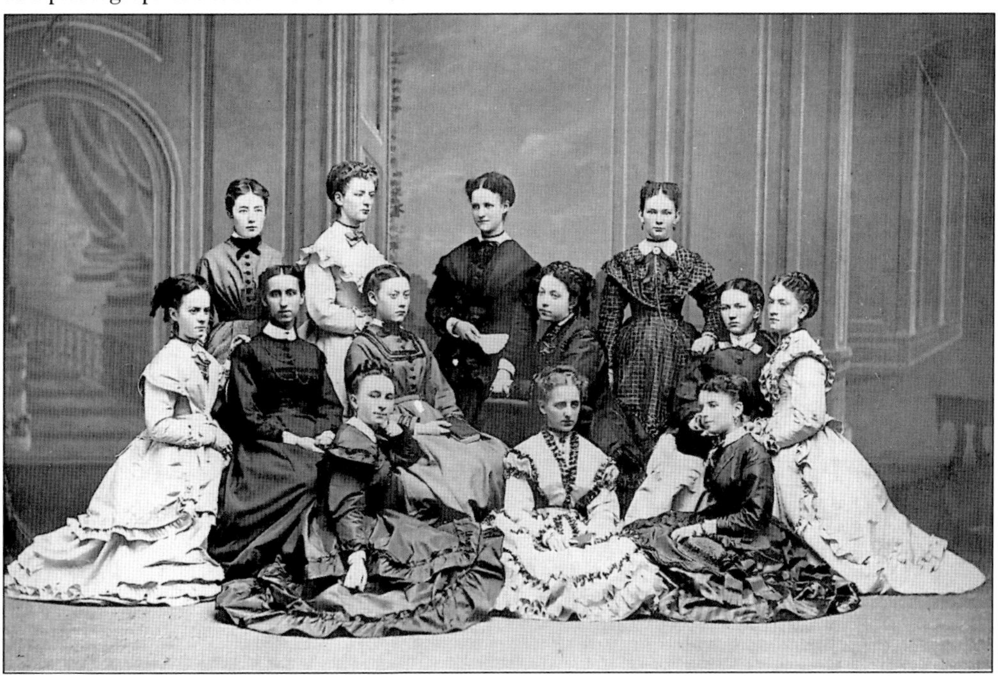

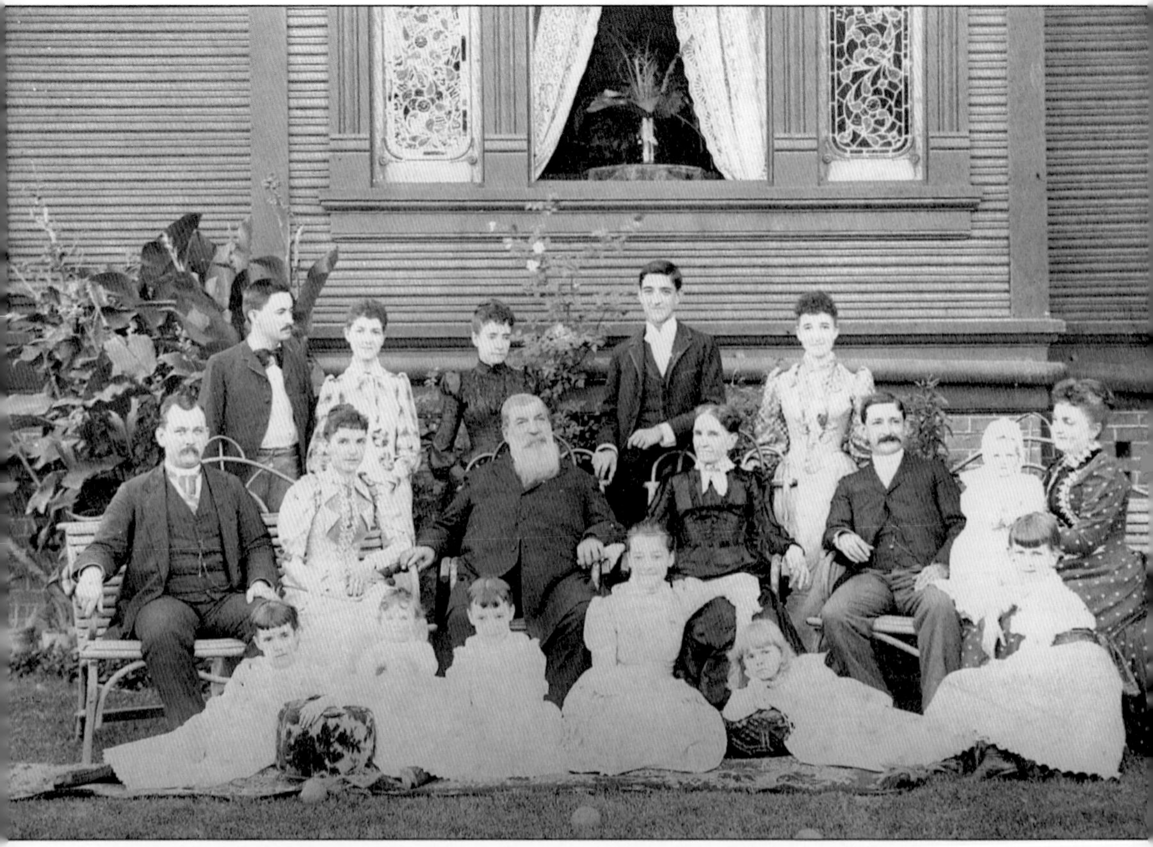

Prominent banker Edward Jacobs and family assemble outside their Travis Street mansion in 1892. Pictured from left to right are (back row) William S. Penick Jr., Sarah Ottelia Jacobs Penick, Weltha Belzora "Lula" Jacobs Alcocke, Ernest Jacobs, and Australia "Tralia" Jacobs Crawford; (middle row) William Everard Hamilton, Myrtle Aurora Jacobs Hamilton, Edward Jacobs, Palestine Livonia Cole Jacobs, Walter Byron Jacobs, baby Frances Ottelia Jacobs, and Mary Frances Abrams Jacobs; (front row) Fay Alcocke, Myrtle Virginia Hamilton, Julia Alcocke, Mabel Alcocke, Annie Frances Jacobs, and Mary Elizabeth Jacobs.

(Right) An early daguerreotype of Edward and Palestine Jacobs with their house servant and two of their children was made around 1860. During the Civil War, Edward (born Ephraim Jacobi in Germany) swore that if the Confederacy lost he would never shave again; he never did. (Below) The Holiday in Dixie Cotillion is the city's premier annual society event. Founded in 1948, the Cotillion Ball was first held at the Washington-Youree Hotel but later moved to the Municipal Auditorium where it remains today. Each year a "royal court" is chosen to rule over the festivities. Shown here are the 1973 silver anniversary King Clarence Yancey and Queen Carolyn Querbes Nelson.

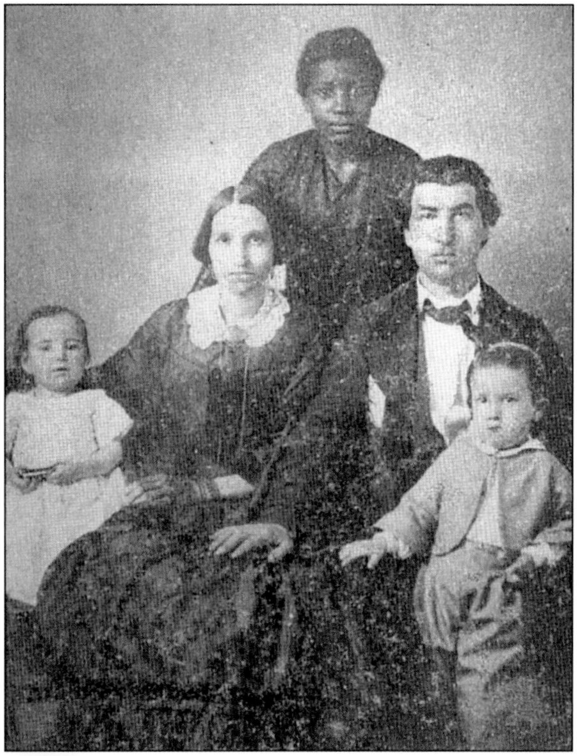

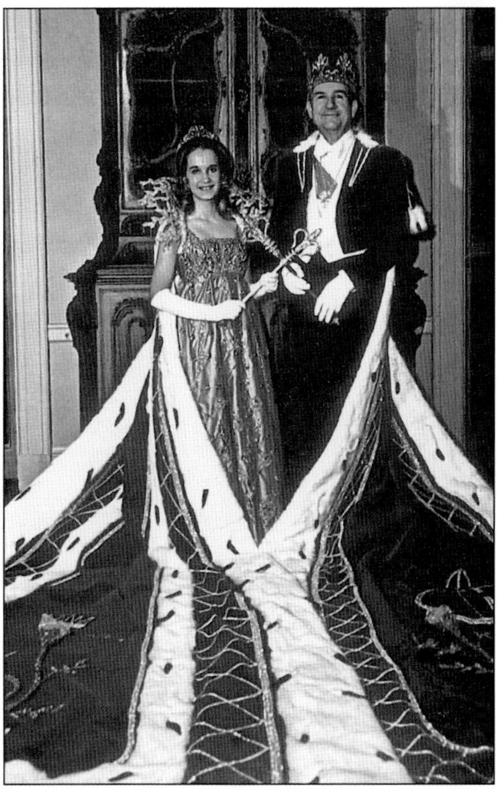

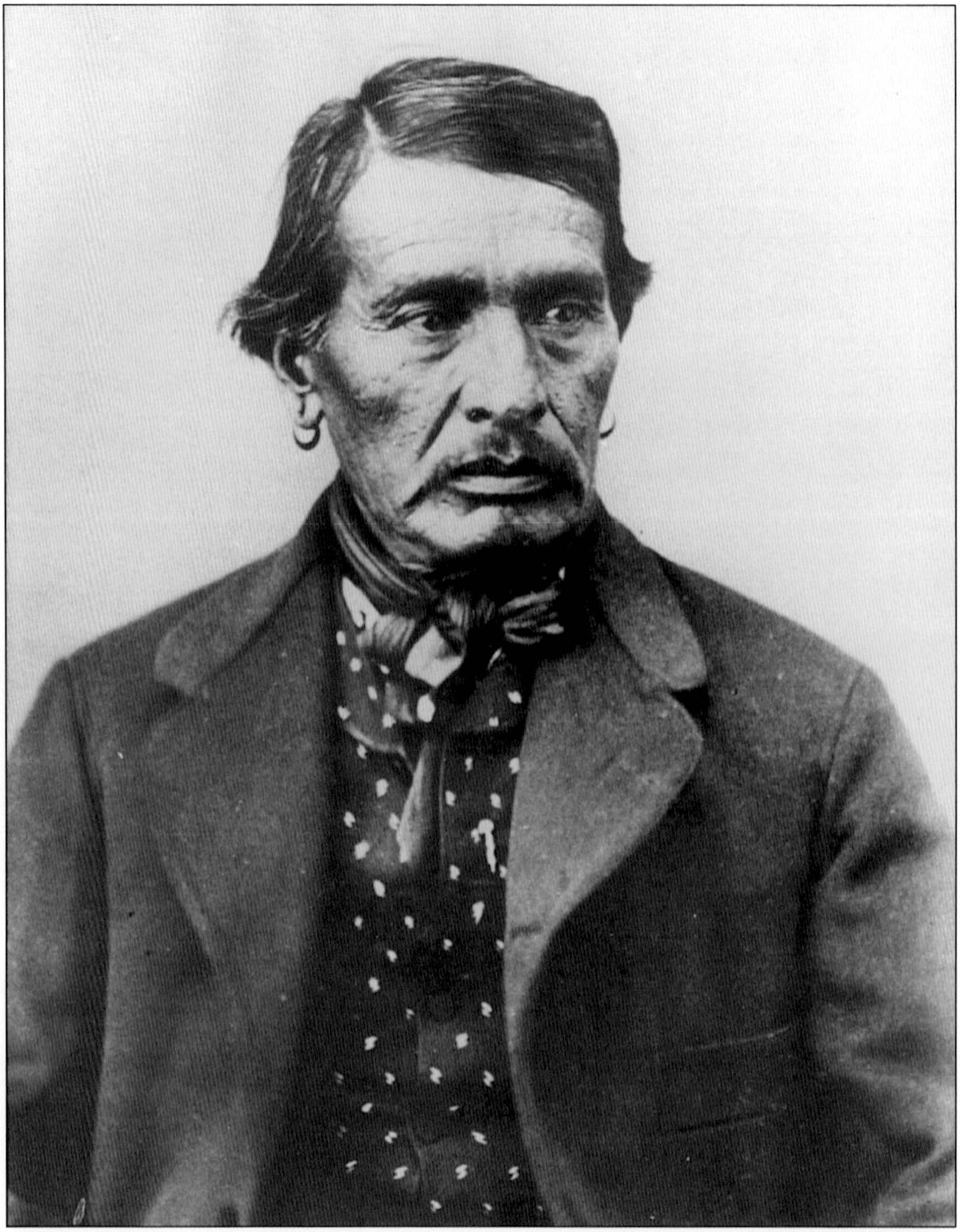

The first residents of the Shreveport area were, of course, the Indians. Caddo Parish takes its very name from the fact that the Caddo Indians once dominated the vicinity. The Caddo Indian Treaty of 1835 ceded the land on which Shreveport now stands to the U.S. Government and opened the door for the city's development. Few early photographs of Caddo Indians exist today. Unfortunately there are none of such notable chiefs as Tarshar or Tsauninont, who were principals in the Caddo Treaty negotiations. One of the only images of a Caddoan from that early era is this one, of the middle aged Caddo chief Sho-E-Tat dressed in American attire. He also favored using an American name, one he chose for himself: George Washington. Alex Gardner, noted photographer of American Indians, created this portrait in Washington, DC.

Four

Artists, Entertainers, and Other Celebrities

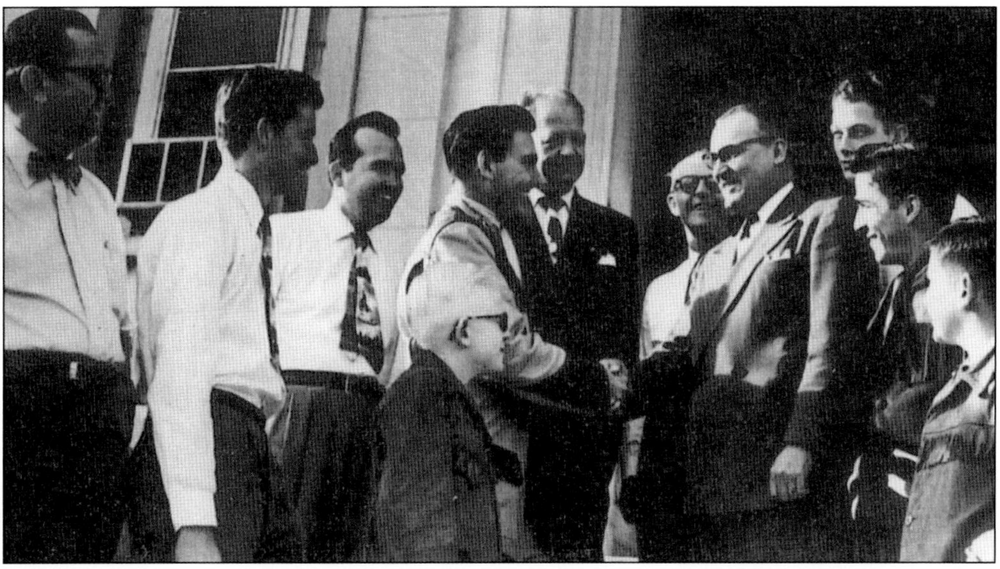

Shreveport has been home to many well-known individuals, and still more have gotten their starts here. Indeed, Shreveport's "Louisiana Hayride" program, a nationally broadcast radio program featuring country and rockabilly entertainers, came to be known as "The Cradle of the Stars." In this 1952 photo taken with local politicians on the steps of the Municipal Auditorium are several notable musicians. Pictured from left to right are accordionist Soko Sokoloski, pianist Floyd Cramer, guitarist and producer Tillman Franks, 12-year-old guitarist Terry Nottgress, guitarist and vocalist Webb Pierce, Public Safety Commissioner Cotton Morris, drummer Jimmy Burrage, Shreveport Police Chief E.G. Huckaby, violinist Jackie Kay, vocalist Faron Young, and 11-year-old guitarist Jerry Kennedy. The Hayride was a weekly live radio show broadcast from 1948 to 1960 and monthly thereafter through the 1960s.

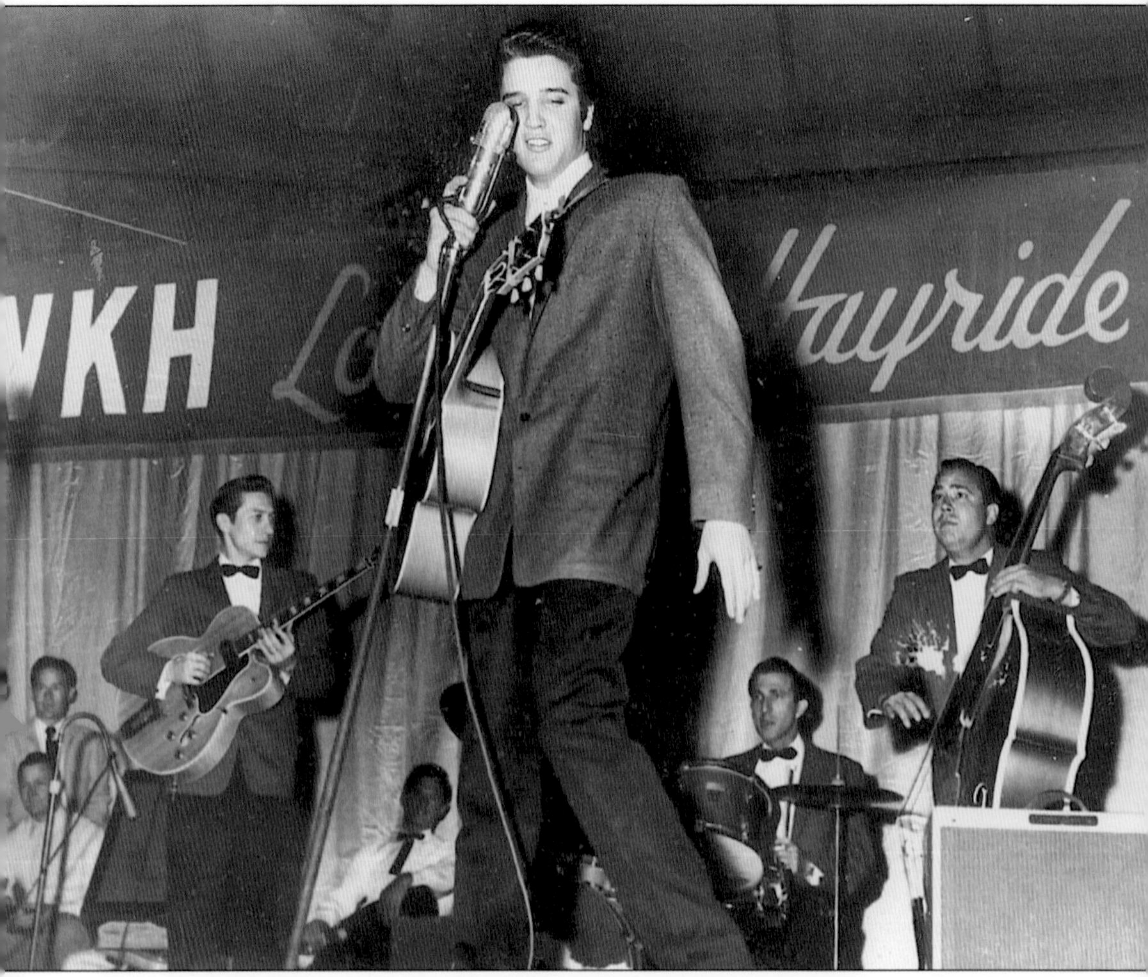

Elvis Aron Presley, a young truck driver from Memphis, made his national radio debut from the stage of Shreveport's Municipal Auditorium on October 16, 1954. The performance was broadcast over KWKH radio on the Louisiana Hayride program. Thereafter through December 1956, Elvis had a contract with the Hayride and resided much of the time in Shreveport and Bossier City. The image above is of Elvis's last Hayride show on December 15, 1956, held at the Hirsch Memorial Coliseum at the Fairgrounds (it could accommodate the crowd better than the Municipal could). Scotty Moore plays guitar at left, Bill Black plays bass at right, and D.J. Fontana plays drums. Following the performance Elvis exited immediately and shouts for an encore elicited the now-famous reply from announcer Horace Logan: "Ladies and gentlemen, Elvis has left the building."

An earlier Elvis performance took place at the Municipal Auditorium in 1955.

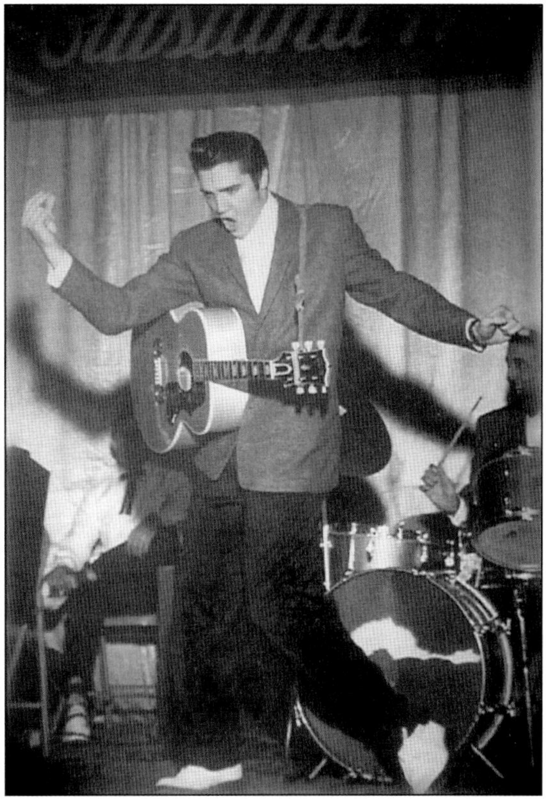

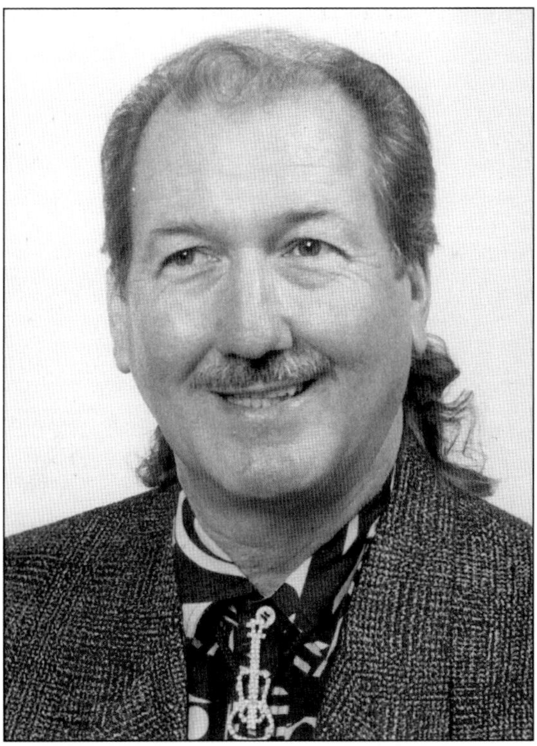

Elvis's principal backup guitarist James Burton, a member of the Rock 'n Roll Hall of Fame, still resides in Shreveport and still regularly plays the guitar in public performances. Among other notable Hayride figures from the Shreveport area are Jim Reeves, Red Sovine, Jimmy Martin, Kitty Wells, and Gene Austin.

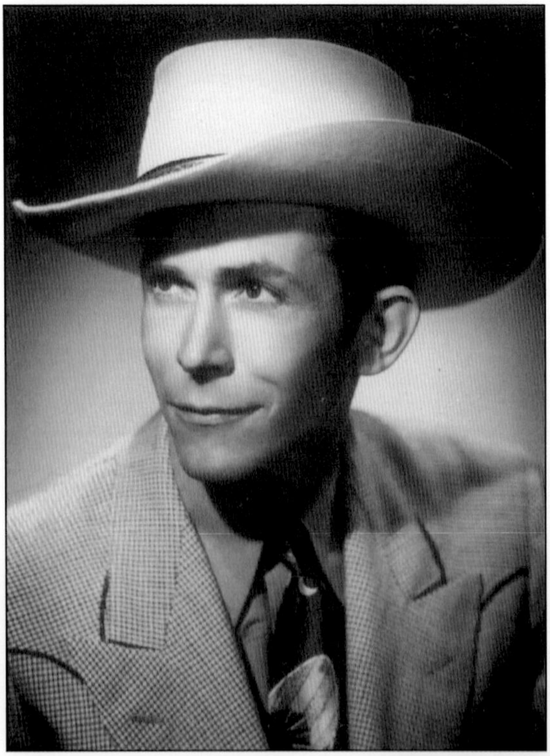

Another important Hayride performer was Hank Williams, who came to Shreveport in 1949. Here he twice married and here his son, Hank Williams Jr., was born.

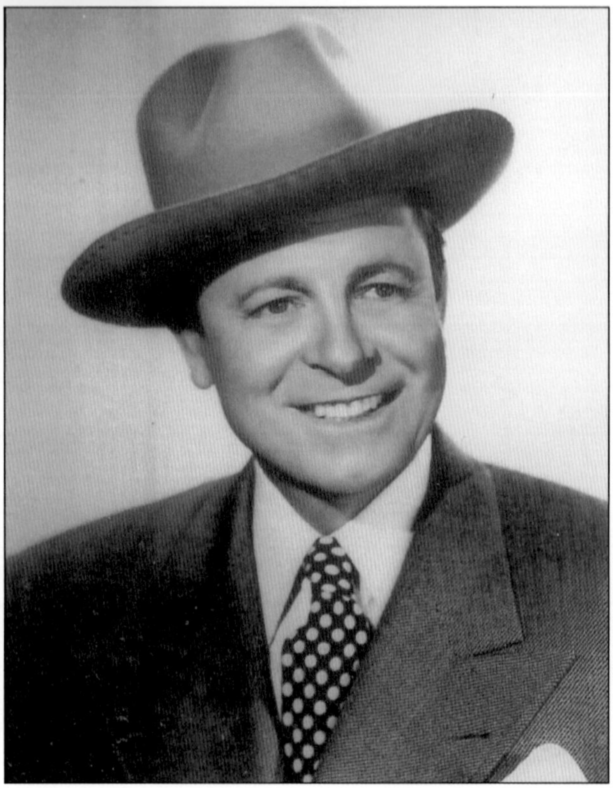

Jimmie Davis, in addition to being a notable singer, songwriter, and guitarist in his own right, was also a Hayride regular and served twice as governor of Louisiana.

(Right) Guitarist and vocalist Tex Ritter from nearby Carthage, Texas, was a regularly featured Hayride star. His son, John Ritter, went on to become a well-known television actor. (Below) Hayride regulars Johnny Cash and Linda Brannon are seen in the late 1950s. Linda Brannon married former child prodigy guitarist Jerry Kennedy. Their son Gordon is a well-known songwriter today.

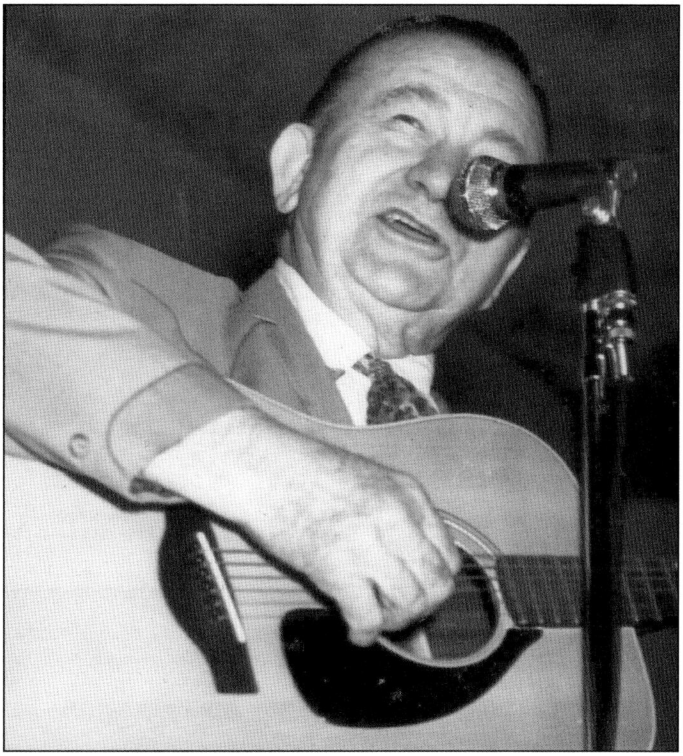

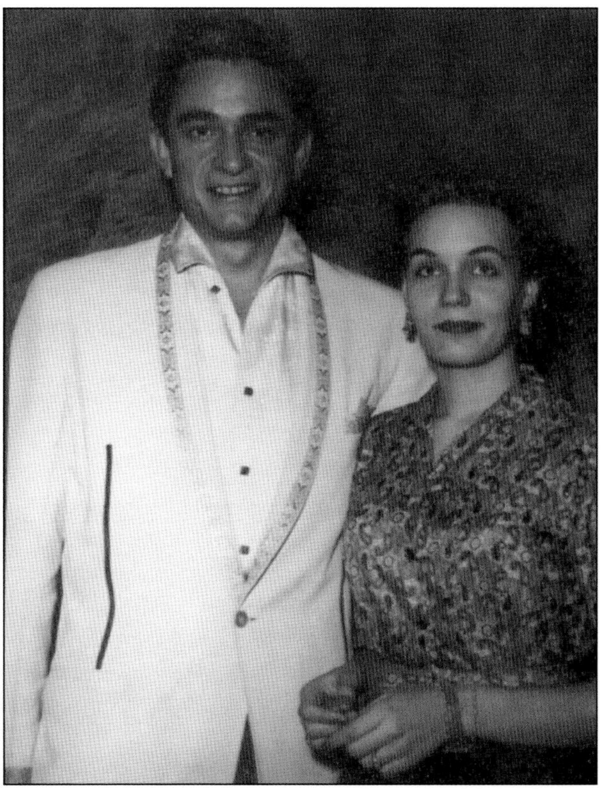

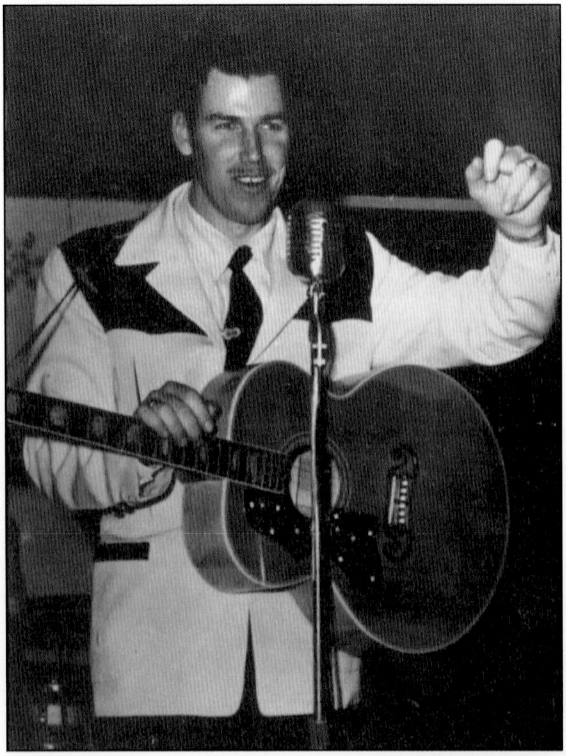

(Left) Guitarist/vocalist Slim Whitman resided in Bossier City and was a mail carrier in Shreveport's Queensborough neighborhood when not on stage at the Louisiana Hayride. (Below) Three Hayride regulars in the late 1950s were (from left to right) electric guitarist Tommy Tomlinson, vocalist Johnny Horton, and guitarist/bassist Tillman Franks.

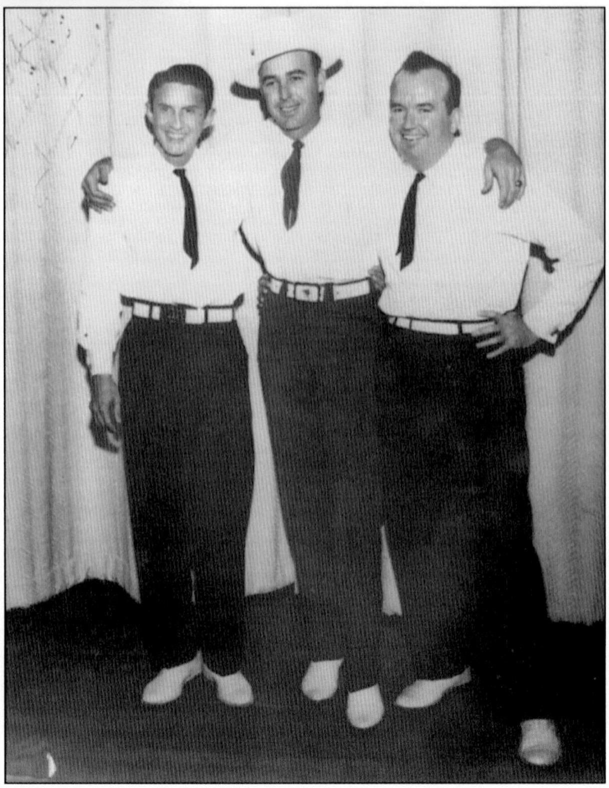

(Right) Johnny Horton was one of the Hayride's top stars at the time of his death in an auto accident in 1960. The 35-year-old singer left a widow (who was also the widow of Hank Williams) and an infant daughter. His last residence was on Audubon Drive in Shreveport's Broadmoor area. He is buried at Hillcrest Cemetery in Haughton. (Below) Vocalist Margaret Lewis, another Hayride star, is seen here at the finale of a performance in the late 1950s. Behind her is guitarist Mira Smith, founder of Ram Records. Lewis later married Smith's cousin, Alton Warwick.

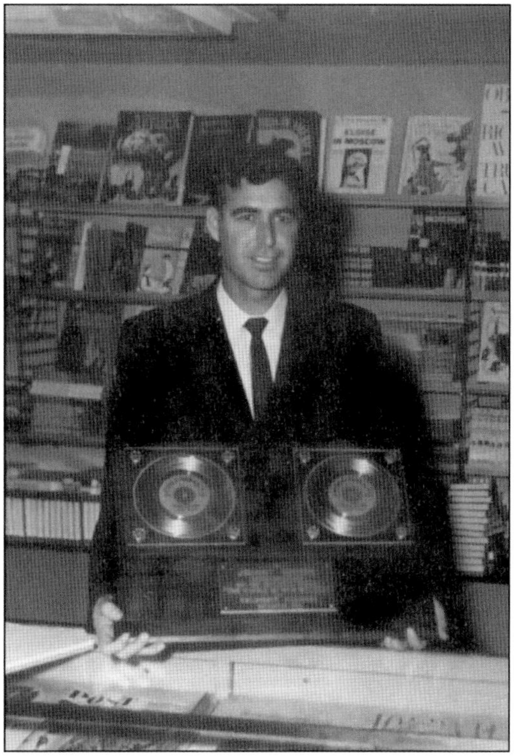

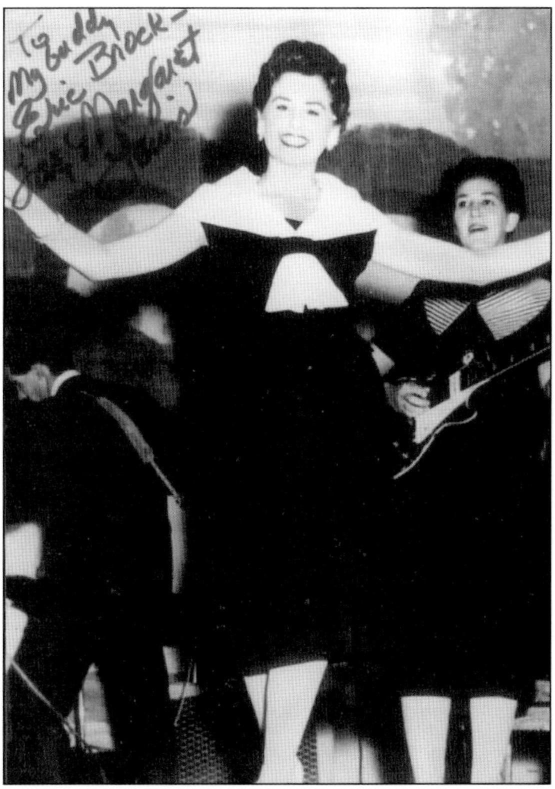

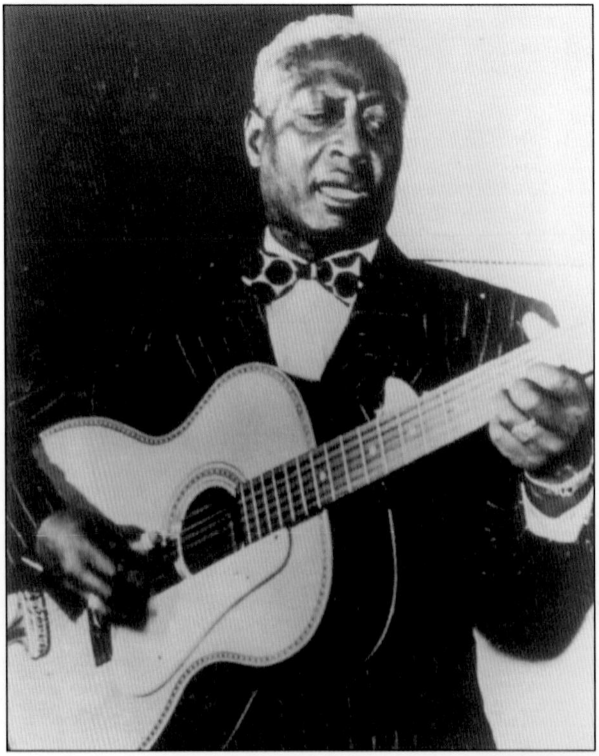

(Left) Huddie "Lead Belly" Ledbetter was one of the South's foremost blues guitarists and composers. Born at Mooringsport, he spent his formative years in Shreveport where he had run-ins with the law but continued to play, sing, and compose. He died in 1949 and is buried at Shiloh Cemetery near Cross Lake. (Below) Another important blues guitarist from Shreveport was Jessie Thomas, who recorded as "Babyface" Thomas as a young man. Like Lead Belly, Thomas (who died in 1995) was internationally recognized as were fellow Shreveport bluesmen "Kid" West, Joe Harris, and Oscar "Buddy" Woods. Today local blues guitarists Kenny Wayne Shepherd and Joe Nadeau are widely recognized as well.

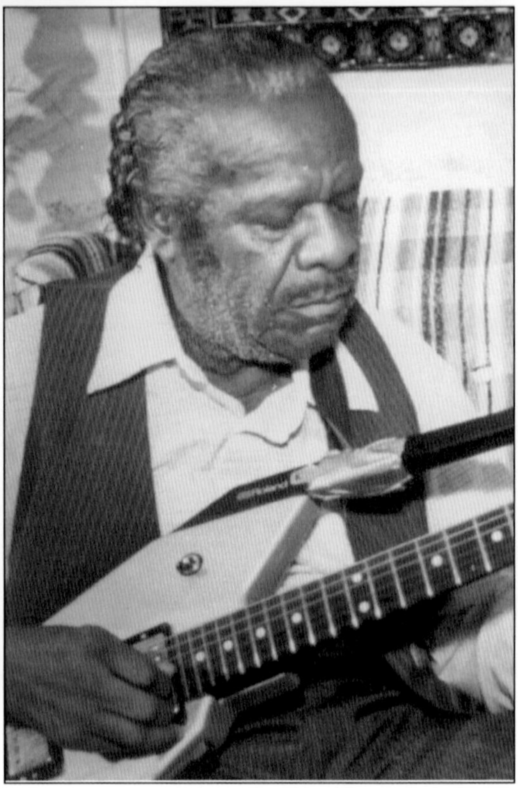

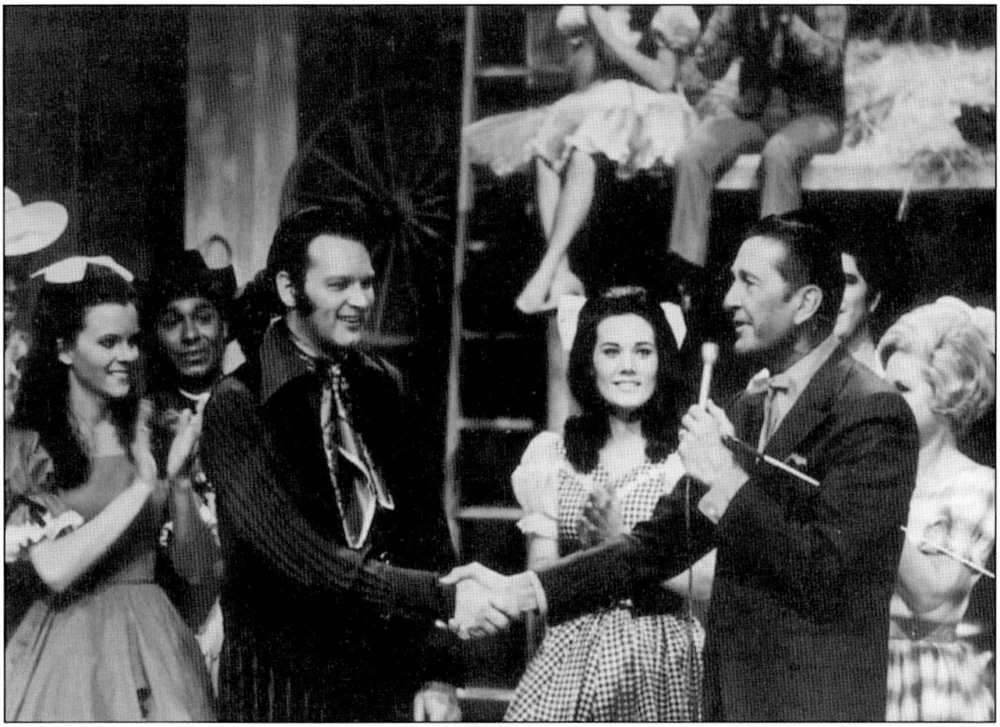

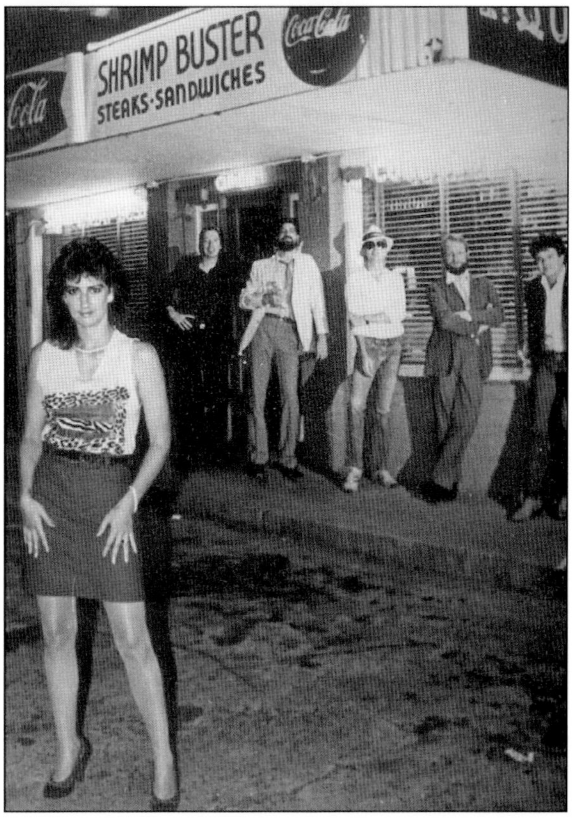

(Above) David Houston of Bossier City got started on the Hayride and went on to win multiple grammies and international recording fame. Here he appears with Lawrence Welk in 1970. (Left) The pop band "A Train" was a one of the most notable groups to emerge from Shreveport in the 1980s. Posed in front of Herby K's on Pierre Avenue are lead vocalist Miki Honeycutt (left) and band members Bruce Flett, David Egan, Buddy Flett, John Howe, and Paul V. Griffith.

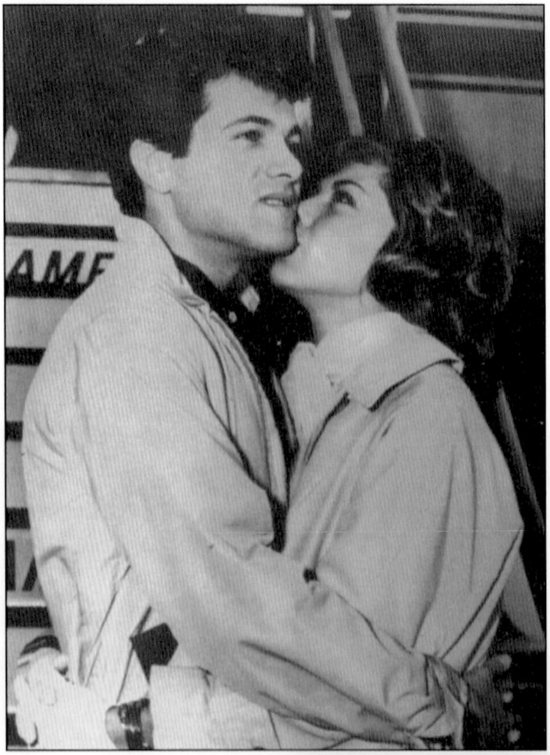

Shreveporter Tommy Sands became hugely popular as a recording artist during the late 1950s. He even appeared in several movies and was considered a rival for Elvis Presley's popularity. In 1961 he married Nancy Sinatra in Las Vegas; the two are seen together in this photo made shortly after the wedding. They were later divorced and Nancy's father Frank Sinatra was successful in wrecking Sands' career.

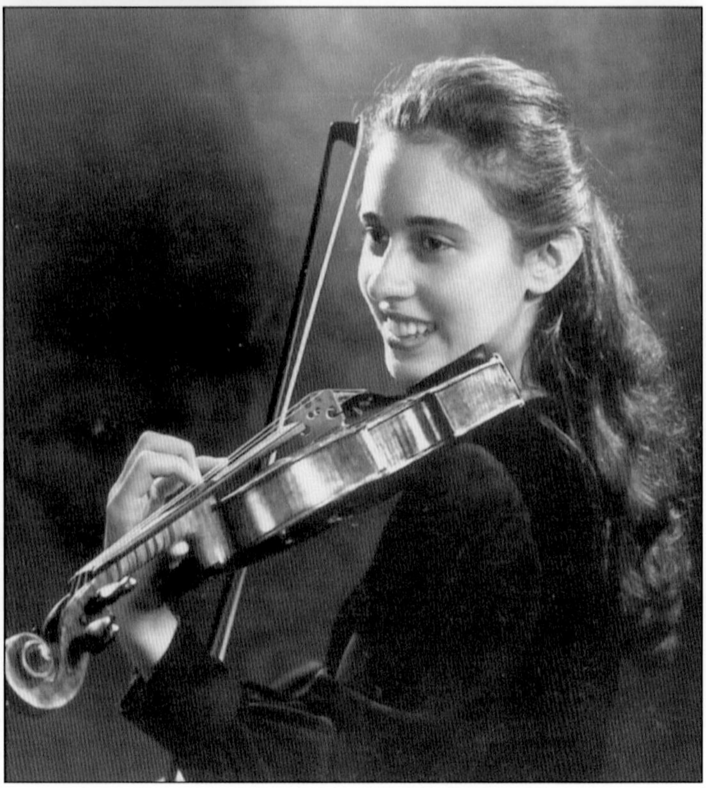

Internationally recognized violinist Zina Schiff of Shreveport has been compared in the international press to the great violinist Jascha Heifetz. She has played and recorded with numerous orchestras and on multiple labels. Her CD debut was with the Israel Philharmonic.

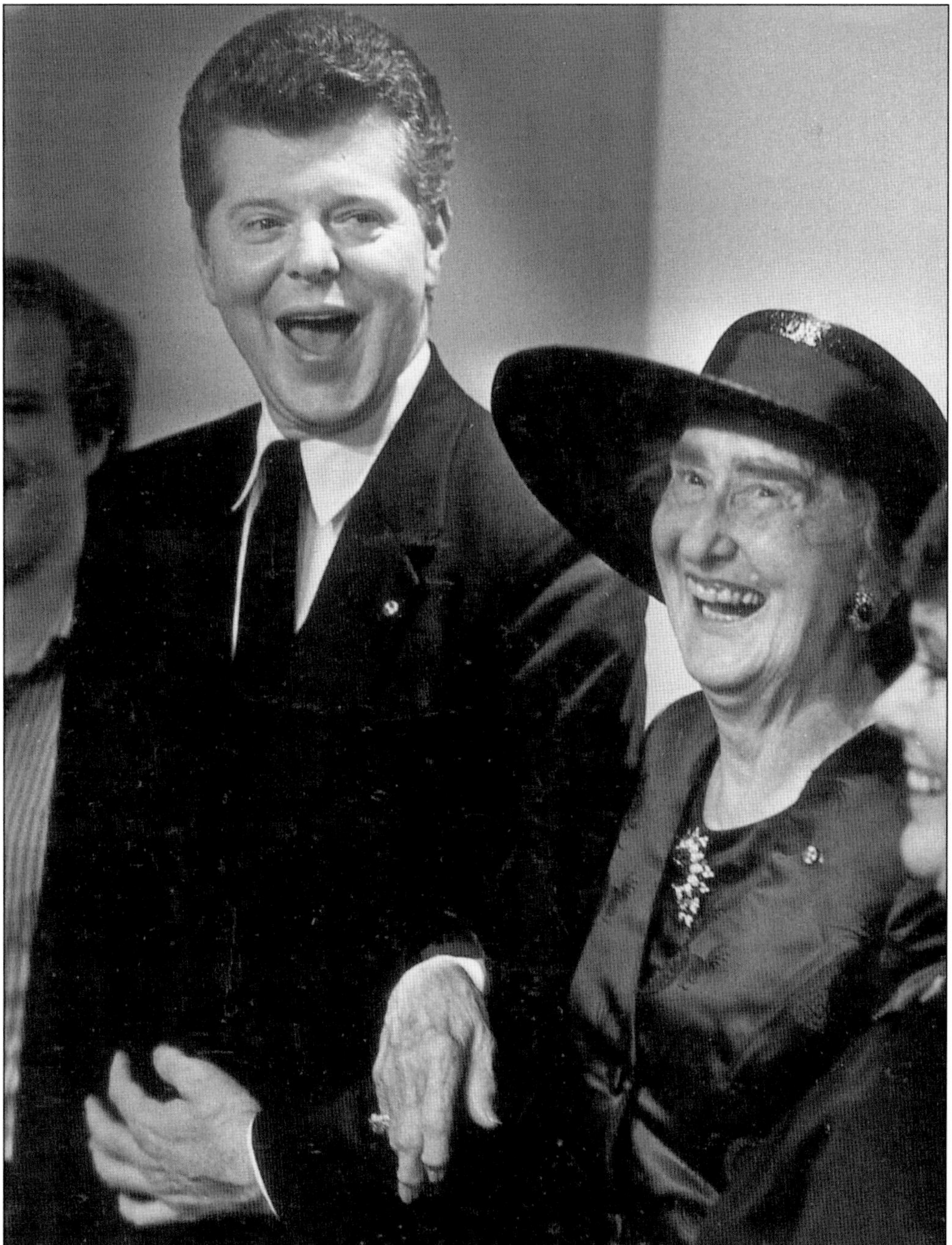

Harvey LeVan Cliburn, better known as Van Cliburn, grew up in Shreveport and also spent part of his childhood in nearby Kilgore, Texas. Today the legendary pianist maintains homes in Shreveport's South Highlands neighborhood as well as in Fort Worth, Texas. Cliburn, who helped break Cold War barriers by performing in the USSR at the very height of international tensions, may well be the most famous living American pianist. Here he is seen with his mother, the late Rildia B. Cliburn, at an event at Centenary College in the 1970s. Noted pianist Art Ferrente has also called Shreveport home.

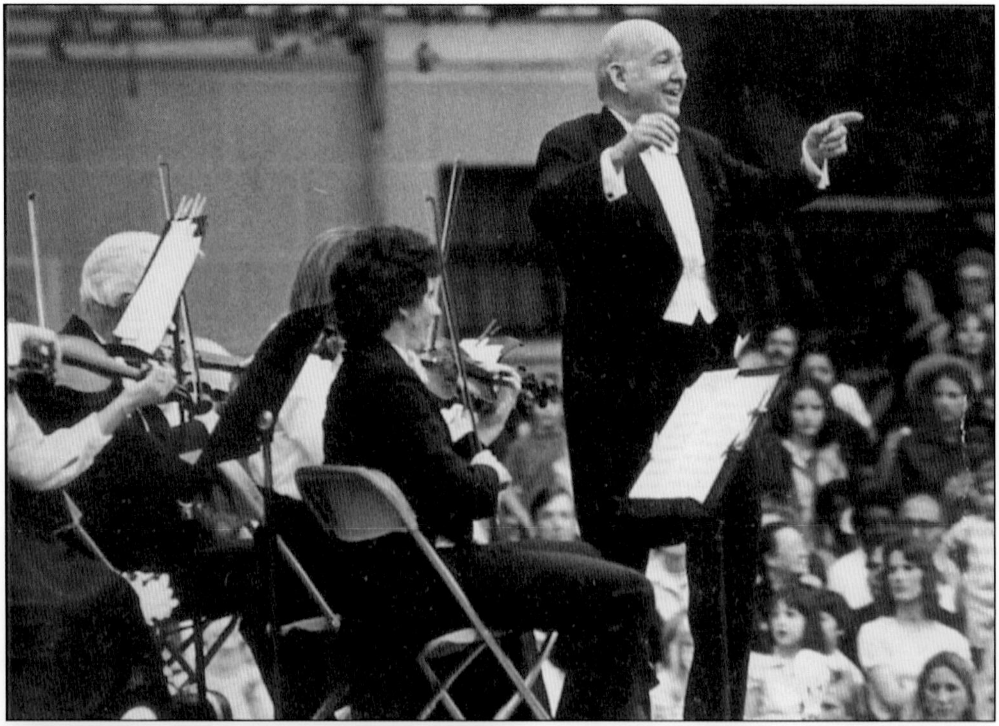

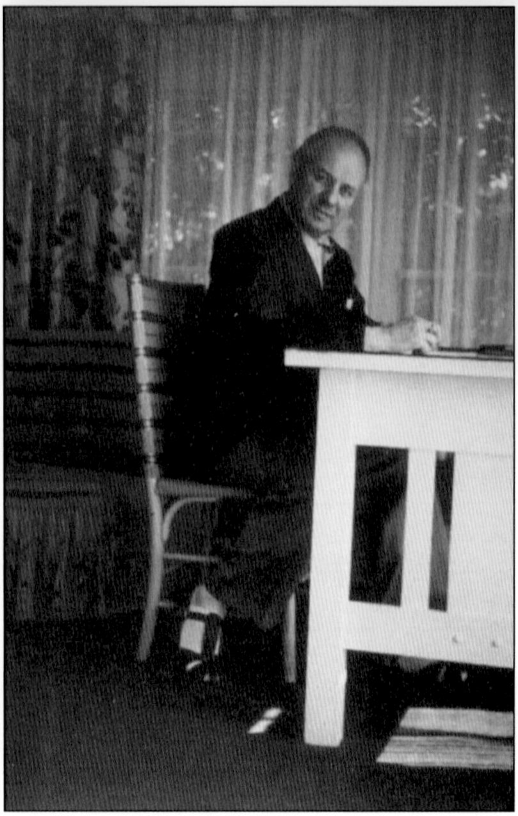

(Above) The Shreveport Symphony was formed in 1948, though there had been an earlier, short-lived incarnation at the beginning of the 20th century. Its first conductor was John Sheneaut, who remained with the symphony for many years and is conductor emeritus today. (Left) Another notable conductor who resided in Shreveport was Fausto Magnani, a colorful figure who claimed to be connected to the Romanovs. Magnani had conducted at LaScala in Milan and with the Los Angeles Philharmonic among others. He settled in Shreveport's South Highlands area after his wife's death, coming here at the invitation of friends. He is buried at Forest Park Cemetery.

Through the years Shreveport has had its share of celebrity visitors, especially while movies were being made here or for the Holiday in Dixie festival. (Right) Miss America Mary Ann Mobley is made an honorary citizen by Holiday in Dixie president Jim Griffith on April 29, 1959. (Below) Actress Mamie Van Doren poses with the Byrd High School football team in September 1953.

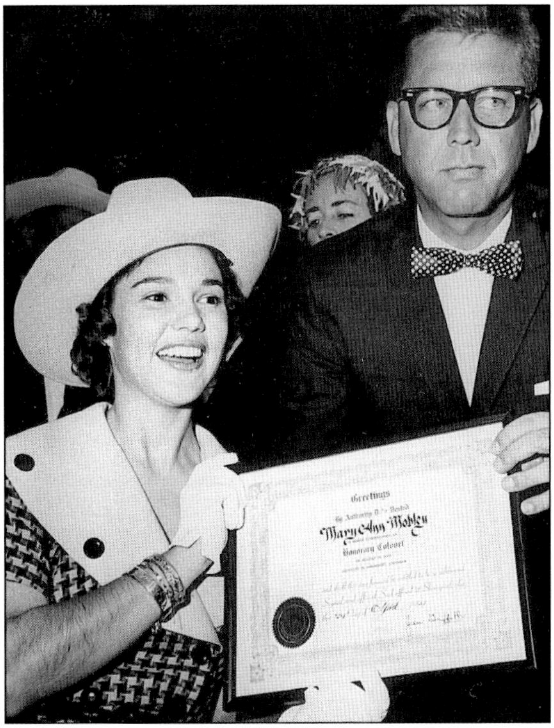

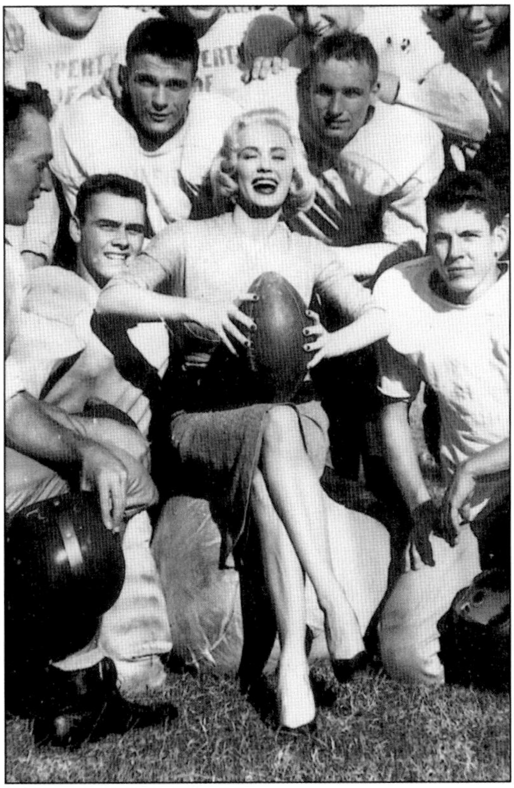

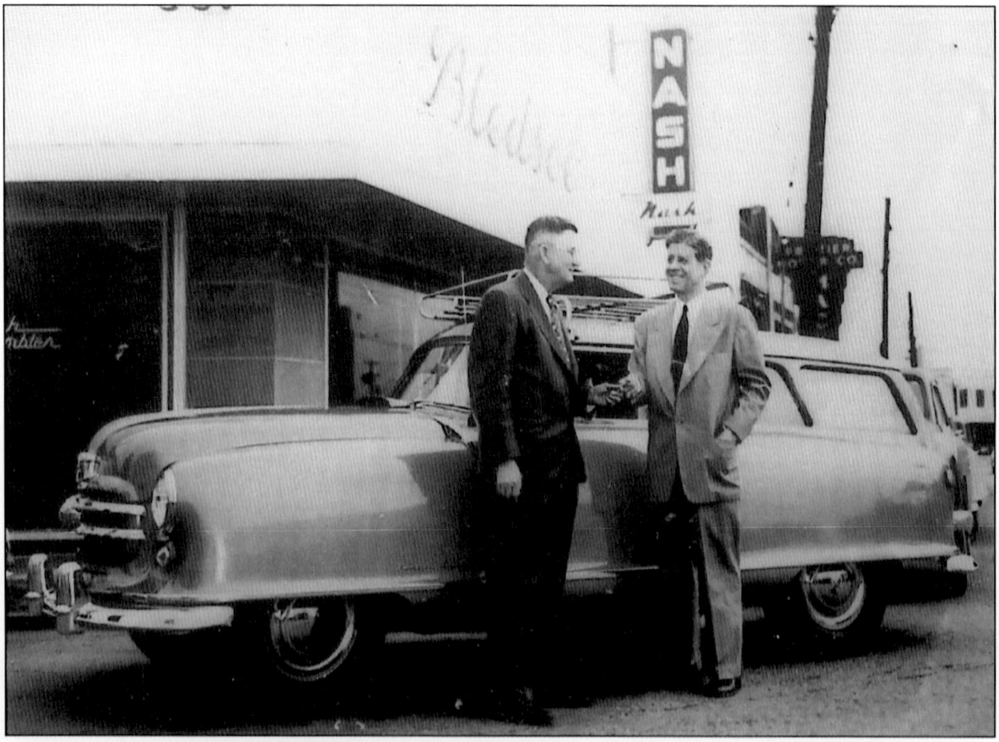

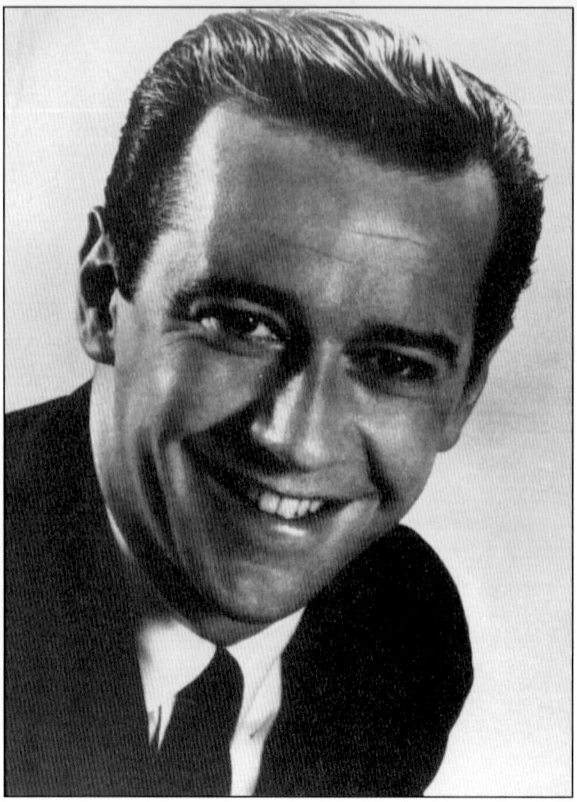

(Above) Actor Rudy Vallee (right) purchases a Nash Rambler station wagon from W. Raines Bledsoe (left) of Bledsoe Motors on Texas Avenue during a March 1952 visit to Shreveport. (Left) This is comedian George Carlin at the beginning of his career. Carlin got his start in radio as a disk jockey on Shreveport's KJOE radio station in 1958. Nationally noted disc jockey Wolfman Jack also got his start in Shreveport.

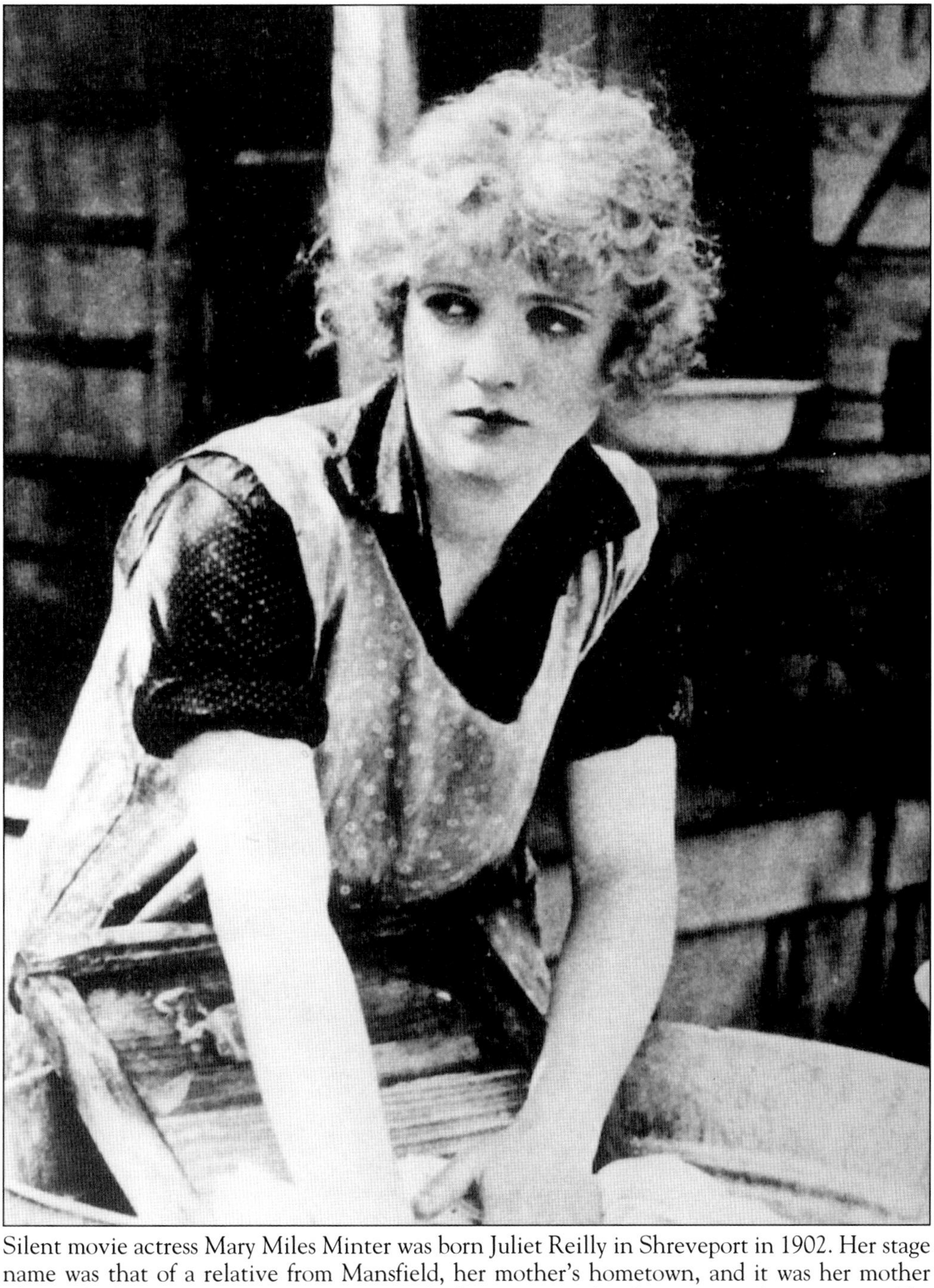

Silent movie actress Mary Miles Minter was born Juliet Reilly in Shreveport in 1902. Her stage name was that of a relative from Mansfield, her mother's hometown, and it was her mother who pushed Mary's acting career. By 1912 little Mary was already acting in the movies and by 1920 she had made 51 films. In 1922 Mary's director and lover William Desmond Taylor was murdered in Hollywood and Mary's mother came under suspicion. Though the case was never solved Mary's career was irreparably damaged by the scandal when her three-year affair with the much older Taylor became public. Mary Miles Minter's last film was made in 1923. She later split with her mother and married a Los Angeles real estate broker. She died in 1984.

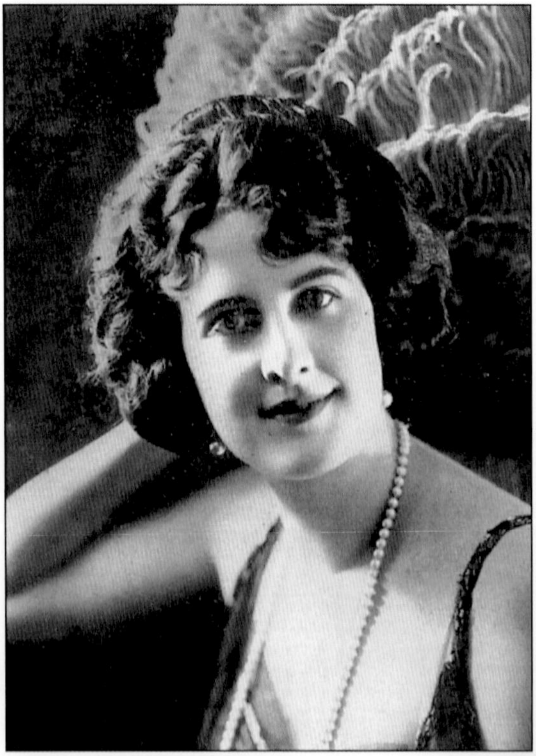

After her retirement from the silent screen, actress Edith Pennington became a Shreveport minister, pastoring the Full Gospel Temple at Line and Pierremont for many years. Other notable silent movie figures who made their homes in Shreveport include Kneipton Greene and Jack Ponder.

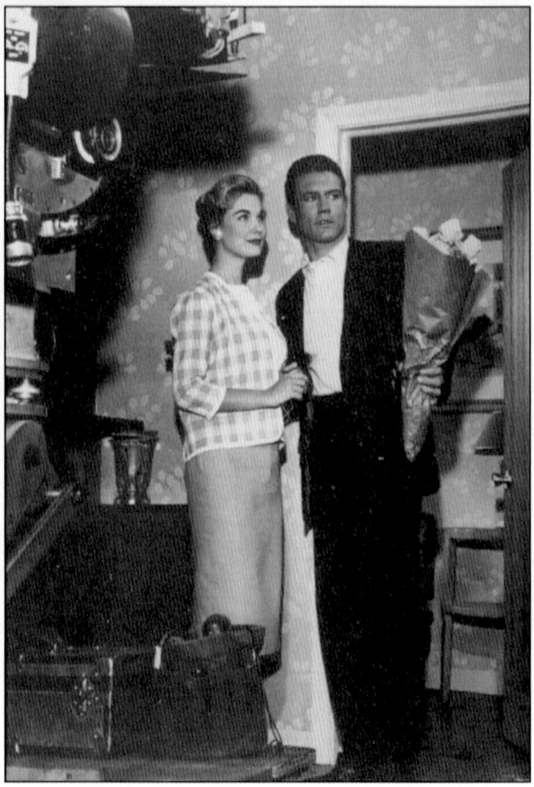

Bossier City's Eurlene Howell was Miss USA 1958. Becoming Arlene Howell LeCava, she went on to an acting career in Hollywood. Here she is seen on the set of the early television show *77 Sunset Strip*. Other local names in acting include Jack Prince, Martin Salisbury, Reggie Smith, Pat Studstill, Pat Carroll, Gwen Hajek, Virginia Hewitt, Marcella Morton, Tricia O'Neil, Brenda Sykes, Monica Tidwell, Julia Wall, Lisa and Ashley Welch, Carole Wells, Jimmy Stewart, and Dennis Weaver.

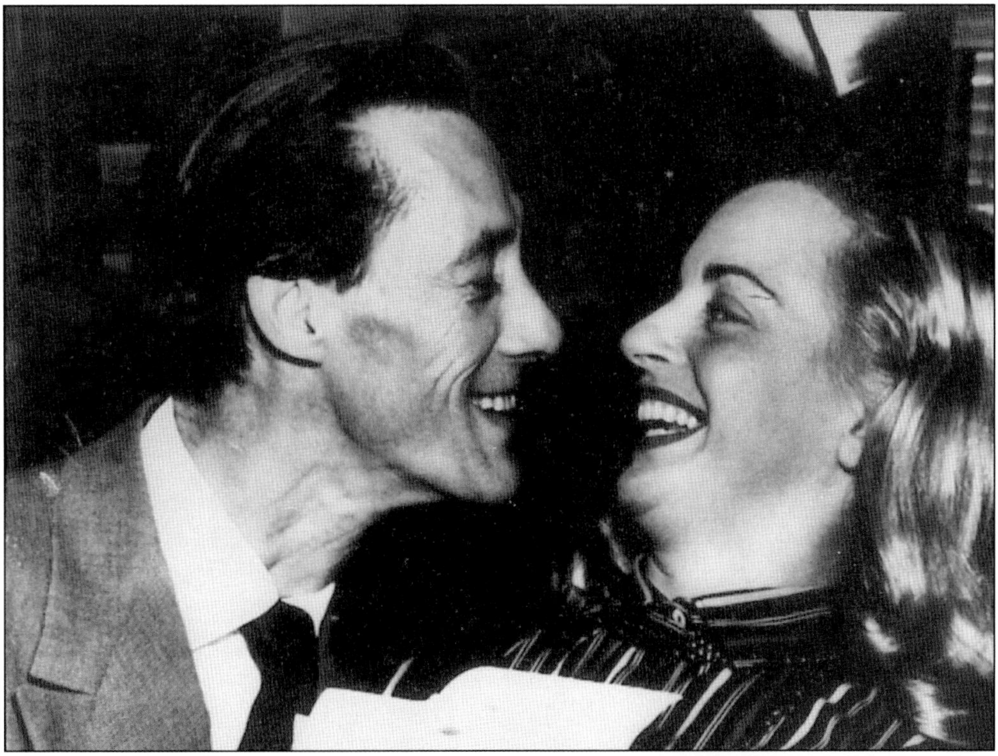

(Above) Actor John Carradine, seen here with his wife, got his start on the stage of the Shreveport Little Theatre in the 1920s. (Right) Television actor Alan Autry, best known for his supporting role on the series *In the Heat of the Night*, grew up in the Highland neighborhood. More celebrities who have called Shreveport home include Lynn Herring (of *General Hospital*), Valerie Bertinelli, Snookie Lanson, and Sinbad. Additionally, singer Perry Como made his radio debut while working as a barber at Shreveport's Washington-Youree Hotel.

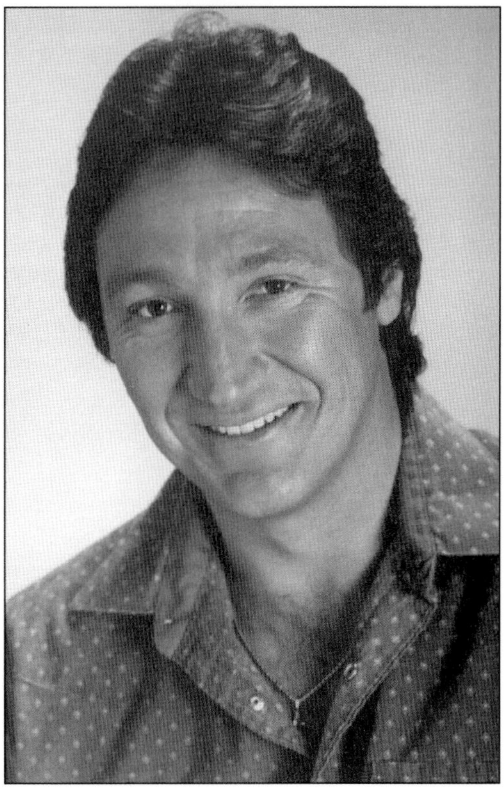

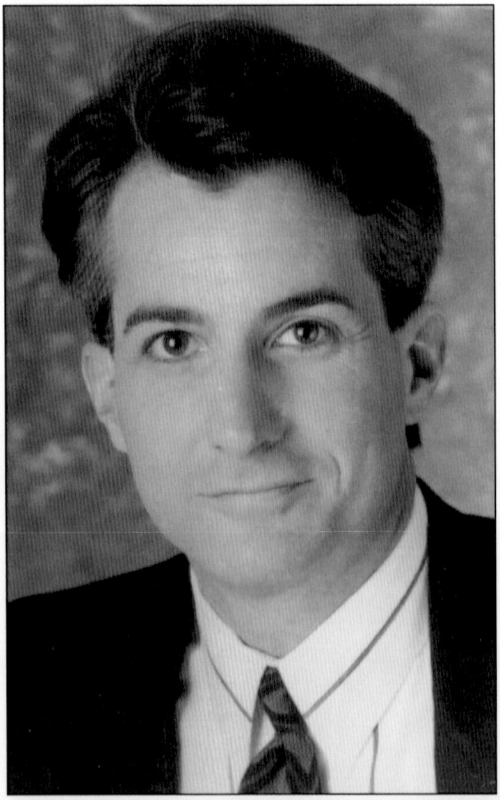

(Right) Screenwriter Richard R. Hawkins got his start as a writer for *The Carol Burnett Show* and later wrote for *The Love Boat*, *Punkie Brewster*, and others. He was also the creator of *Mama's Family*. (Below) Author and illustrator William Joyce is creator of numerous children's productions including *Rolie Polie Olie* and *Toy Story*. Other native screenwriters and producers include John William Corrington, Judi Mason, Tia Texada, Charles B. Pierce, Drew and Andy Sidaris, W. Zolley Lerner (a.k.a. Thomas Z. Loring), and Jim McCullough.

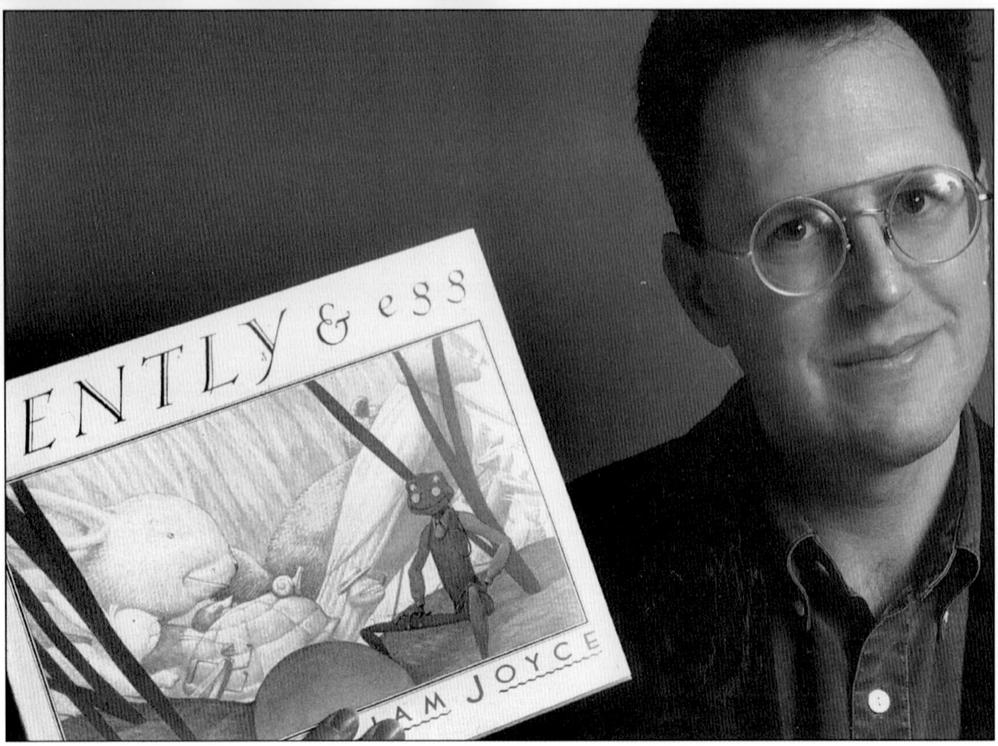

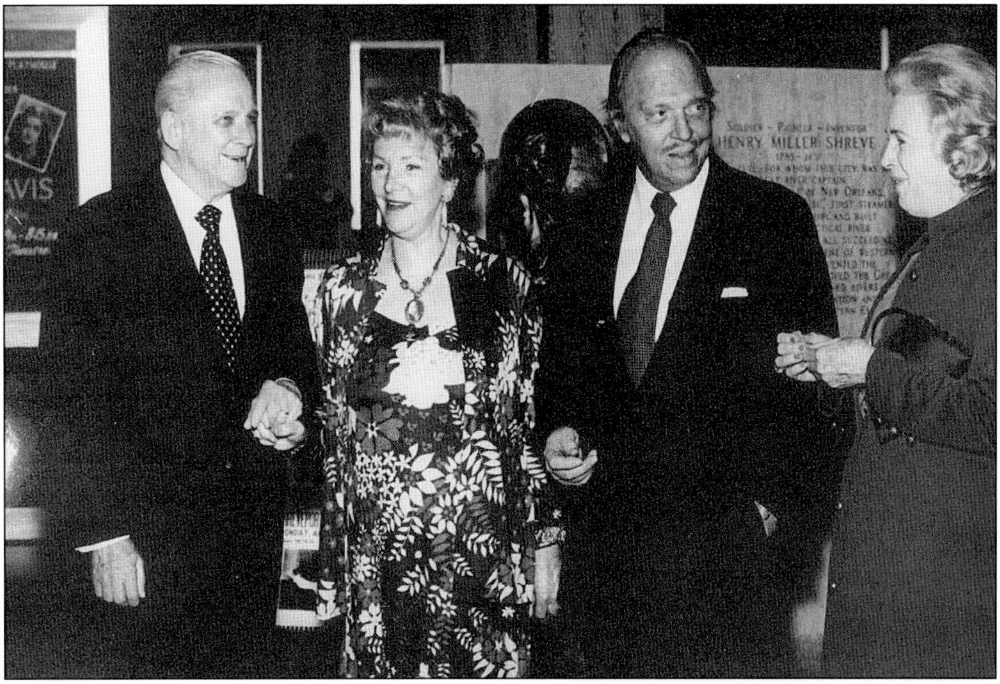

Broadway director/producer Josh Logan (second from right) and his wife (second from left) chat with Dr. Walter Colquitt and wife Eleanor (Logan's cousin) at the Shreveport Civic Theatre. Logan grew up in Shreveport and in nearby Mansfield.

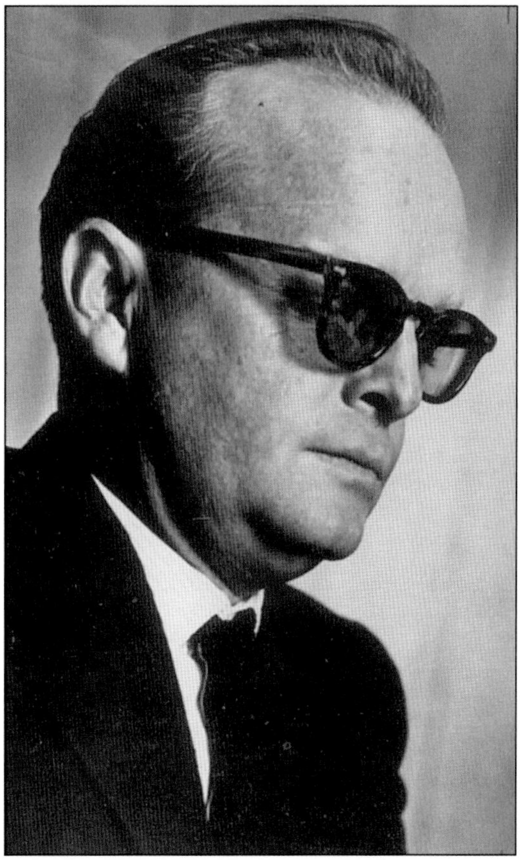

Writer Truman Capote was born Truman Persons in New Orleans but his father was a Shreveporter and Capote maintained connections to the city. Arch Persons, his father, resided in Queensborough and later in Highland and was visited there by his famous son. Persons is buried at Forest Park Cemetery. Other writers connected to Shreveport include poet Cleanth Brooks, playwright Lee Arthur (Arthur Lee Kahn), dramatist Ada Jack Carver, and Pulitzer Prize–winning playwright Roark W.W. Bradford.

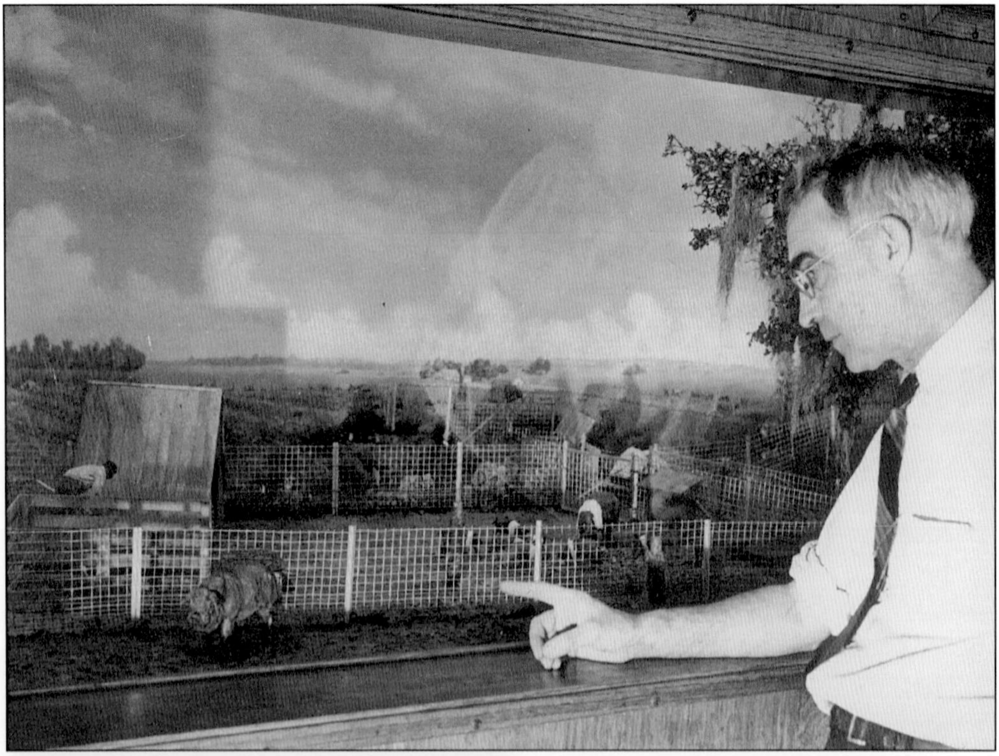

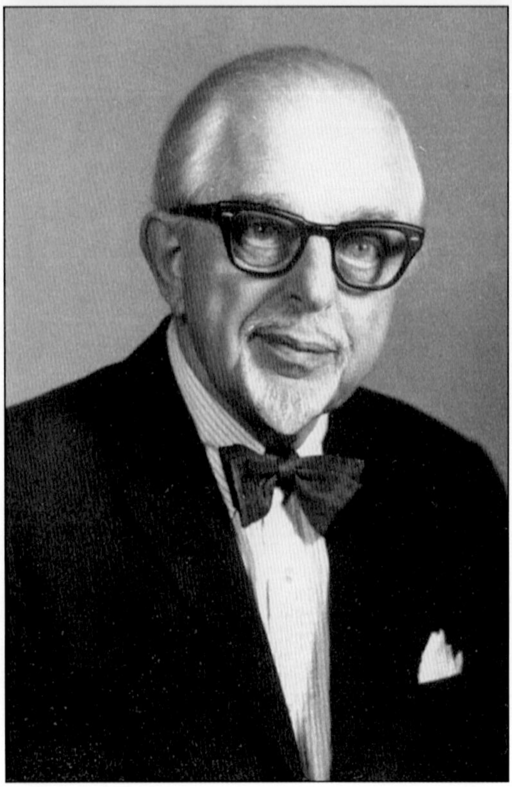

(Above) H.B. Wright, longtime director of the Louisiana State Exhibit Museum at Shreveport, designed and sculpted the museum's remarkably detailed and meticulously rendered dioramas beginning in the late 1930s. Here Dr. Wright is seen in the 1950s pointing out details of one of the dioramas depicting Louisiana agriculture. (Left) One of Shreveport's most noteworthy architects was Samuel G. Wiener, whose local creations range from the Municipal Auditorium of the 1920s to buildings constructed in the 1970s. Wiener and his brother William Wiener Sr. were among the American pioneers of the International Style and were internationally recognized for their work. Among other local architects of note were Julian Sokoloski, Seymour Van Os, Edward F. Neild, Edward F. Neild Jr., and Theodore Flaxman.

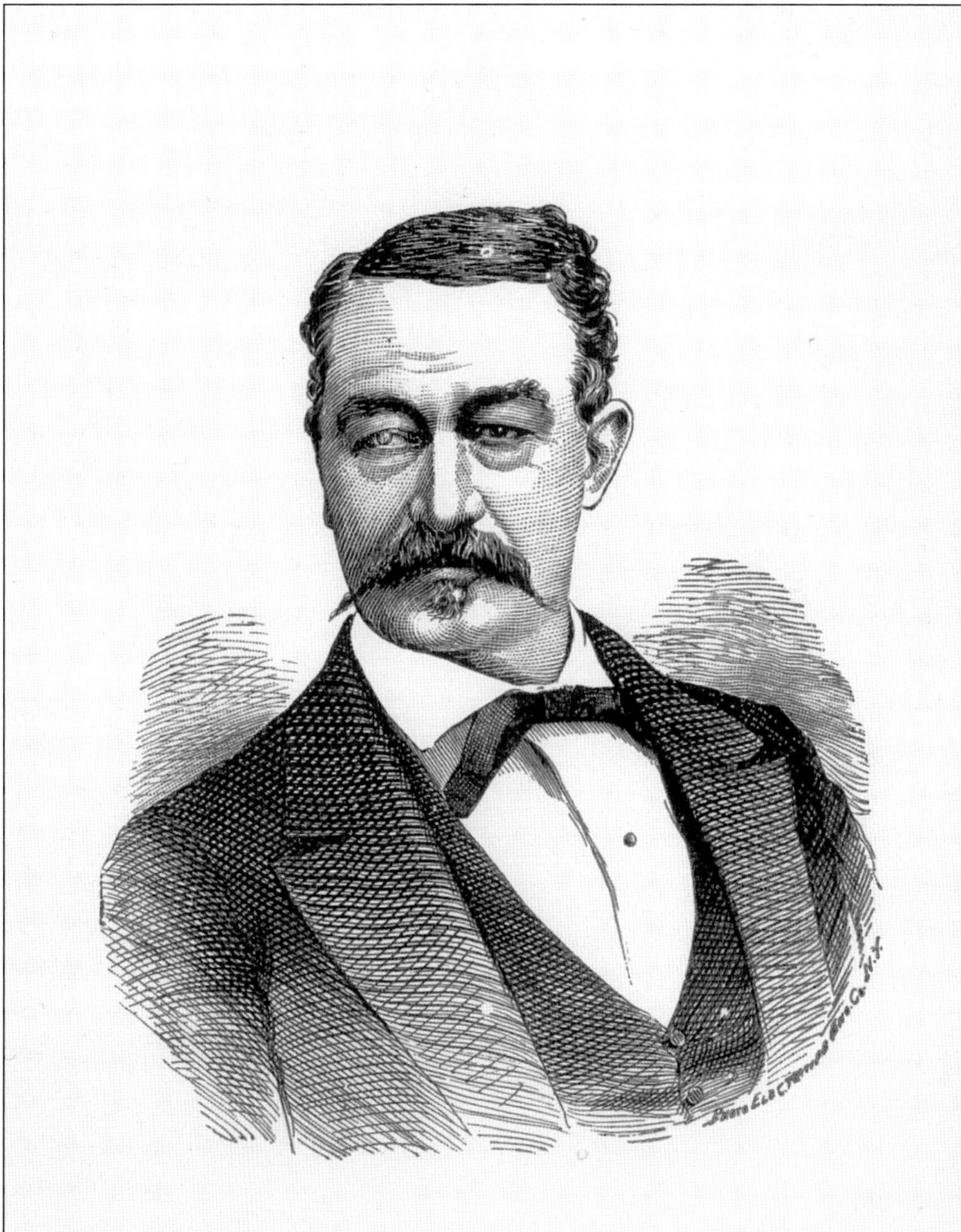

Perhaps the most notable of Shreveport's architects was Maj. Nathaniel Sykes Allen, whose career began just after the Civil War and extended into the 1920s. Most of the city's first public schools and many early public buildings were Allen designs. In all he designed almost 400 local structures, including virtually all of the city's most extravagant Victorian homes. Indeed, Allen was famous throughout the South for his residential designs, which ranged from simple houses to wildly flamboyant mansions. Some of the homes and other buildings he designed remain standing today in towns across Louisiana, Texas, Maryland, and elsewhere, though only five verifiable Allen designs still stand in his home city of Shreveport. Allen died in 1922 at the age of 93 and is buried at Forest Park Cemetery.

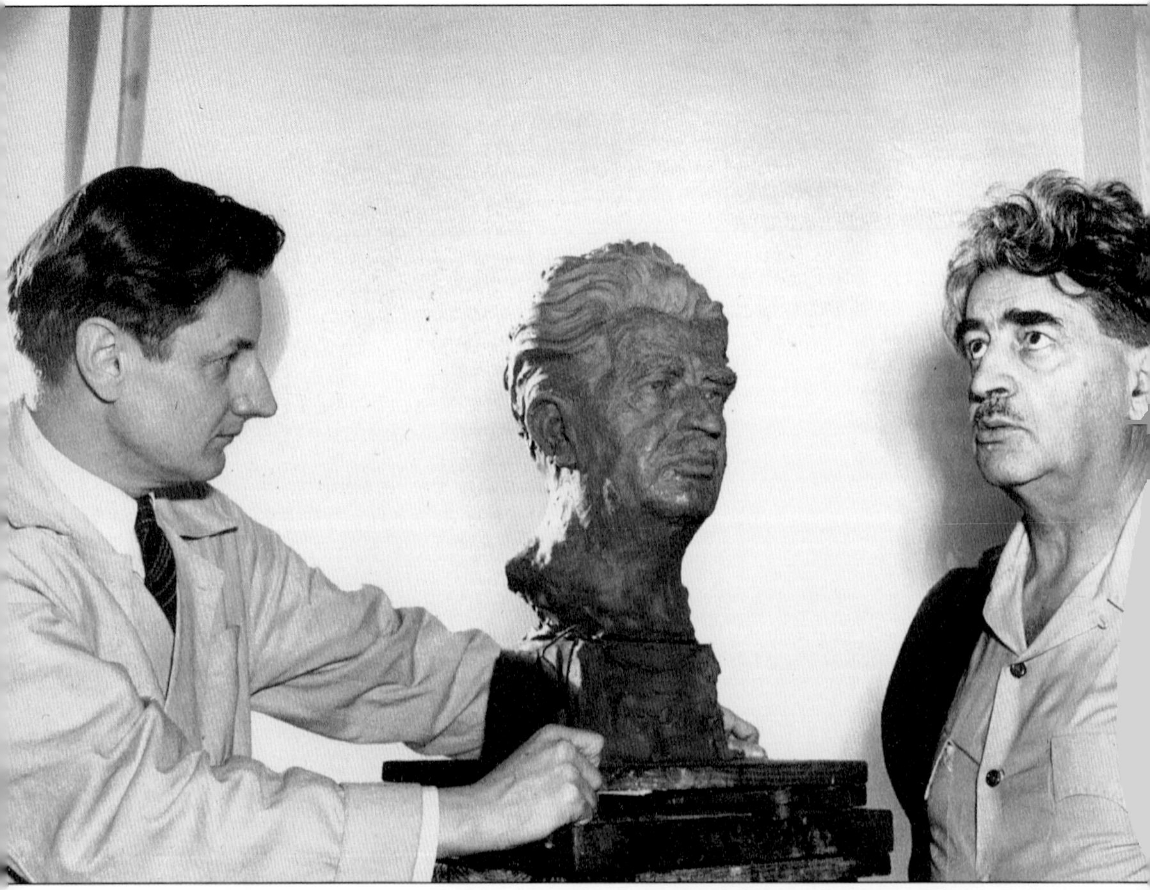

Sculptor Arthur C. Morgan, whose work is in the U.S. Capitol rotunda among other prominent locations, is seen here in the 1940s displaying a bust of fellow Shreveporter Jean Despujols. Despujols, himself a noted painter, poses at right beside the likeness. Arthur Morgan and his wife Gladys founded the art department at Centenary College. Nationally noted sculptors Karl Gerhardt and Clyde Connell also made their homes in the Shreveport area.

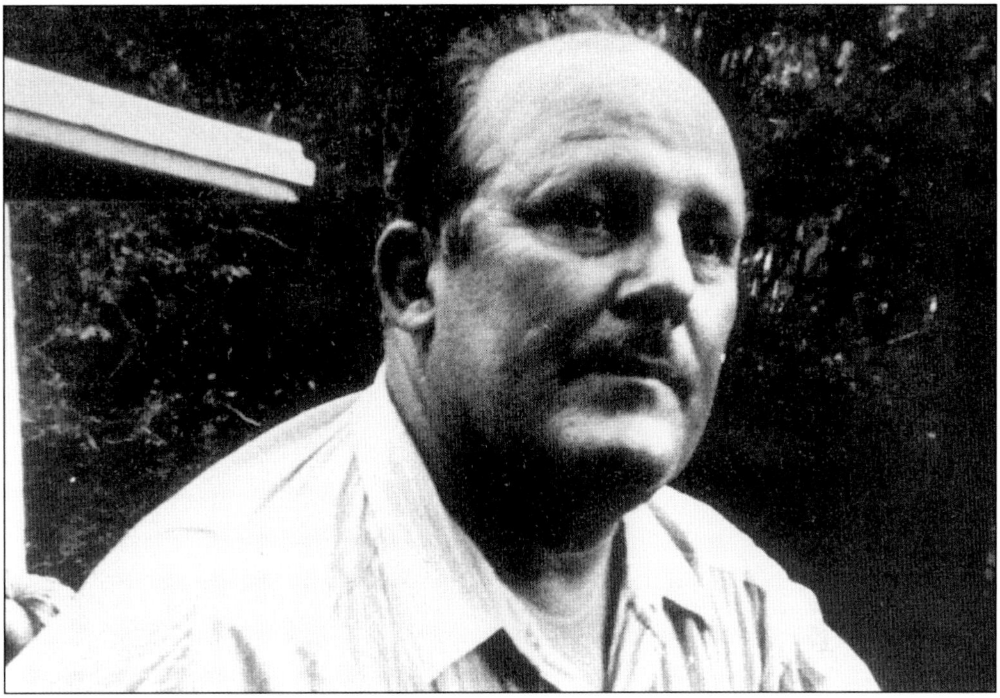

Outstanding among local visual artists were Don Brown (above), longtime art professor at Centenary and a respected Southern painter in his own right, and Louis Sicard (below). Other noted local visual artists include James L. Kendrick III, whose New Orleans and South Louisiana images are well known; Theo Minge Rendell, who was part of the Bohemian set of Taos and later of New Orleans; and Jean-Pierre Pique, painter and designer who studied under Erte in Paris and resided in Manhattan for many years. Additionally, fashion designer Geoffrey Beene is a native of nearby Haynesville.

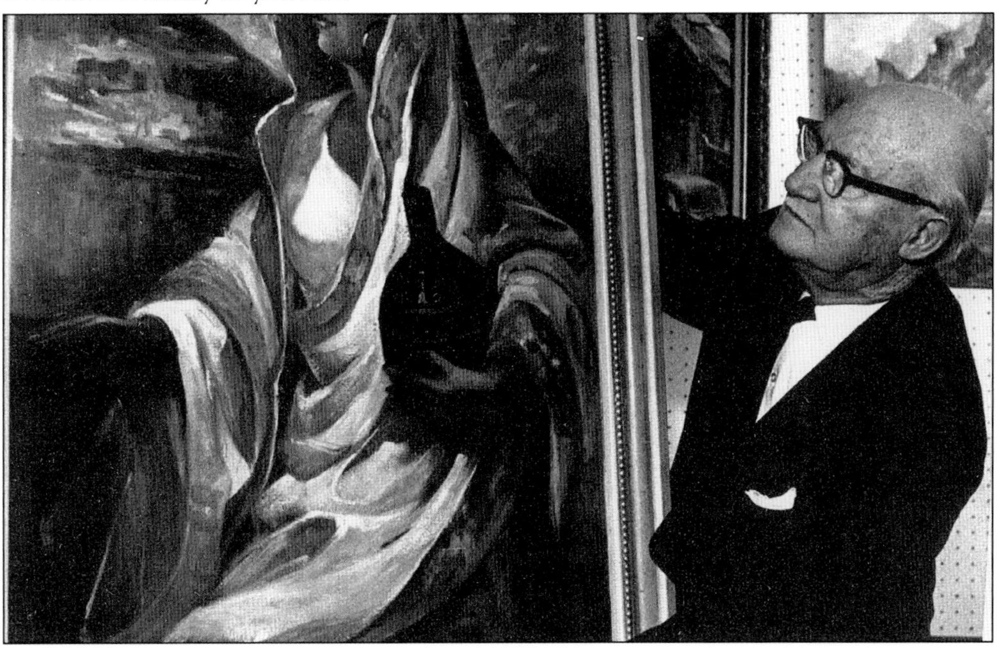

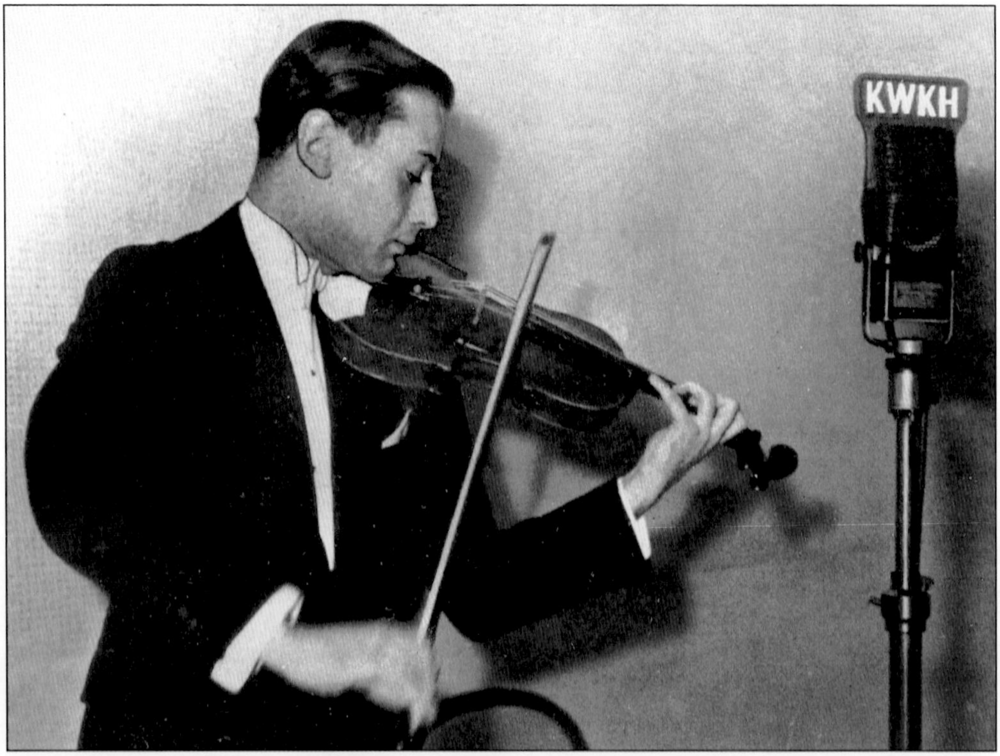

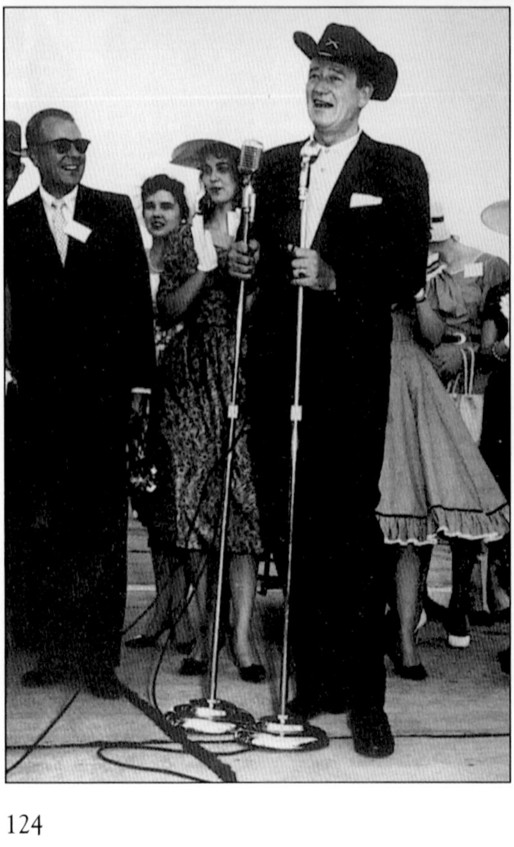

Albert Martini, Centenary music professor and noted violinist, performs a solo for KWKH radio in 1937. Aside from those mentioned earlier in this chapter, famous local musicians include singers Joe Stampley, Victoria Williams, Trace Adkins, Kix Brooks, and William Oliver Swofford, better known simply as Oliver; the rock group the Newbeats; blues composer Percy Mayfield; opera singer Lester Senter Wilson; cellist Charlotte Moorman; music agent Tom Ayres; singer/composer Stuart Hamblin; and pioneer recording artist Vernon Dalhart as well as big band leader Jan Garber (see page 24).

John Wayne visits Shreveport in 1960 during the making of *The Horse Soldiers*, which had its world premiere at the Strand Theatre. Wayne, who was made an honorary citizen of Shreveport, called it one of his "favorite cities" and visited numerous times during his notable career.

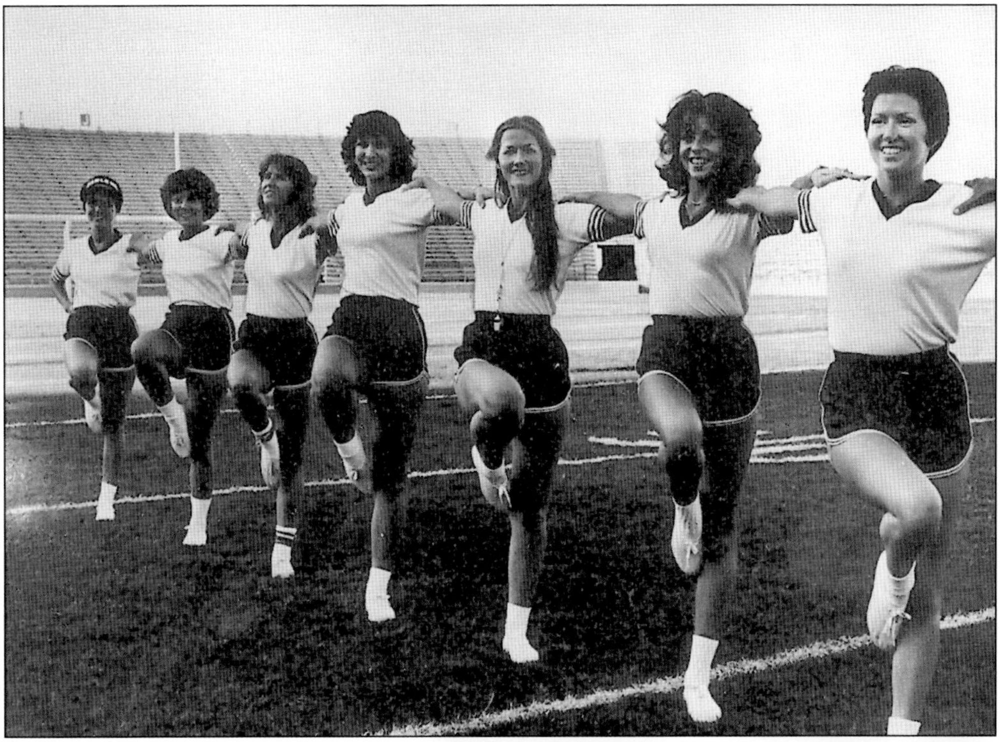

Cheerleaders of the Shreveport Steamers, Shreveport's short-lived professional football team, practice at Independence Stadium in 1980.

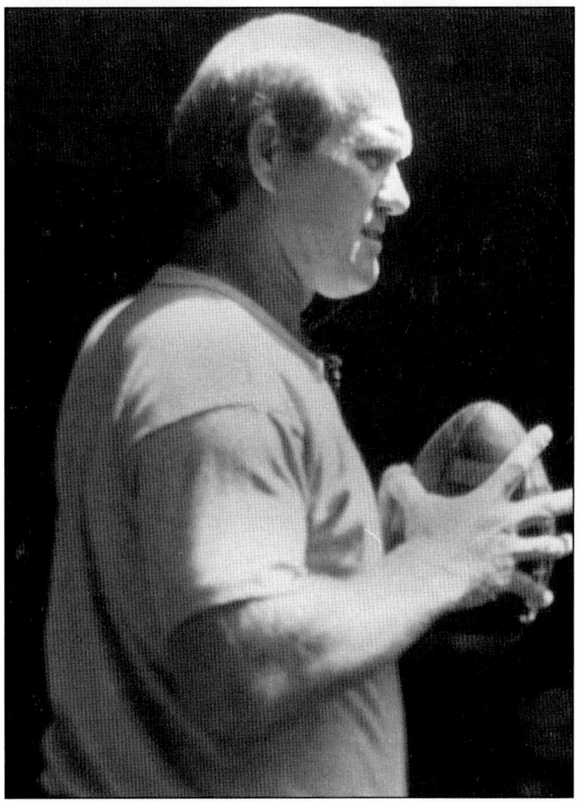

Shreveport native and resident Terry Bradshaw, formerly of the Pittsburgh Steelers football team, is one of the area's most notable sports figures. Others include Tommy Davis (San Francisco 49ers), Joe Ferguson (Buffalo Bills), David Woodley (Miami Dolphins), Bert Jones (Baltimore Colts), golfers Hal Sutton and David Toms, racer Freddie Spencer, skater Scot Baronet, track star Evelyn Ashford, tennis stars Venus and Serena Williams, gymnast Kathy Johnson, basketball stars Robert Parish (Boston Celtics) and Karl Malone (Utah Jazz), and baseball star Vida Blue (Oakland As).

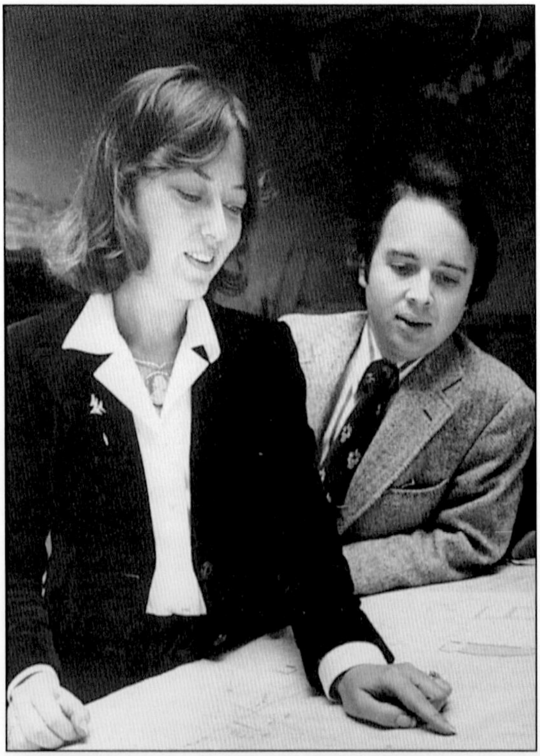

(Left) Pat Thatcher and Judd Tooke look over plans for the restoration of Shreveport's historic Strand Theatre. Closed in 1977, the Strand was nearly demolished and might have been were it not for concerned citizens such as Thatcher, Tooke, Jim Montgomery (see page 41), and Virginia Shehee (see page 45), who realized its cultural potential and fought to save it. In 1974 the Strand reopened as the city's premier venue for quality entertainment. (Below) Actress Kitty Carlisle Hart, widow of composer Moss Hart, is today a cultural leader of New York City. The granddaughter of Mayor Ben Holzman (see page 6), Mrs. Hart spent part of her childhood and youth here and still considers herself a Shreveport daughter.

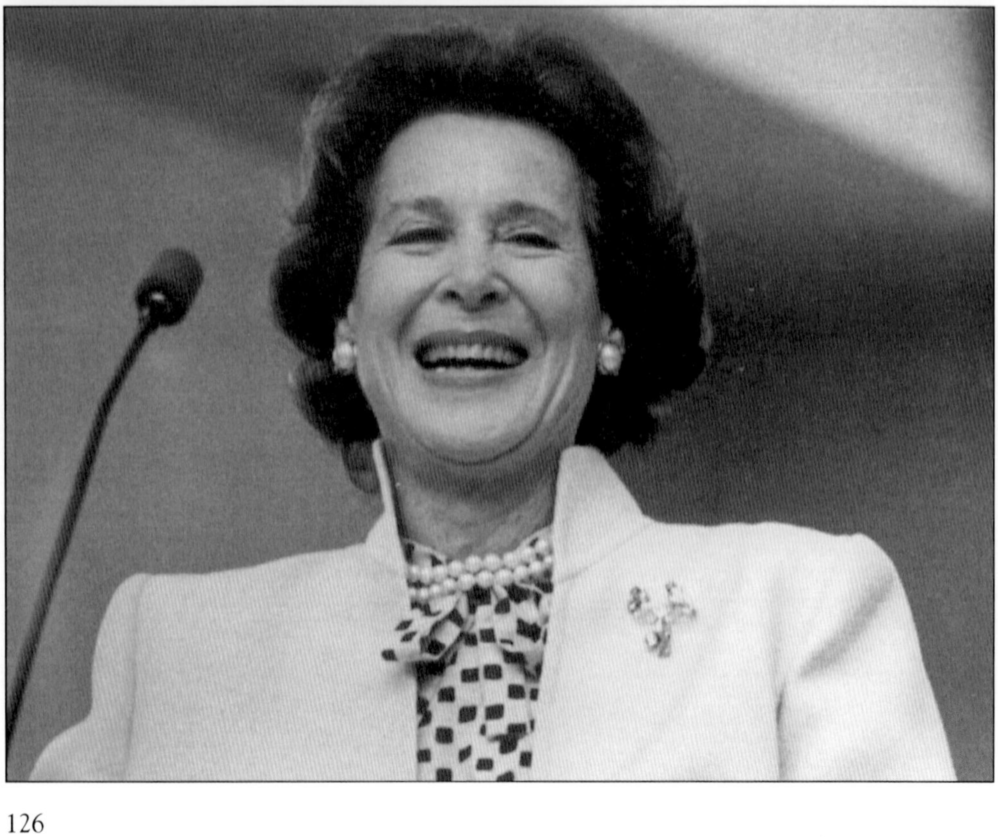

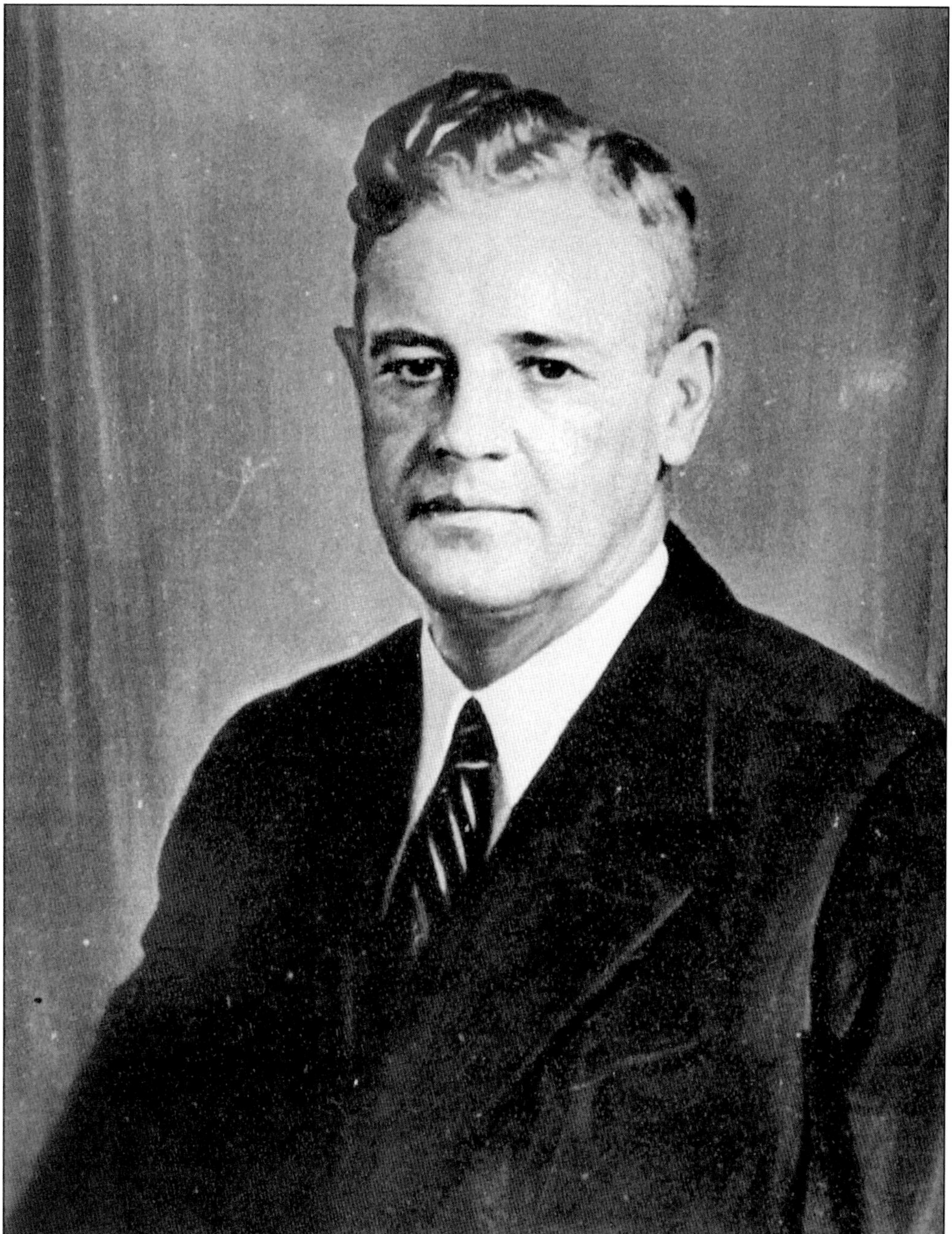

Oilman Richard William Norton was a collector of paintings, sculptures, rare books, and other *objects d'art*. The R.W. Norton Art Gallery, arguably Shreveport's most important cultural institution, was founded by Norton and his immense collection, some of which was housed in the Smithsonian before returning to Shreveport, forms the nucleus of the museum. Shreveport's rich cultural legacy owes an enormous debt of gratitude to philanthropists such as R.W. Norton, Justin Gras, the Community Foundation of Shreveport-Bossier, and other individuals and organizations who have worked so hard and done so much to improve the quality of life in the Shreveport metro area and the Northwestern Louisiana region.

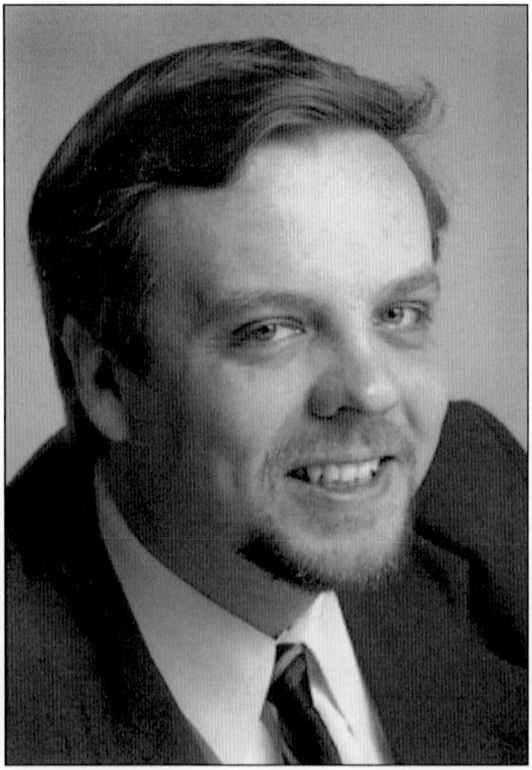

About the Author

Eric J. Brock is the author of eight previous books on Shreveport and Louisiana subjects including six for Arcadia. Additionally he is the author of numerous newspaper, magazine, and academic journal articles including his present column, "A Look Back," published in Shreveport's *Forum News* Magazine. Mr. Brock is president of Historic Preservation of Shreveport and of the Oakland Cemetery Preservation Society, as well as being active in numerous other cultural, historical, and preservation-related organizations, both on the regional and national levels.

Acknowledgments

Special thanks for support and assistance go to Archivist Laura Conerly and the staff of the LSU-Shreveport Noel Memorial Library Archives; to Special Collections Director Pat Ferguson and the staff of the Department of Special Collections, Shreve Memorial Library; and to librarian Martha Matlock and the library of the *Shreveport Times*. I wish also to thank all of those who have assisted with this project in any way and especially the many fans of my work who have been so very loyal and supportive over the past decade.